Cloud and Fog Computing Platforms for Internet of Things

Chapman & Hall/CRC Cloud Computing for Society 5.0
Series Editor
Vishal Bhatnagar and Vikram Bali

Digitalization of Higher Education using Cloud Computing
Edited by: S.L. Gupta, Nawal Kishor, Niraj Mishra, Sonali Mathur, Utkarsh Gupta

Cloud Computing Technologies for Smart Agriculture and Healthcare
Edited by: Urmila Shrawankar, Latesh Malik, Sandhya Arora

Cloud and Fog Computing Platforms for Internet of Things
Edited by: Pankaj Bhambri, Sita Rani, Gaurav Gupta and Alex Khang

For more information about this series please visit: https://www.routledge.com/Chapman--HallCRC-Cloud-Computing-for-Society-50/book-series/CRCCCS

Cloud and Fog Computing Platforms for Internet of Things

Edited by
Pankaj Bhambri
Sita Rani
Gaurav Gupta
Alex Khang

CRC Press
Taylor & Francis Group
Boca Raton London New York

CRC Press is an imprint of the
Taylor & Francis Group, an **informa** business

A CHAPMAN & HALL BOOK

First edition published 2022
by CRC Press
6000 Broken Sound Parkway NW, Suite 300, Boca Raton, FL 33487-2742

and by CRC Press
4 Park Square, Milton Park, Abingdon, Oxon, OX14 4RN

CRC Press is an imprint of Taylor & Francis Group, LLC

Library of Congress Cataloging-in-Publication Data
Names: Bhambri, Pankaj, editor. | Rani, Sita, editor. | Gupta, Gaurav (Computer science professor), editor. | Khang, Alex, editor.
Title: Cloud and fog computing platforms for Internet of Things / edited by Pankaj Bhambri, Sita Rani, Gaurav Gupta, Alex Khang.
Description: First edition. | Boca Raton, FL : CRC Press, 2022. | Series: Chapman & Hall/CRC cloud computing for society 5.0 | Includes bibliographical references and index. | Summary: "Today, relevant data are typically delivered to cloud-based servers for storing and analysis in order to extract key features and enable enhanced applications beyond the basic transmission of raw data in order to realize the possibilities associated with the impending Internet of Things (IoT). To allow for quicker, more efficient and much more privacy-preserving services, a new trend called fog computing has emerged: moving these responsibilities to the network's edge. Traditional centralized cloud computing paradigms confront new problems posed by IoT application growth, including high latency, limited storage and outages due to a lack of available resources. Fog computing puts the cloud and IoT devices closer together to address these issues. Instead of sending IoT data to the cloud, the fog processes and stores it locally at IoT devices. Unlike the cloud, fog-based services have a faster reaction time and better quality overall. Fog computing, Cloud Computing and their connectivity with the IoT are discussed in this book, with an emphasis on the advantages and implementation issues. It also explores the various architectures and appropriate IoT applications. Fog Computing, Cloud Computing and the Internet of Things are being suggested as potential research directions"-- Provided by publisher.
Identifiers: LCCN 2021059202 (print) | LCCN 2021059203 (ebook) | ISBN 9781032101507 (hbk) | ISBN 9781032276182 (pbk) | ISBN 9781003213888 (ebk)
Subjects: LCSH: Internet of things. | Cloud computing.
Classification: LCC TK5105.8857 .C63 2022 (print) | LCC TK5105.8857 (ebook) | DDC 004.67/8--dc23/eng/20220124
LC record available at https://lccn.loc.gov/2021059202
LC ebook record available at https://lccn.loc.gov/2021059203

ISBN: 978-1-032-10150-7 (hbk)
ISBN: 978-1-032-27618-2 (pbk)
ISBN: 978-1-003-21388-8 (ebk)

DOI: 10.1201/9781003213888

Typeset in Palatino
by SPi Technologies India Pvt Ltd (Straive)

Contents

Preface

Recent developments in Micro-Electro and Micro-Mechanical Systems innovation, remote intersections, and computerized devices have enabled the development of low-cost, multipurpose sensor hubs that are easy to use, consume little power, and transmit data wirelessly across short distances. When used as an IoT segment, intelligent sensors turn a current reality factor that they're predicting into an electronic information stream that may be transmitted to a gateway for further processing. Whether for city structures, plants, or wearable devices, Internet of Things (IoT) technologies rely on a wide range of sensors to collect data, which is then transmitted via the Internet to a nearby, cloud-based calculating asset.

IoT and cloud computing have altered how computing, networking, and services are delivered in today's world of smart devices. The current generation of computing devices, especially in a mobile context, cannot meet stringent requirements of applications with cloud computing and IoT, which include issues of latency-sensitive, safety, or geographically restricted applications, scheduling as well as power management, heterogeneous nature of devices.

IoT and fog technologies have grown in importance in recent years as a powerful tool for revolutionizing the way information and communication networks work. Platforms in 'Fog Computing' provide computation, storage, and networking services to end devices and traditional data centers from a cloud-based infrastructure. Manufacturing, smart cities, linked transit, smart grids, e-health, and oil and gas are expected to have a high demand for fog computing applications.

Computer programs that conduct investigations reduce the massive amounts of generated data into useful data for clients while also retracing the orders given to actuators in the field. Different firms have benefited enormously from the merging of the three. Using IoT, cloud, and fog computing, the book sheds light on these and other cutting-edge technologies. This book covers a number of today's scientific and technical problems, including how to turn the IoT concept into a workable, technically possible, and commercially viable product. Fog computing and cloud computing are introduced as key enablers for the IoT's sensing and computation backbone. CRC publications gave us the opportunity to publish the book, and we are grateful for it. Thanks to our families and loved ones for their support as well.

Aimed at academics, postgraduates, and practitioners in Cloud Computing, Internet of Things, intelligent systems, and fog computing, this book has a broad readership of interested parties.

Editor Biography

Dr. Pankaj Bhambri is an Assistant Professor in the Department of Information Technology at Ludhiana's Guru Nanak Dev Engineering College. He also serves as the Institute's Coordinator, Skill Enhancement Cell. He has almost 18 years of experience as a teacher. He earned an M.Tech. (CSE) and a B.E. (IT) with honors from the I.K.G. Punjab Technical University, Punjab, India, and the Dr. B.R. Ambedkar University, Uttar Pradesh, India, respectively. Dr. Bhambri earned a doctorate in computer science and engineering from the I.K.G. Punjab Technical University, Punjab, India. His research has appeared in a variety of prestigious international/national journals and conference proceedings. Dr. Bhambri has authored numerous textbooks and also filed several patents. He has supervised many undergraduate/postgraduate research projects/dissertations and is now supervising multiple Ph.D. research work as well. He organised numerous courses while receiving funding from the AICTE, TEQIP, and others. Machine Learning, Bioinformatics, Wireless Sensor Networks, and Network Security are his areas of interest. He serves as an editor, reviewer, and member of prominent national/international organisations' technical committees.

Dr. Sita Rani is working as a Professor – Computer Science & Engineering and Deputy Dean (Research) at Gulzar Group of Institutions, Khanna (Punjab). She has completed her B.Tech and M.Tech degrees in the faculty of Computer Science and Engineering from Guru Nanak Dev Engineering College, Ludhiana. She earned her Ph.D. in Computer Science and Engineering from I.K.Gujral Punjab Technical University, Kapurthala, Punjab in the year 2018. She has more than 19 years of teaching experience. She is an active member of ISTE, IEEE and IAEngg. She is the receiver of ISTE Section Best Teacher Award- 2020, and International Young Scientist Award-2021. She has contributed to the various research activities while publishing articles in the renowned journals and conference proceedings.She has published three international patents also. She has delivered many expert talks in A.I.C.T.E. sponsored Faculty Development Programs and organized many International Conferences during her 19 years of teaching experience. She is the member of Editorial Board of many international journals of repute. Her research interest includes Parallel and Distributed Computing, Machine Learning, and Internet of Things (IoT).

Dr. Gaurav Gupta is currently serving as Assistant Professor at Punjabi University, Patiala(Pb), India after completing his Ph.D., M.Tech, and B.Tech in Computer Science & Engineering from the University. He has more than 18 years of teaching experience and has supervised more than 45 M.Tech dissertations. He is also supervising 5 Ph.D. research scholars. He has contributed 93 articles in many reputed journals besides participating in some international conferences. His research interests include Machine Learning, Data Science, Data Mining & Warehousing, Big Data, CRM, Information Systems, Knowledge Management, Cloud Computing and DIP. He is a member of UACEE, IAENG, IACSIT, and SDIWC. He is on editorial board of various Journals. Before joining Punjabi University, he served Chitkara University and RIMT University. He had delivered many Expert talks and headed workshops on Data Mining and its techniques in different colleges and universities. He also headed many committees at department and university level.

Dr. Alex Khang PH (Prof. of Information Technology) has over 20 years of non-stop teaching and researching at VIUST in Vietnam; VUST Virginia, USA; Global Research Institute of Technology and Engineering, North Carolina, USA.

He is Session Chair for many Universities in the world and Editorial Board Member for ISSN of 2582-7464-CI Machine Learning, 0976-1136- A.I.I.F.J Organization; Globsyn Management Journal (GMJ), ISSN: 0973-9181, and member of Intl. International Advisory Committee for many International Conferences-VOL XIV, Issue 1 & 2 and ISSN: 0973-9181 Tradepreneur Global Academic Platform UK, and Group of CT University, Amity University, India USA and UK. He has published 48 best-seller IT books since 2001 to 2012 at domestic market, four specialized technology IT books in the University; editor of fourAI Books of CRC (978-0-367-70210-6, 978-1-032-10150-7, 978-1-032-21624-9, 978-1-032-17079-4), and calling chapters for two AI Books of CRC, and some IT books in English on Amazon.

He also has reviewed and evaluated more than 120+ journal papers, book chapters, and science articles in AI, Data Science, IoT, Blockchain and Cloud Computing for CRC, Springer, Elsevier, Emerald, IGI-Global, and InderScience Publishers and some essays and thesis which come from Ph.D. students and scholars in the world since 2010 up to now. He is a specialist of Data Science and Artificial Intelligence in IT Corporation and also in the contribution stage of knowledge and experience into the scope of tech talk, consultant, lecturer in full time and part-time, and evaluation on the sides of contents and engineering for the research, editor, Master/Ph.D. thesis for local and international institutes and schools of Technology. He also has over 25 years of non-stop working in the field of Computer Science and specialized in the Software Engineering, Data Science, and Artificial Intelligence fields for foreign corporations from Sweden, USA, Germany, Singapore, and Multi-nations.

Contributors

Anil B. Malali
Acharya Institute of Graduate Studies
Bengaluru, India

Arun Kumar Sivaraman
Vellore Institute of Technology
Chennai, India

Arunava Chatterjee
Raghunathpur Government Polytechnic
Purulia, India

Avita Katal
University of Petroleum and Energy Studies
Dehradun, India

Bindu Madavi K.P.
Dayananda Sagar University
Bengaluru, India

Biswarup Ganguly
Meghnad Saha Institute of Technology
Kolkata, India

Chandrashekhar Azad
National Institute of Technology
Jamshedpur, India

Debabrata Sarddar
University of Kalyani
Nadia, India

Dhanabalan Thangam
Acharya Institute of Graduate Studies
Bengaluru, India

Dhanalakshmi R.
KCG College of Technology
Chennai, India

Enakshmi Nandi
University of Kalyani
Nadia, India

Gopalakrishnan Subramanian
Acharya Institute of Graduate Studies
Bengaluru, India

Jenitha R.
Kalasalingam Academy of Research and
    Education
Virudhunagar (Dt), India

Jin Yong Park
Konkuk University
Seoul, South Korea

Jithendra H.N.
Vellore Institute of Technology
Chennai, India

Jose Anand
KCG College of Technology
Chennai, India

Kalpana Murugan
Kalasalingam Academy of Research and
    Education
Virudhunagar (Dt), India

Krishna Sowjanya K.
Dayananda Sagar University
Bengaluru, India

S. K. Mouleeswaran
Dayananda Sagar University
Bengaluru, India

Nainsi Soni
The LNM Institute of Information
    Technology
Jaipur, India

Nazeer Haider
National Institute of Technology
Jamshedpur, India

Opeyemi Osanaiye
Nile University of Nigeria
Abuja, Nigeria

P. Vijayakarthik
Sir M. Visvesvaraya Institute of Technology
Bengaluru, India

Pankaj Bhambri
Guru Nanak Dev Engineering College
Ludhiana, India

Payel Ray
University of Kalyani
Nadia, India

Prateek Kalia
Masaryk University
Brno, Czech Republic

Rachna
CT University
Ludhiana, India

Ranjan Kumar Mondal
University of Kalyani
Nadia, India

Rekha D.
Vellore Institute of Technology
Chennai, India

Saurabh Kumar
The LNM Institute of Information
     Technology
Jaipur, India

Sita Rani
Gulzar Group of Institutions
Ludhiana, India

Steve Adeshina
Nile University of Nigeria
Abuja, Nigeria

Vitesh Sethi
University of Petroleum and Energy
     Studies
Dehradun, India

Yogesh Chhabra
CT University
Ludhiana, India

1

Resource Allocation Techniques in Cloud Computing

K. Krishna Sowjanya and S. K. Mouleeswaran
Dayananda Sagar University, Bengaluru, India

CONTENTS

1.1 Introduction

Cloud Computing manages, stores, and provides access to many resources such as storage, network, and computing resources over the Internet using a pay-as-use policy. Using this technology, users don't have to manage a computer's hard drive or physical servers for themselves. These servers and resources can be accessed over the Internet along with the software and databases that run on those servers. All these resources are maintained, upgraded, and run by the cloud servers which are spread across the world through data centers. The Cloud Computing overview is represented in Figure 1.1.

All the computing resources such as storage, processing, and applications are provided to the users on-demand through the Internet services by Cloud Computing. Many organizations nowadays tend to operate their business transactions in a way that reduces the cost by accessing the resources over the Internet. Cloud Computing provides efficient computing by centralizing all the resources and making them available for the users in three ways. First is by providing the computing resources along with storage and network. Second is by providing a platform to develop the products. Third is by providing the application software which is maintained by the cloud. In addition to that, it also provides four ways

DOI: 10.1201/9781003213888-1

1

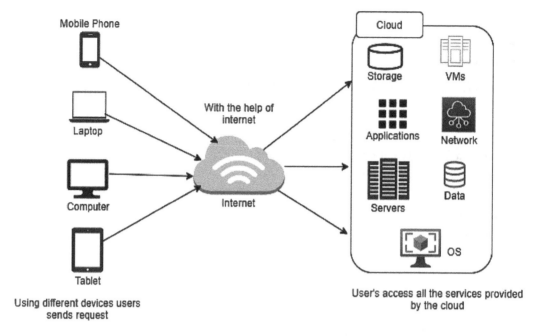

FIGURE 1.1
Cloud Computing overview.

to deploy the cloud. First, where only the organization can access, i.e., private model; second, all the people can access without any restriction, i.e., public model; third, the combination of private, and public, i.e., hybrid model; and fourth, a model shared by many and different organizations, i.e., community model. It also provides on-demand virtualized services with dynamic computing infrastructure which are represented in Figure 1.2.

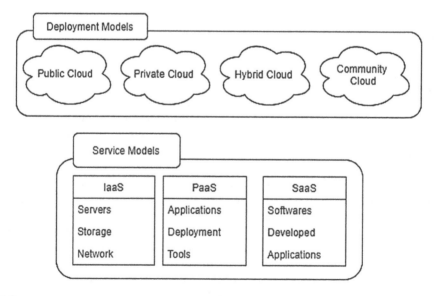

FIGURE 1.2
Deployment and service models in Cloud (Metwally, 2016).

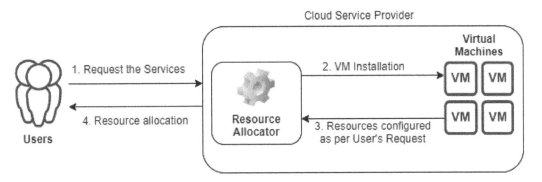

FIGURE 1.3
Process of resource allocation.

The gaining popularity of the cloud had increased requests from users tremendously. To meet the requirements of the client and also to boost the cloud's performance, all the virtualized resources provided as a service in the cloud need to be optimized. Resource Allocation (RA) is a mechanism to assure the fair and equal distribution of requests to the servers to avoid the situation of over usage (requests accessing the same machine) and under usage (idle machines) of resources, shown in Figure 1.3. This mechanism also ensures the satisfaction of the user by providing the requested configuration details by the service provider. It balances the load effectively by scaling the resources to achieve optimal utilization of the resources, thereby increasing the response time and also reducing the cost.

Cloud Computing is developing rapidly. The gaining popularity of the cloud mainly depends on few important technologies such as virtualization and resource management.

1.2 Resource Management

Resource management includes the overall maintenance of the heterogeneous resources, allocation of the resources to requests, and also maintaining the overall process of request servicing. As there is an increase in cloud users, there will be an increase in the requests also. To maintain the balance between user demands and resource supply, a proper strategy for RA is needed through resource management. Resource management is based on the user's request the service provider allocates the required resources to the customer.

Before doing that, a series of steps are involved in the process of RA. The customer and the service provider agree about the resource provisioning called SLA (Service Level Agreements). Based on the terms specified in SLA, the mapping of the resources and requests is done. If the number of requests is increasing, dynamically the resources are adjusted to serve the surge of incoming requests, and RA is done. After allocating the resources, the machines are modeled virtually to meet the requirements specified by the user, and the processing of the request is scheduled. The entire process of resource management is depicted in Figure 1.4.

In the schedule of processing the request, the appropriate resources for the process completion are identified and apt resources among them are selected by the scheduler.

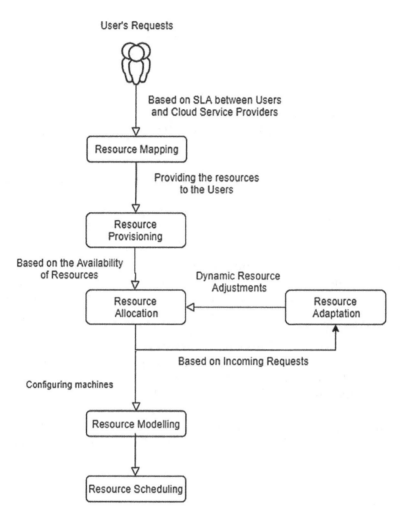

FIGURE 1.4
Resource management in the Cloud.

In addition to that, the scheduler should also try to approximate the future requests and should be ready to process those upcoming requests also.

RA can be done effectively with the approach called virtualization. After allocating the resources, based on the user configurations a separate machine is set up and it is provided to the user for the requested service.

1.3 Virtualization

Virtualization is a process of allocating the required resources for users virtually via VMs. The resources that can be allocated are the operating system, CPU, storage devices, network, etc. Instead of giving the real hardware/physical resources, virtualization takes care of providing the resources logically to the user by creating an abstraction layer over the bare metal hardware. The layer over the hardware called a hypervisor or VM monitor takes care of creating several replicas of machines. Using the concept of virtualization, multiple copies of VMs with different configurations can be created and also can be hosted on a single machine to serve multiple requests. Once the user submits the specific requirements, the VM monitor ensures the suitable allocation of the VMs for the execution.

Few scenarios must be considered while allocating the VMs to the user. They are as follows:

1. Limited resources: Many times, the requests from users will be more. But with limited resources, all the incoming requests will create a bottleneck situation which leads to the degradation of the overall performance.
2. Utilization: Based on the pre-defined configurations of the VMs, few VMs will be loaded more with requests and few will be idle without any request which will also be a factor for the underperformance of the cloud due to more requests in the waiting list.
3. Load balance: The incoming load must be equally partitioned across all the VMs to enhance the performance and should also support the scalability of resources if there is a sudden rise in the incoming requests.
4. User satisfaction: Overall, users who send the requests must be satisfied by the services provided by the cloud service provider. Cost and QoS (Quality of Service) are the two main factors that fulfill user satisfaction.

Based on above all factors/scenarios, optimal VMs should be configured to provide service for the user as well as to enhance the performance of the cloud.

1.4 Resource Allocation Algorithms

RA ensures the proper and fair allotment of the required requested specifications to users. For the efficient allocation of resources, there are a few challenges to overcome. They are the prediction of the requests by the user, obtainability of the resources at the data centers of the clouds, meeting the SLA requirements, avoiding the over-provisioning and under-provisioning situations, and reducing the cost and power consumption. So, a reliable, efficient, flexible RA strategy is needed to overcome these challenges. RA is a two-step process: first, predicting the resource requirement of the users and second, allocating the necessary resources using allocation strategies.

The various RA techniques illustrated in Figure 1.5 are proposed by various authors based on different parameters. Some techniques meet few parameters such as low cost, user satisfaction, and some techniques meet the parameters such as efficiency, performance, and time taken to respond to the request. Based on all these parameters, the algorithms for allocating the resources are broadly classified as follows.

1.4.1 Priority-Based Resource Allocation Algorithm (PB-RA Algorithm)

This algorithm is a pre-emptive technique in which the tasks or requests are scheduled or executed based on the priority value assigned to it. The priority value is given to a task

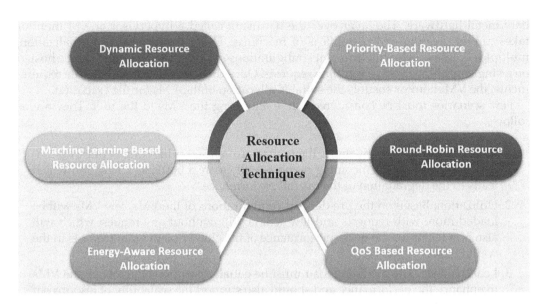

FIGURE 1.5
Types of resource allocation techniques.

depending on various metrics such as the cost of the resource, type of the task, memory requirement, storage requirement, number of processors required, etc. (Savani Nirav 2014) proposed an algorithm that takes priority of the requests for effective usage of the resources. This technique collects the user's requests and divides them into tasks based on the resources required. Based on the resources such as memory, storage, and processing unit the task is assigned a priority by comparing it with the tasks which are already in the queue. When two tasks arrive with the same priority level, preference is given to the task that came first. The priority for a task is given by AHP (Analytical Hierarchy Process). Abid et al. (2020) performed an analysis on a similar PB-RA Algorithm which uses the combination of two algorithms that consider the minimum time of execution and lists them to set priority for the task. When the user's request arrives at the cloud, it is divided into tasks based on the requirements. Later, appropriate VMs and resources are prepared and allocated to the requests using CLS. If the required resources are not available, the proposed method uses the CMMS technique to book the resources in advance to avoid contention and thus by utilizing the resources efficiently. The Priority-based RA algorithms are analyzed and depicted using Table 1.1 using three important parameters such as cost, resource utilization, and execution time and are tabulated as follows:

TABLE 1.1

Analysis of Various PB-RA Algorithms

Referred Paper	Cost	Utilization of Resources	Time Taken for Execution
Savani Nirav (2014)	High	High	Low
Abid et al. (2020)	High	Medium	Low

1.4.2 Round-Robin-Based Resource Allocation Algorithm (RRB-RA Algorithm)

This algorithm equally distributes the computing time of the resources to the requests based on time quantum or time slices. To consider the time quantum or slice, it considers various parameters such as queue length, number of tasks, and execution times. It addresses all the requests without starving them by providing equal time slices for execution Alnowiser et al. (2014) considered weights of the requests to distribute the resources. This technique uses weighing coefficient queues that define several tasks and forwards this task to the scheduler to assign to the queue. To lessen the energy consumed, this method uses a voltage that is dynamic and also with scaling that is frequent. However, resource utilization is reduced. However, Elmougy et al. (2017) set a threshold value to segregate the incoming requests into two. One having the requests with less time of execution and one with more time of execution. The optimal time quantum is calculated by taking a median of the requests. If the request is less than the threshold, it is placed in a short queue else it is placed in a long queue. Later SJF is implemented to execute two tasks from the short queue and one from a long queue by reducing the waiting and turnaround time. However, this technique has not addressed the parameters such as cost and resource utilization. Pradhan et al. (2016) calculated the quantum time based on the average of the sum of the request times. This model has an impact on the system's efficiency and response time. The different papers on the Round-Robin method are analyzed and tabulated in Table 1.2 as follows.

1.4.3 QoS-Based Resource Allocation Algorithms (QoSB-RA Algorithms)

QoS is the prominent factor of Cloud Computing when it comes to customer satisfaction. QoS is completely based on SLAs, in which the users specify the expectations and requirements from the cloud service providers. If the SLA terms are met, that leads to QoS and vice versa. Sun et al. (2016) used domain-specific language to describe configurations specified by the user. This technique automates the entire process of configuration collection and configuration allocation by testing it under various configuration details to achieve optimal conditions to meet the QoS. Mireslami et al. (2017) proposed an optimization algorithm that focuses on multiple objectives such as cost, performance, and QoS. It uses the branch and bound technique to find the suitable and best combination of available resources to meet the user's expectations. However, this method did not specify the resource utilization and also it is incompatible in a multi-cloud scenario. Abid et al. (2020) analyzed a paper on heuristic-based design that uses the help of load-balancing algorithms to meet the user requirements specified by allocating VMs and resources. By doing so, the SLA requirements are easily met without any penalty. This method did not address the response time of the user's request. The different papers on QoS-based RA techniques are analyzed and are tabulated in Table 1.3.

TABLE 1.2

Analysis of Various RRB- RA Algorithms

Referred Paper	Cost	Utilization of Resources	Time Taken for Execution
Alnowiser et al. (2014)	Medium	High	Medium
Elmougy et al. (2017)	High	High	High
Pradhan et al. (2016)	Medium	High	High

TABLE 1.3

Analysis of Various QoSB-RA-Based Algorithms

Referred Paper	Cost	Utilization of Resources	Time Taken for Execution
Sun et al. (2016)	High	–	Medium
Mireslami et al. (2017)	Low	–	Low
Abid et al. (2020)	Low	High	–

1.4.4 Energy-Aware-Based Resource Allocation Algorithms (EAB-RA Algorithms)

The cloud performs operations at data centers that are distributed all around the world. These datacenters to perform computing-intensive operations consume more power and energy. To optimize the usage of energy consumed by cloud data centers, Meshkati and Safi-Esfahani (2019) implemented the combination of two natural phenomenon algorithms: namely, Bee Colony and Particle Swarm algorithms. This hybrid meta-heuristic technique includes scheduler that maintains the homogenous resources and turns them off if the load is less. Based on the requests, the workload analyzer starts analyzing the request. If the request is like the previous one which requires the same number of resources, then the consumed energy is calculated and allocated to the request. Kumar et al. (2018), to reduce energy consumption, have implemented the two-level Ant Colony Optimization (ACO) technique. VM allocation happens in the first level and physical machine allocation happens in the second level. Based on the request, dynamic provisioning of the physical machines is done at the second level. However, this chapter did not address the cost metrics. Abid et al. (2020) analyzed a paper on Artificial Bee Colony to minimize the consumption of energy. Every node maintains a threshold. If that threshold exceeds, then no other work is assigned to that node. This method has addressed various QoS parameters. The different papers on EAB-RA Algorithms are analyzed and are tabulated in Table 1.4.

1.4.5 Machine Learning-Based Resource Allocation Algorithms (MLB-RA Algorithms)

ML-based RA algorithms do efficient RA by predicting the user requirements. So earlier prediction helps in avoiding congestion and bottleneck of the user requests focused on predicting the required resources for allocation and also for reducing the power consumption. Alsadie et al. (2018) predicted that the required resources are done based on the history of the computing resources used. This method used k-means clustering for clustering the data and using them for training the data to estimate the required resources for future requests. Liu et al. (2017) implemented a two-tier architecture for RA and power consumption reduction using Google cloud trace. First-tier focuses on allocating the required VMs and resources considering various configurations using deep learning techniques. Second-tier focuses mainly on workload prediction, power consumption management, and has

TABLE 1.4

Analysis of Various EAB-RA Algorithms

Referred Paper	Cost	Utilization of Resources	Time Taken for Execution
Meshkati and Safi-Esfahani (2019)	Low	Medium	High
Kumar et al. (2018)	–	Medium	Low
Abid et al. (2020)	Low	High	Low

TABLE 1.5

Analysis of Various MLB-RA Algorithms

Referred Paper	Cost	Utilization of Resources	Time Taken for Execution
Alsadie et al. (2018)	High	Medium	Low
Liu et al. (2017)	Medium	High	Medium
Saidi et al. (2020)	Low	Medium	Low

succeeded in reducing the energy consumption but could maintain the latency only till a threshold. Instead of predicting and allocating the resources runtime, Saidi et al.(2020) used a method that can estimate the workload based on the earlier usage knowledge and adapt based on the present requirements. Along with that, genetic algorithms are also used for the workload distribution among the resources. However, the energy consumption is more in this methodology. The different papers on MLB-RA algorithms are analyzed and are tabulated in Table 1.5.

1.4.6 Dynamic Resource Allocation Algorithms (DRA Algorithms)

Dynamic algorithms allocate the resources dynamically based on the user's demand and request. Before allocating the resources to the user's demands, dynamic algorithms first check whether the resources are available or not. If the resources are not available, it will not allocate the resources and denies the request. Requisition of the requests and allocation happens dynamically. X. Liu and Buyya(2020)

analyzed a technique that balanced the incoming requests and their associated RAs to avoid over-provisioning or under-provisioning conflicts. Statistics of time taken for the arrival of request and time taken to process the request are maintained at regular intervals by the manager and the average of those statistics is taken to either allocate or de-allocate a resource. If the processing rate is high, more resources are allocated and if the processing rate is low, few resources are allocated dynamically. Similar work has been analyzed by Alashaikh et al. (2021) by defining the properties of the resources such as the amount of available memory, type of the hypervisor, type of the resource, etc., and a priority is given to the resources depending on the properties. Based on the request, appropriate resources are allocated and the priority value is counted. If any two requests are having the same value, the algorithm is repeated for request processing. In addition to that, a static VM migration is done to support the RA. To enable the smooth migration of VMs at IaaS, Lakhwani et al. (2019) analyzed a method that is completely based on load per VMs. Depending on the user's request, the controller will add or delete the VM. The allocation is done based on the availability of CPU and connections based on the user configuration. Similarly, an instance of VM is deallocated after processing the request and its related resources are also released. The different papers on dynamic RA techniques are analyzed and are tabulated in Table 1.6.

TABLE 1.6

Analysis of Various DRA Algorithms

Referred Paper	Cost	Utilization of Resources	Time Taken for Execution
Liu and Buyya (2020)	High	High	Low
Alashaikh et al. (2021)	Medium	High	Low
Lakhwani et al. (2019)	High	High	Low

1.5 Resource Allocation Factors

RA takes care of the proper and equal distribution of the resources/services for the requests generated by users. To meet the specified user requirements, there are so many factors to be considered. They are the cost of the entire services, utilization of the resources, energy consumption, SLAs, QoS, time taken for the response, and satisfaction of the user. All these factors are presented in Figure 1.6.

Factors such as the user satisfaction, resource utilization, and QoS should have high values, whereas the factors such as cost, energy consumption, and response time to meet the user's requirements should have the low values. Based on the different algorithms discussed in this chapter, main factors such as cost, utilization of the resources, and time taken to give the response are considered, and analysis is represented in Figure 1.7 as a graph.

From the above graph, mentioned RA algorithms focused more on increasing resource utilization benefitting the service provider end. For instance, RRB-RA, DRA, MLB-RA, and QoS algorithms achieved almost optimal performance in terms of resource utilization. In an ideal Cloud Computing environment, the satisfaction of both the parties, i.e. service provider and service consumer, must be considered equally important. Based on the analysis, the above-mentioned RA algorithms failed to meet a few service consumers/user's requirements such as cost and execution time. In addition to the above analysis, few more parameters such as consumption of energy, the performance, satisfaction of the user, and quality of the service provided are also considered and tabulated in Table 1.7. The table emphasizes which algorithm has addressed or not addressed the above-mentioned parameters. (✓) represents that the parameter has been addressed in the chapter, whereas (✗) represents that the parameter has not been addressed in the algorithm.

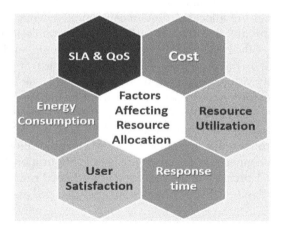

FIGURE 1.6
Factors affecting resource allocation.

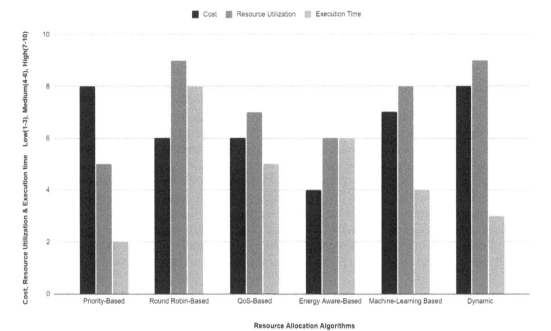

FIGURE 1.7

Analysis of RA algorithms based on resource allocation factors.

TABLE 1.7

Analysis of Various Resource Allocation Algorithms

Referred Paper	Energy Consumption	Performance	User Satisfaction	QoS
Alsadie et al. (2018)	✓	✗	✗	✗
Saidi et al. (2020)	✗	✗	✗	✗
Liu et al. (2017)	✓	✗	✗	✗
Alashaikh et al. (2021)	✗	✓	✓	✓
Liu and Buyya (2020)	✗	✓	✓	✓
Lakhwani et al. (2019)	✗	✗	✓	✓
Alnowiser et al. (2014)	✓	✗	✗	✗
Elmougy et al. (2017)	✗	✓	✗	✗
Pradhan et al. (2016)	✗	✓	✓	✓
Sun et al. (2016)	✗	✗	✓	✓
Abid et al. (2020)	✓	✗	✗	✗
Mireslami et al. (2017)	✗	✓	✓	✓
Abid et al. (2020)	✗	✗	✓	✓

1.6 Conclusion and Future Works

RA is very prominent for the efficient functionality of the computing resources provided by the cloud. Depending on the performance of the cloud, SLA terms are met, and QoS is provided to the users. At the same time penalty for not meeting the SLA can also be reduced. Cloud service providers take the requirements of the users, SLA into consideration to obtain optimal performance. Various RA techniques such as PB-RA, RRB-RA, QoSB-RA, EAB-RA, MLB-RA, and DRA are analyzed based on RA factors. These algorithms focused mainly on obtaining maximum resource utilization and minimum execution time. Resource utilization and execution time are the primary factors for the efficient performance of the cloud. At the same time, there are few more parameters such as cost, consumption of energy, and response time. Many of the discussed algorithms failed to meet these extra parameters that are equally important. Cost and energy consumption are important metrics that will result in user satisfaction. Hence, there is a need for an efficient algorithm that can address as many factors as possible without impacting the process of RA and execution time. In addition to this, future algorithms can also focus on security aspects, fault tolerance, and effective VM migration while addressing the requests.

References

Abid, A., Manzoor, M. F., Farooq, M. S., Farooq, U., & Hussain, M. (2020). Challenges and issues of resource allocation techniques in Cloud Computing. *KSII Transactions on Internet and Information Systems*, 14(7), 2815–2839.https://doi.org/10.3837/tiis.2020.07.005

Alashaikh, A., Alanazi, E., & Al-Fuqaha, A. (2021). A survey on the use of preferences for virtual machine placement in cloud data centers. *ACM Computing Surveys*, 54(5). https://doi.org/10.1145/3450517

Alnowiser, A., Aldhahri, E., & Alahmadi, A. (2014). Enhanced weighted round robin (EWRR) scheduling with DVFS technology in cloud. *Proceedings - 2014 International Conference on Computational Science and Computational Intelligence, CSCI 2014*, 1, 320–326. https://doi.org/10.1109/CSCI.2014.62

Alsadie, D., Tari, Z., Alzahrani, E. J., & Zomaya, A. Y. (2018). Dynamic resource allocation for an energy efficient VM architecture for Cloud Computing. *ACM International Conference Proceeding Series*. https://doi.org/10.1145/3167918.3167952

Elmougy, S., Sarhan, S., & Joundy, M. (2017). A novel hybrid of Shortest job first and round Robin with dynamic variable quantum time task scheduling technique. *Journal of Cloud Computing*, 6(1). https://doi.org/10.1186/s13677-017-0085-0

Kumar, A., Kumar, R., & Sharma, A. (2018). Energy aware resource allocation for clouds using two level ant colony optimization. *Computing and Informatics*, 37(1), 76–108. https://doi.org/10.4149/cai_2018_1_76

Lakhwani, K., Kaur, R., Kumar, P., & Thakur, M. (2019). An extensive survey on data authentication schemes in cloud computing. *Proceedings - 4th International Conference on Computing Sciences, ICCS 2018*, 17(9), 59–66. https://doi.org/10.1109/ICCS.2018.00016

Liu, N., Li, Z., Xu, J., Xu, Z., Lin, S., Qiu, Q., Tang, J., & Wang, Y. (2017). A hierarchical framework of cloud resource allocation and power management using deep reinforcement learning. *Proceedings - International Conference on Distributed Computing Systems*, 372–382. https://doi.org/10.1109/ICDCS.2017.123

Liu, X., & Buyya, R. (2020). Resource management and scheduling in distributed stream processing systems: A taxonomy, review, and future directions. *ACM Computing Surveys*, 53(3). https://doi.org/10.1145/3355399

Meshkati, J., & Safi-Esfahani, F. (2019). Energy-aware resource utilization based on particle swarm optimization and artificial bee colony algorithms in Cloud Computing. *Journal of Supercomputing*, *75*(5), 2455–2496. https://doi.org/10.1007/s11227-018-2626-9

Metwally, K. (2016). *A Resource Management Framework for IaaS in Cloud Computing Environment*. http://www.ruor.uottawa.ca/handle/10393/34951

Mireslami, S., Rakai, L., Far, B. H., & Wang, M. (2017). Simultaneous cost and QoS optimization for cloud resource allocation. *IEEE Transactions on Network and Service Management*, *14*(3), 676–689. https://doi.org/10.1109/TNSM.2017.2738026

Pradhan, P., Behera, P. K., & Ray, B. N. B. (2016). Modified round Robin algorithm for resource allocation in cloud computing. *Procedia Computer Science*, *85*(Cms), 878–890. https://doi.org/10.1016/j.procs.2016.05.278

Saidi, K., Hioual, O., & Siam, A. (2020). Resources allocation in cloud computing: A survey. In *Lecture Notes in Networks and Systems* (Vol. 102). https://doi.org/10.1007/978-3-030-37207-1_37

Savani Nirav, M.(2014). Priority based resource allocation in cloud computing. *International Journal of Engineering Research & Technology*, 3(5), 855–857.

Sun, Y., White, J., Eade, S., & Schmidt, D. C. (2016). ROAR: A QoS-oriented modeling framework for automated cloud resource allocation and optimization. *Journal of Systems and Software*, *116*, 146–161. https://doi.org/10.1016/j.jss.2015.08.006

2

Transforming Healthcare through Internet of Things

Dhanabalan Thangam, Anil B. Malali, and Gopalakrishnan Subramanian
Acharya Institute of Graduate Studies, Bengaluru, India

Jin Yong Park
Konkuk University, Seoul, Korea

CONTENTS

DOI: 10.1201/9781003213888-2

2.1 Introduction

As the whole world is alluring with information and communication technologies (ICTs), a lot of advancements have happened in all spheres, and thereby they influence our lives from birth to death. Further, a sequence of technological advancements leads to changes in the lifestyle of the people and connects the nuke and corner of the world with the growth and development of Internet technologies and its enabled digital devices. Thus, these technologies have transformed almost all industries including healthcare. Because, in the recent days, though the world is good at in various technological advancements on one side, there is a health crisis on the other side due to the hectic lifestyle and hassled working environment. Hence, it is essential to maintain the good healthy condition of the people with the help of advanced health technology (Shrimali, 2021). In recent times, the health sector is moving forward with the technology called the Internet of Things (IoT), as it is collecting and analyzing a huge volume of data in a short span with more accuracy and faster. As a result, it has the prospective to transform the way health service is provided. It also permits the people and devices to be attached at all times, in all the places, with everything and everybody, can idyllically using network and all the service. The growth and development of the IoT are only because of smart devices such as Smartphones, tablets, and related digital technologies. These smart gadgets act as a gateway to the world of IoT. As it has the potential to carry out the multi-tasks for the patients and doctors, it seems like a superpower technology (Shockloss, 2021). The growth and development of smartphone technology are approaching other physical devices to monitor and collect the necessary data and store it impeccably with cloud storage. Thus, this technology enables the collection of huge volumes of data by connecting and conversing with number devices. This outburst of data requests to be accumulated, sorted, and evaluated with multifaceted data analytic methods to present the actual and essential data to the patients and doctors. As a result, IoT is being one of the major productive technologies for health service providers, and lessens the treatment costs for the patients and helps to get better quality of health services. The less cost and a range of accessible sensors along with the cross-device connectivity system enable to capture, safeguard, and examine the patients' data automatically; by this way this technology speed ups the medical services on-time along with efficiency (Philips, 2019). In a manner, the IoT has a lot of advantages, and thereby it minimizes the errors happening in the health sector by diagnosing the patients accurately; further, it ensures the safety of the patients from wrong treatments, human incapability to take action quickly, and other errors resulting from carelessness of the medical staffs and other related factors. Moreover, this technology specially cares the age-old patients, individuals who are anguish from unending diseases, and patients in need of regular monitoring. Thus, this technology provides a lot of advanced solutions such as gathering, storing, and analyzing health data collected from the various real-time health monitoring gadgets (Umanenko, 2020). It is ensuring better treatment based on more exact data, reaching a wider range of healthcare providers, enabling the patients to care remotely through audio and video stream, alarming health notifications to the family members and doctors during urgent, monitoring and checking the medicinal process, and sharing those details with doctors from across the country or other regions of the world, and also overseeing and recuperating the sanatorium assets for the patients and doctors. Thus, this technology has transformed the way of doing health services in modern times (Forgan, 2021).

2.2 Application of IoT in Healthcare

The application of IoT in the health sector is witnessing a lot of progression in various areas. Healthcare units in the recent days showing interest to invest a lot toward the IoT-enabled gadgets or technologies such as Wi-Fi or Bluetooth-facilitated X-ray equipment to various wearables like smartwatches, smart bands, and other bio-sensors gadgets, and they supply significant health data to the medical practitioners to take necessary actions in the relevant field. Even though IoT is comparatively emerging in the healthcare sector, the pace is altering fast, so much as the whole health landscape is called the 'Internet of Medical Things' (Matthews, 2019). A company called CISCO systems guesstimated that by 2025 IoT-enabled health applications or gadgets would consist of 50 billion devices that will be connected to the Internet directly. This growth would offer new insight into IoT's potential. IoT-enabled health devices are changing healthcare in multifaceted areas. Smart health devices are linked to worldwide information and communication networks that can be retrieved at all times and in all places (Leewayhertz.com, 2020). The IoT-enabled hospitals can keep tabs on the health gadgets of patients and individuals. IoT-enabled health systems and their relevancies contain many other systems such as Artificial Intelligence, cloud computing, Machine learning, grid computing, and big data, linked networks, and other wearable technologies. IoT-enabled gadgets augment competency by minimizing treatment costs and also offer new insights into patient care (Zerone-consulting.com, 2020).

2.3 IoT-Enabled Technologies and Medical Devices

The IoT-enabled technologies have helped a lot to the health sector by offering health services even in remote places, particularly the place where the hospitals, doctors, or related service providers are not available or approachable. Entrenched medical or health devices decrease the time taken for diagnosing the diseases and provide care for more patients in less time, as this technology works with high speed, and it also has alarms for reminding the healthcare staff about the end of the process through the multifaceted operating system interface (Biospectrumindia.com, 2020). Entrenched health devices are operating along with the hardware to the number of diseases taken for inspection. Most health devices are coming up with a touchscreen interface for particular users to enter the data for processing and testing. Further, these systems can process a large number of files, any number of users feed the data into the system, and it compares and correlates those data automatically based on the various signs existing on the file, and the same compare with the input again. It is a kind of way through which the device reacts to the data and thus suggests the actions that need to be done for a disease. This is how the IoT-enabled technologies are working on health devices (DCHS, 2019).

2.4 IoT and its Potential Transformations in Healthcare

The application of IoT in the health sector is transforming it massively by making the treatment cost cheaper and making available the health devices handier. Further, it makes it easier to supervise the patients all 24 hours with and without the presence of the healthcare staff. As a result, several companies have started to focus on the manufacturing of IoT-enabled digital health gadgets and to provide patient care, by using smart mobile devices, wearable, and other digital gadgets (Sermakan, 2014). By these technologies, healthcare service providers may access data in real-time and thus it may improve the healthcare conditions by providing exact treatments. With the help of IoT, healthcare staffs feel easy and convenient as this technology helps to gather and incorporate data from these gadgets resulting in swift and enhanced services to the patients. Apart from the patient's care, hospital or sanatorium administration is yet another area where this IoT is contributing a lot by putting into practice. The IoT-enabled solutions are more useful for handling the medical equipment with the cloud technology and by collecting the concurrent data of that equipment. Thus, this technology enhances the capabilities of hospitals by the optimum utilization of the available equipment to provide sufficient care when necessary. As a result, this technology is operating with the intelligence to detain and analyze data, which was not possible previously, and it offers new insights into earlier untreatable diseases and also makes the possibility of full-fledged as well as customized health services. Apart from these, the IoT has also been transforming the health sector in the following ways (Sermakan, 2014).

2.4.1 Continuous Monitoring of Hospital Routines

IoT-enabled devices will continuously monitor, gather, and transmit various health data such as blood pressure, sugar level, and Electro Cardio Grams (ECGs). In this way, this technology helps to supply these data to patients, medical staff, medical labs, and insurance companies wherever necessary without considering the time and place. It is also ensuring 24×7 real-time monitoring of the patients during various emergencies such as breathing troubles, diabetes, heart attack, asthma, etc. In such times, the IoT-enabled medical gadgets help to determine and observe the data in real-time. It also ensures personalized care for the patients, based on their health conditions, and thereby it also recommends best suit medicinal solutions. Further, this technology also averts the diseases likely to happen and treats well the present ones. Thus, IoT technology will segregate each health issue carefully and accurately to identify the best solution in the health science sector (OpenSystems Media, 2019).

2.4.2 Safety and Adherence Tools

Patients safety is the prime concern of the health sector, particularly while dealing with patient's health data such as blood test reports, maximum security should be given. This is a major challenging task for the medical staff principally for the multispecialty hospitals. IoT-enabled devices are available at low cost along with cutting-edge technology to observe the activities every day. Thus, both doctors and patients can track and contact each other for instant support such as dispensing medicines to the patients whenever required. Billions of IoT-enabled health gadgets and sensors are available in the health science market, and thus it ensures well-personalized services to the patients ever before (OpenSystems Media, 2019).

2.4.3 Quality, Compliance, and Monitoring

IoT in the health sector helps to reduce the treatment cost, augment patients' safety, and enhanced data collection techniques, more trustworthy examination of data, and extraordinary and immediate patient–doctor consultation and response. Through these ways, more benefits are available to the patients ranging from first-class patient care to instantaneous data collection and analysis, and proper updations in the patients' health files or the reports.

2.4.4 Closed-Loop Diagnosis for Treatment

Due to the availability of IoT-enabled technologies, patients can contact and communicate with the medical staff seamlessly, irrespective of time and place, as this technology keeps on recording the patients' real-time data in the hospital records. Thus, it ensures enhanced health checkups and distributes suitable medicine, and drugs according to the patients' health condition. Though it is a low-cost technology it enables cost-effective treatments through monitoring patients' health remotely along with proficient diagnosis, and thus improves the quality of life of the patients (Zerone-consulting.com, 2020).

2.4.5 Real-World Data and Environments

IoT-powered healthcare gadgets are sharing patients' data to the cloud servers directly through a secure service layer (SSL). It is not possible to collect, store, and process a huge volume of data manually and it is a tough task too. But the IoT-enabled devices are doing these tasks by collecting and analyzing the raw data, with the potential to prepare the final reports along with pictorial representation like charts, and graphs. In this way, IoT technology provides essential health information, and thereby it comes up with up-to-date conclusions to take appropriate decisions with a minimum of error as much as possible.

2.4.6 Digital Biomarkers to Capture Disease Symptoms

Being alert is an important one during health emergencies, but sometimes it may not happen. In such times IoT-enabled devices such as smartwatches, smart bands, and smart rings conveying real-time data to medical staff or doctors by observing the symptoms so that the medical staff can diagnose the problems thoroughly and prescribes medicines for the same. This can also aid in monitoring the dangerous chronic disease like COVID-19, and considerate significant determinants in health, and providing a reliable and accurate health report (Medicaldevice-network.com, 2020).

2.5 IoT and Its Advantages to the Health Sector

IoT has changed the outlook of the health sector with its powered devices by accommodating those with the healthcare network and ensures utmost patients care with a higher standard. The application of IoT in health sectors allows for the automation of health services that have earlier taken time and human error. At the present time, many hospitals use attached devices to manage the airflow, trips level, and hotness in operating theatres. Thus, the benefits of IoT in health sectors are never-ending, but here's just a small number of the benefits are as follows.

2.5.1 Cancer Treatment

IoT-powered gadgets have been helping a lot of cancer patients, and it has proved through a clinical trial was conducted by the American Society of Clinical Oncology (ASCO), 2017, randomly with 300 patients who suffered head and neck cancer and have undergone treatment for the same. In that clinical trial, blood-pressure cuff and Bluetooth enabled scale for measuring weight along with an application for following symptoms. Through these smart monitoring devices such as CYCORE, they could identify the cancer symptoms easily while evaluating the patients who are consulting the doctor every week. Through this analysis, the report concluded that IoT-enabled smart technologies make simpler care for patients by examining the rising side-effects and rapidly and lessening the workload of the doctors and treatment cost for the patients.

2.5.2 Diabetes Management

IoT-enabled smart devices have to monitor the diabetic patients' glucose level at particular time intervals and these techno loges are called Continuous Glucose Monitors (CGM) that assist to provide appropriate treatment to patients. There are CGMs such as Freestyle Libre and Ever sense collect and send the data about the glucose level in the blood to various applications installed on different devices such as smartphones and smartwatches. In the same manner, there are devices to monitor the levels of Insulin through Insulin pens such as InPen, Esysta, and Gocap have the potential to record the insulin level, time, amount, and type of insulin used in a particular dose, and based on these details it recommends insulin injection with the correct type and on correct time. Followed by in 2014, a subsidiary unit of Google's parent company Alphabet called Verily also developed a smart contact lens to compute glucose from the tears, and it is helping a lot to more patients (Aniket, 2020).

2.5.3 Treatment of Asthma

IoT-powered smart devices ensure detailed insight by identifying the symptoms of asthmatic patients effectively and start treating them through smart inhalers technology greater than before. A company called Propeller Health is playing a major role in producing smart inhaling technology massively. This smart inhaler works with a sensor or Bluetooth-enabled technology that is coupled with the applications installed in Smartphones or smartwatches and these smart devices help people safeguard themselves from the diseases asthma and Chronic Obstructive Pulmonary Disease (COPD).

2.5.4 IoT in Mental Healthcare

World Health Organization (WHO) carried out a study worldwide on psychiatric patients in the year 2003, and the study found that more than 50% of the medicines have not been taken as per the prescription of the psychiatrist. To solve such issues the company named Proteus system has come up with pills that melt in the abdomen and generates small signs that are collected by the sensor-enabled technologies worn on the body. Numbers of trials have also been done on this process by providing medicines to treat a range of psychological illnesses. For assessing the cognitive disorder and to measure Major Depressive Disorder (MDD), a smart technology-enabled health platform has been developed by the joint efforts of Cognition Kit Limited and Takeda Pharmaceuticals, and it can be used through smartwatches. It was found through the technology found by these companies that a high level of conformity in the treatment of a lot of cognitive disorders and other psychological problems (Sheldon, 2020).

2.6 Challenges of IoT in Healthcare

Though the IoT-enabled smart devices provide lots of advantages to the health sector, it is not free from some of the challenges, and all these need to be checked thoroughly. Although the IoT technology is extremely resourceful and ground-breaking; but many technical problems are also being experienced among many parts of the world. Adaptation and maintenance of this technology is not so easy; thus, all such issues are needed to be resolved. Apart from these, the following are some of the challenges that exist with IoT (Intellectsoft.net, 2020).

2.6.1 Data Security and Privacy

Data security and privacy is the major problem of the IoT, as almost all IoT technologies collect real-time data many of them being deficient in adherence to data etiquettes and principles; there should be a proper code of conduct for dealing with the data. Further, there is also a lack of clarity regarding data possession and directive. Hence, the data accumulated in IoT-enabled gadgets are having the possibility to misuse and theft of data and it also leads to the data more inclined to cybercrimes that may hack from the stored devices to compromise patients' health data. This issue also leads to misuse of the patients' data for generating fake health claims and the conception of fake patient IDs for buying and selling drugs.

2.6.2 Integration of Multiple Devices and Protocols

The incorporation of various types of devices creates an impediment to the operational effectiveness of IoT in the health sector. Because the manufacturers of these devices have not followed the communication standards and protocols properly in many cases, there impedes the health sector. In some cases, it is found that each manufacturer has been following their manufacturing ecosystem of the IoT gadgets and these gadgets will not work with other gadgets manufactured by the competitors. In such a circumstance, there is no possibility for following the synchronization protocol that could be pursued for the aggregation of data. This uneven process sluggish downs the speed of data transfers and lessens the performance of IoT in healthcare.

2.6.3 Data Overload and Accuracy

Owing to the non-consistency of data and improper communication procedures, it is hard to collect the required data for imperative insights and investigation. As IoT devices collect billions of data, and it needs to be sorted in chunks for proper data analysis, with no congestion with clear-cut accuracy for better and enhanced outputs. Congestion of data may slow down the decision-making practice in the health sector over the long run period.

2.6.4 Investment

IoT-enabled technologies, although reduces the treatment cost and helps the patients, involve a higher amount of investment while developing healthcare applications. However, the costs are completely worth it if the IoT implementation solves a genuine problem.

2.6.5 Existence of Obsolete Software Infrastructure

Though ICT technologies are growing day-by-day, still many hospitals use obsolete IT systems, since the installation cost are high. It's a result there is no proper incorporation of IoT technologies. For that reason, hospitals should try to use the up-to-date healthcare facilities available recently. So that it can ensure world-class treatment with better healthcare ecosystems. Meantime, they should also grab the benefits of virtual health technologies along with Software Defined Networking (SDN), and Network Functions Virtualization (NFV), and superfast mobile networks such as Long-Term Evolution (LTE) or 5G.

2.7 Future of IoT in Healthcare

IoT-enabled devices in the health sector help to get better healthcare gadgets or services. It would also improve the applications used in the health sector, such as patient monitoring, disease diagnosing, telemedicine, medication administration and management, imaging, and general workflows in hospitals. Thus, it would create a new health ecosystem for treating various diseases. The application of IoT is not only helping for the health centers, but also for surgical units, health-related research centers, and even for various governmental institutions involved in the research. IoT technologies alone do not function in the health sector; they need to be integrated with some other related technologies so that the healthcare data can be transferred in a significant manner. For the congenial data transmission, IoT technologies should be incorporated with high-speed Internet technologies along with appropriate data security protocols. Moreover, the availability of 5G networks also helps to speed up the collection and mobility of data through the IoT in the health sector is in need. Artificial Intelligence (AI) generated solutions will help to identify the data leakages from the data collection gadgets (Pande, 2014). Big Data analytics approaches will also be using such AI algorithms to explore data in instantaneous and help to make significant decisions needed for healthcare. The latest technologies such as SDN and NFV will also help to minimize or avoid the obsolete ICT infrastructure in hospitals and ensure world-class healthcare facilities. IoT-enabled technologies have almost occupied all spheres of the health sector and helping to evolve further, and this development will keep on continue in the days to come. As a result, both the health sector and IoT will become indivisible, and completely it will transform the present health sector (BioSpectrum Bureau, 2015).

2.8 Conclusions and Future Scope

As mentioned in this chapter, all the IoT-enabled applications will work flawlessly with device-to-device and human-to-device interaction. This type of interaction is an advantage for the health sector, wherever the health manipulating factors both inner and outer to the human body can be examined effectively. These technologies along with the genetic inputs will make it promising to forecast the health conditions and allergies of a man or woman; thereby these technologies can offer personalized advices on appropriate bodily activities, diets, etc. Thus, the role played by the IoT technologies in transforming the health sector cannot be destabilized or unfasten. The advancements of this technology have replaced the old systems and their process with continuous innovation. This technology has almost occupied society too at each stage of its progress. Industry 4.0 and its platforms have created a route through IoT-enabled technologies, which would generate new boulevards and create a brunt on a global level. Further, the IoT-enabled applications are designed not to replace the doctors, but to work together with the doctor. In this move toward complement the doctor with the new technology-enabled inputs, accordingly the new trends in IoT have the ability to transform the way the healthcare service is provided to the patients. On the other hand, for the developing world, IoT-enabled health devices bring modernized health services with high-quality at a reasonable cost. Proposal of IoT-enabled health devices for the growing human races is far-flung consulting, handheld analytical devices for identifying pandemics such as COVID, malaria, and cholera. These IoT-enabled devices shall have the extreme and wider reach compared to the conventional healthcare methods. It is evident that IoT-enabled devices will make new healthcare service delivery models in the future for all the problems prevailing at present, and all the world irrespective of developing and developed.

References

Aniket. (2020, April, 17). The role of IoT in healthcare: Applications and implementation. *finoit.com*. https://www.finoit.com/blog/the-role-of-iot-in-healthcare-space

Bio Spectrum Bureau. (2015, April, 15). Transforming healthcare through IoT. *biospectrumindia.com*. https://www.biospectrumindia.com/features/75/6863/transforming-healthcare-through-iot.html

Biospectrumindia.com. (2020, April, 29).Transforming healthcare through IoT. *biospectrumindia.com*. https://biospectrumindia.com/features/75/6863/transforming-healthcare-through-iot.html

Deloitte Centre for Health Solutions. (2019, April, 29). Medtech and the Internet of Medical Things how connected medical devices are transforming health care. *deloitte.com*.https://www.deloitte.com/global/en/pages/life-sciences-and-healthcare/articles/medtech-Internet-of-medical-things.html

Forgan, Ben. (2021, April, 26). How IoT is transforming healthcare. *forbes.com*. https://www.forbes.com/sites/forbestechcouncil/2021/03/31/how-iot-is-transforming-healthcare/?sh=3331f63e67e5

Intellectsoft.net. (2020, April, 19). IoT in healthcare: Benefits, use cases, challenges, and future. https://www.intellectsoft.net/blog/iot-in-healthcare/

Leewayhertz.com. (2020, May, 12).How IoT is transforming healthcare. *leewayhertz.com*. https://www.leewayhertz.com/how-iot-transforming-healthcare/

Matthews, Kayla. (2019April, 29). 6 exciting IoT use cases in healthcare. *iotforall.com*. https://www.iotforall.com/exciting-iot-use-cases-in-healthcare

Medicaldevice-network.com. (2020, April, 17). Bringing the Internet of Things to healthcare. https://www.medicaldevice-network.com/comment/bringing-Internet-things-healthcare/

Open Systems Media. (2019, May 21). How IoT is transforming healthcare. *embeddedcomputing.com*. https://www.embeddedcomputing.com/application/healthcare/how-iot-is-transforming-healthcare

Pande, Prajakta. (2014). Internet of Things - A future of Internet: A survey. *International Journal of Advance Research in Computer Science and Management Studies*, 2, pp.18–24.

Philips. (2019, April, 27). Five ways in which the Internet of Five ways in which the Internet of Five ways in which the Internet of Things is transforming healthcare. *philips.com*. https://www.philips.com/a-w/about/news/archive/blogs/innovation-matters/20191107-five-ways-in-which-the-Internet-of-things-is-transforming-hea

Sermakan, Vijayakannan. (2014, April, 29). Transforming healthcare through Internet of Things. *pmibangalorechapter.in*. https://pmibangalorechapter.in/pmpc/2014/tech_papers/healthcare.pdf

Sheldon, Amyra. (2020, April, 19). IoT in healthcare: Benefits, challenges and applications. *valuecoders.com*. https://www.valuecoders.com/blog/technology-and-apps/iot-in-healthcare-benefits-challenges-and-applications/

Shockloss, Wayne. (2021, April, 29). The Internet of Medical Things is transforming healthcare and creating opportunity. *connectorsupplier.com*. https://www.connectorsupplier.com/the-Internet-of-medical-things-is-transforming-healthcare-and-creating-opportunity/

Shrimali, Rahil. (2021, April, 29). How IoT is transforming the healthcare industry. *mbeddedcomputing.com*. https://www.embeddedcomputing.com/application/healthcare/telehealth-healthcare-iot/how-iot-is-transforming-the-healthcare-industry

Umanenko, Anna. (2020, April, 28). How Internet of Things is transforming healthcare. *Onix-systems.com*. https://onix-systems.com/blog/Internet-of-things-in-healthcare

Zerone-consulting.com. (2020, May, 12). How IoT is shaping the future of the healthcare industry. *Zerone-consulting.com*. https://www.zerone-consulting.com/wp-content/uploads/2020/02/White-paper-How-IoT-is-shaping-the-future-of-the-healthcare-industry.pdf

3

IoT Motivated Cyber-Physical and Industrial Internet Systems

Saurabh Kumar and Nainsi Soni

The LNM Institute of Information Technology, Jaipur, India

CONTENTS

3.1 Introduction

In the past few decades, a continuous evolution of industrial processes has been observed. Industrial processes may be understood as the use of chemical, physical, electrical, or mechanical ways to help in the manufacturing of intended products (Metzger & Polakow, 2011). In addition to this, the production must be done on an enormous scale. For example, by observing the evolution of computer systems with respect to the invention of transistors, the size of computers is reduced significantly. The transistors helped in the manufacturing of an integrated circuit (IC) on a vast scale. In fact, it has evolved in stages from Large Scale Integration (LSI) during the early 1970s, Very Large-Scale Integration (VLSI) during the early 1980s, and Super Large-Scale Integration (SLSI) in the present time, wherein billions of components are added on a single chip during the manufacturing process (Er, 1990). Moreover, in the current scenario, the industrial processes need real-time data processing to be performed to generate the instructions that can be dispensed further to increase

DOI: 10.1201/9781003213888-3

production while maintaining its quality. In this regard, the introduction of computing has played a significant role in improving production in industrial processes.

The current generation of computing needs to explore intelligence in its implementation (Satapathy et al., 2018). The intellect can be achieved through the cooperative efforts by the different intelligent devices. Data processing for real-time applications in the current scenario requires intelligence to be explored in terms of autonomy, gradual learning, and prompt response to the various services (Kumar et al., 2020). In this context, ambient intelligence serves as an emerging discipline and aims to bring intelligence to our daily life activities. The research in ambient intelligence focuses on the use of sensor networks, pervasive computing, and artificial intelligence (Ray, 2016). The sensor networks provide an environment for the heterogeneous sensor devices to work cooperatively to sense and communicate the sensed parameter to its intended location. With the evolving role of data in the current generation applications and the distribution of devices at different locations, it becomes a critical challenge to acquire data from these devices deployed anywhere throughout the terrain. Due to the profound use of devices by the end-users worldwide, there is a need to minimize the user's interaction with the computers and maximize the interaction of one device to another. Thus, the concept of pervasive computing evolved, which addresses the growing trend of embedding computational capability into the objects to communicate effectively to achieve ubiquity (Satyanarayanan, 2001). Thus, pervasive computing helps to realize the potential of Machine-to-Machine (M2M) communication to build an autonomous environment (Wu et al., 2011). The autonomous environment requires the machines to perform their operations without any human intervention. Therefore, there is a need to implement learning on these autonomous devices, which can be explored using Artificial Intelligence (AI) (Dunne et al., 2021).

In the context of AI, the devices are modeled as intelligent agents. These agents are distributed throughout the terrain and perform three essential operations: *sensing, actuation,* and *communication* of the sensed events in the network. These three operations are performed in the environment wherein the devices are deployed. Furthermore, the cyber-physical system (CPS) effectively utilizes the data and information from the deployed agents to integrate the computing, networking, and physical processes, and thus, realizing the vision of ambient intelligence (Rajkumar et al., 2010). The realization of ambient intelligence is crucial for the continuous improvement of industrial processes, especially in the current context wherein, real-time service delivery from anywhere and at any time is a crucial challenge.

The real-time service delivery can be achieved by efficient communication among the cyber-physical devices operating in the network. In this context, the Internet of Things (IoT) evolution has provided a platform that supports communication using IP-based protocol (Pandey & Zaveri, 2018). Since the Internet is accessible worldwide and it has been getting cheaper over some time, communication from anywhere, at any place, by any device, and at anytime is made possible using the IoT. Furthermore, Internet usage has been helping human beings during their day-to-day activities and providing a platform for the industries to grow by implementing the automated manufacturing, delivery, and management of industrial operations.

In the last 300 years, there have been different industrial revolutions (Lasi et al., 2014) observed around the world, which have provided different unique materials and affected the lives of human beings by revolutionizing the work processes and ethics. In this context, the recently introduced fourth industrial revolution focuses on using the Internet and CPS to automate industrial operations so as to increase the output with optimized cost. Moreover, IoT plays a crucial role in industrial processes by integrating the cyber-physical devices with the communication and computation essentials for optimizing the operations in the industries. However, the different entities of the IoT environment must cater to the fundamental challenges, such as heterogeneity, interoperability, power constraints, and real-time communication even in the presence of mobility in the network, robustness, and scalability (Pandey & Zaveri, 2016). In addition to this, the requirements from M2M communication and associated technologies are evolving at a faster rate throughout the world. Thus, there is a need to address the globalization and emerging issues for Industry 4.0 and their significance in achieving ambient intelligence by virtue of AI and IoT.

This chapter introduces ambient intelligence by sensing and actuation technology and the role of agents in communication and networking to realize the vision of a smart world. The role of CPS and next-generation sensors in the field of Industry 4.0 are also discussed in terms of the role of IoT and the challenges associated with their implementation. Further, the significance of IoT in Industry 4.0 is discussed with respect to the business model and reference architectures for lean production systems and their relevance to creating a collaborative platform in achieving improved product lifecycle management. Lastly, unmanned vehicles are becoming a pillar in factory automation and process automation. Thus, the chapter provides a brief discussion on the application of unmanned vehicles in industries to achieve the vision of ambient intelligence using the IoT environment.

3.2 Ambient Intelligence

In the current scenario, the automation of industrial processes requires that the process of data acquisition, data processing, and data communication must be responsive and sensitive to real-time constraints (Robinson et al., 2015). In this regard, the basic building block of ambient intelligence uses the concepts of pervasive computing (Saha & Mukherjee, 2003), ubiquitous computing (Lyytinen & Yoo, 2002), profiling, context awareness (Perera et al., 2013), and human-centric computing. Although the services must be delivered in real-time, these services must adhere to the characteristics such as the level of embedded design, recognition of situational context, tailored to the customers' needs, adaptive, and anticipatory. To realize these characteristics and constraints, the use of deployed devices for achieving intelligence in an M2M environment must be explored. In (Wooldridge, 1999), the devices are modeled to act as the agents for the purpose of sensing and actuation on the environment in which they are operational. The sensors are responsible for perceiving the different parameters from the environment and process them using specific rules and conditions. It results in the set of actions to be performed by the actuators on the environment. For example, in an office, the sensor device can continuously sense the room temperature during the summer season and passes these values in real-time. These values can be used to formularize the actuation conditions based on the threshold value available with the system. If the sensed value is more than the threshold, the air conditioning can be turned on by the actuator, and thus, the automation of process can be performed. The authors in Russell and Norvig (2002) have classified these agents into simple reflex, model-based reflex, goal-based, utility-based, and learning agents on the basis of the complexity of goals. The key components of this whole process are sensors and actuators.

3.2.1 Sensors

In the past two decades, there has been a lot of research done in the fields of sensing and actuation. All these researches focused on the utilization of the sensor and actuator devices in different areas. However, it is found that an efficient operation can result in improvement of the accuracy of these devices in real-time conditions. In this context, the development of these devices must be supported by an underlying understanding of both the sensor and actuator devices at the hardware level.

A sensor device is responsible to detect the presence of a particular physical quantity in the region wherein it is deployed (Kubrusly & Malebranche, 1985). These physical parameters can be temperature, pressure, humidity, gas, pollution level, sound, motion, fire, etc. The performance of a sensor device depends on two essential characteristics: *static* and *dynamic*. The static characteristics describe the change of output with respect to the change in the input to the device. Some of the static characteristics of the sensor devices include accuracy, range, resolution, error, sensitivity, linearity, drift, and repeatability. Similarly, the dynamic characteristics of a sensor device evaluate its transient response with respect to the change in its input. It can be categorized as the zero-order system (response to the input signal with no delay), first-order system (output reaches its final value gradually), and second-order system (generates complex output responses).

The sensor devices can be classified as either passive and active, analog and digital, or scalar and vector. The *passive* sensor cannot independently sense the input. Some examples of passive sensors include accelerometer, soil moisture, water level, and temperature sensors. Similarly, the *active* sensor can independently sense the inputs, for instance, in the cases of radar and sonar. In the case of an *analog* sensor, the response is a continuous function of its input parameters, while in a *digital* sensor, responses are recorded in binary form, and it consists of extra circuitry for the conversion of bits. Lastly, the *scalar* sensor detects the input parameters on the basis of the magnitude only, as observed in the cases of temperature, gas, strain, color, and smoke. On the other hand, the response of a *vector* sensor depends on the magnitude, direction, and orientation of the input parameters, such as that in accelerometer, gyroscope, magnetic field, and motion detection sensors.

3.2.2 Actuators

An actuator can be considered as the part of an intelligent agent that deals with the mechanical action required to fulfill the requirements of the environment (Le et al., 2016). An actuator needs the energy and signals to generate a response, in the form of motion or force, on the environment. The control signal acts as an input to the actuator, and the energy source is used to keep it running to carry out the operation. Some of the examples of actuators include, but are not limited to, electric motor, hydraulic cylinder, piezoelectric actuator, pneumatic actuator, etc. Based on the motion and energy source required for actuation, an actuator can be classified as electric linear, electric rotary, fluid power linear, fluid power rotary, linear chain, manual linear, and manual rotary actuators (Le et al., 2016). Once the sensor and actuator devices are deployed in the terrain, they provide a foundation of the critical infrastructure needed to form the basis of a smart world. This will further help achieve intelligence by implementing a learning platform that supports these devices through networked components known as cyber-physical space, as discussed in the following section.

3.3 Cyber-Physical System

In the current scenario, the automation of industrial processes requires effective communication among the heterogeneous devices deployed for shop-floor activities. The basic idea is to build an environment where all the devices, whether sensor or actuator, co-exist and provide an efficient response for the effective utilization of resources in product development. The most crucial aspect in industrial operations is to generate the solutions timely and support the dynamically changing environmental conditions. In this context, the CPS provides a platform to support ubiquitous computing among the heterogeneous entities responsible for carrying out different activities in the industries and pervasively monitor the flow of data and information, irrespective of the location of these entities (Wolf, 2009).

The CPS can be understood as a system that consists of physical devices connected with each other using the Internet. The CPS can also be understood as the generalization of embedded systems such that they possess compute, communicate and control capabilities while interacting with the physical world through sensors and actuators. Some of the areas where CPS can be utilized are, but are not limited to, medical instrumentation, transportation vehicles, defense systems, robotic equipment, industrial process monitoring, and factory automation system (Wolf, 2009).

As shown in Figure 3.1, the architecture of CPS consists of three domains: *physical space*, *network space*, and *cyberspace* (Rajkumar et al., 2010). The physical space maps the object domain to the real space. The real space consists of all the objects around us that can be seen and need monitoring. Some of the objects in real space include, but are not limited to, human beings, houses, factories, transportation vehicles, etc. The object domain consists of devices such as mobile phones, cameras, microwave ovens, washing machines, refrigerators, wireless devices, etc. These devices either need to be controlled or used to monitor and control the objects kept in the real space. Similarly, the network space consists of all the networking devices used to connect the devices in the object domain with the network. The network devices may include routers, switches, hubs, wireless access points, etc. Once the devices are connected to the network, the cyberspace provides the communication platform among these devices. As the name suggests, the cyberspace provides Internet

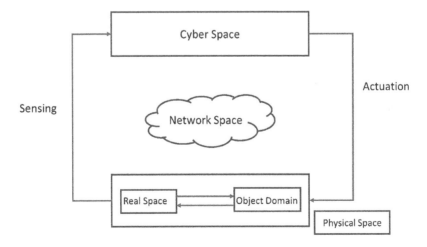

FIGURE 3.1
Architecture of cyber-physical systems (Saha & Mukherjee, 2003).

connectivity to the devices so that they can communicate among themselves. The cyber-space also consists of the servers responsible for receiving the sensed information from the devices in the physical space. These high-end servers are responsible for generating the action plan on the physical space, and thus, helps in the actuation operation.

Although the CPS utilizes smart communication among the devices, it is different than the embedded systems (Rajkumar et al., 2010). First, the embedded devices have information processing systems embedded into them, whereas the CPS is a complete system having physical components and software. Second, the embedded system is usually confined to a single device, while CPS is a networked set of embedded systems. Third, the embedded system suffers from limited resources for performing a limited number of tasks, while the CPS is not resource-constrained. Finally, the embedded systems have main issues related to real-time response and reliability, whereas the main issues in a CPS are timing and concurrency.

Certain features of CPS help in effective utilization of the resources to improve communication and computation capability among heterogeneous devices (Marwedel, 2021). The first among them is that the CPS offers reactive computation, which entails the interaction with the environment in an ongoing manner for the sequence of observed inputs and outputs at a particular instant of time. Second, the CPS supports concurrency among the multiple processes that exchange the information to achieve the desired result using both the synchronous and asynchronous modes of operation. Third, the CPS is equipped with control systems with a feedback loop. This helps the intelligent agents in recognizing the gap between the set of actions implemented and how much near those actions have taken the environment to the goal. Fourth, the real-time computation is also supported by the CPS so that the time-sensitive autonomous operations such as coordination and resource allocation can be performed among the devices effectively. Finally, the CPS help develop a precise model and validate the designed model prior to the actual development, which helps produce the safety-critical applications. Although the CPS have the potential to build an environment where the processing can be performed for heterogeneous applications with their respective requirements, the most crucial aspect of such systems is the utilization of sensors and their level of intelligence, as discussed in the following section.

3.4 Next-Generation Sensors

In the previous discussion, the role of ambient intelligence is identified in a smart world while focusing on the usage of CPS to achieve the same. However, there is a need to improve the potential of sensor devices which are an integral part of such systems, and forms the basic building block to achieve the efficiency of these systems. Thus, there is a need to improve the inherent accuracy of these sensor devices to cater to the real-time sensing and communication requirements in a smart environment. In this context, it must be understood that the characteristics of the sensor devices differ for different manufacturers. Thus, there is a need for interoperability of networks, transducers, and control systems of these heterogeneous devices. It adds to the need for compatibility of sensors with multiple bus standards, which helps in the reduction of wiring cost and complexity of physical connection among the components present in these devices. Moreover, with time, the digital networks have evolved wherein the analog transducers exist and operate for different services. The interconnection of these analog transducers with the evolving digital networks must be established for efficient communication at the physical layer. The reasons mentioned above outline the need for next-generation sensor devices to be built, which offer better services than the existing sensor devices.

Due to the increasing usage of existing networks, instead of proposing newer standards to build a smart environment, smart sensors play a crucial role. A smart sensor integrates sensors, actuators, processors, and the communication module on a single device. As defined in IEEE 1451 standard, *a smart sensor is the sensor with small memory and standardized physical connection to enable the communication with processor and data network in which it is operating* (K. Lee, 2000). Some of the key functionalities provided by these sensors include self-calibration, communication, computation, multi-sensing, and cost improvement. However, the smart sensors suffer from certain limitations such as the problem with customization due to pre-defined embedded functions, it works with narrow application spectrum, difficulty to perform sensor data acquisition, need of external processor to perform sensor calibration, and the use of basic communication protocols which are either not suitable or suitable with limited scope in the current real-time networking. To overcome these limitations and challenges, the next-generation sensors are evolved.

As shown in Figure 3.2, the intelligent sensors, also known as next-generation sensors, can process the sensed data to perform pre-defined functions by processing data. It provides the feature to customize the embedded algorithms in on-the-fly mode (Yurish, 2010). It is also capable of managing and controlling the operations of external sensors or other devices. Generally, an intelligent sensor consists of a sensor, a microcontroller, a memory unit with flash memory, RAM and ROM, and a platform that helps run the sensor applications. Some of the key advantages of using the intelligent sensors include, but are not limited to, optimized data communication, reduced power consumption, the customization of sensor nodes specific to the intended applications, a way to continuously calibrate and monitor the working on the sensors, adaptive sampling rate and sleep-wake cycles, use of a shorter software development time, and the improved compatibility and interoperability of sensors to cater to the different application needs (K. Lee, 2000).

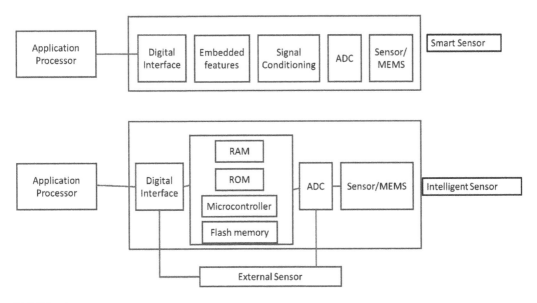

FIGURE 3.2
Architectures of smart sensor and intelligent sensor (K. Lee, 2000; Yurish, 2010).

3.5 Industrial Internet of Things

In the last few years, the Industrial Internet of Things (IIoT) has evolved as one of the pillars of current generation smart industrial operations (Kumar et al., 2020). The industrial processes, in the current generation, need to improve upon their operational efficiency by the virtue of advanced analytics, ubiquitous operation, and utilization of effective tools and methodologies offered by Information Technology (IT) (Lyytinen & Yoo, 2002). The Internet of Things (IoT) provides an environment wherein the heterogeneous devices, irrespective of whether they are sensor or IoT devices, support the communication and computation essentials by getting connected among themselves always using the Internet. This has helped improve upon the applications where the data can be acquired, processed, and actuated upon from anywhere, instant, and with increasing speed and accuracy.

Industrial IoT can be considered as a branch of IoT and utilizes the application of IoT in the fields of manufacturing, logistics, marketing, production and other industrial processes with the goal to enhance the working conditions, increase machine life, and optimize operational efficiency (Cheng et al., 2018). Although the IIoT is one of the key enablers associated with automation, it is quite different from automation utilized in the industries for a few decades. IIoT focuses on ubiquitous sensing to help in advanced data analytics using the current generation IT tools and methodologies. In the traditional automation process, the sensors and actuators are used to monitor and control the critical industrial elements, whereas IIoT utilizes sensors and actuators everywhere to control, enhance, and optimize the various industrial operations such as monitoring machine health, track various operations, emergency systems, etc. Ubiquitous sensing acts as an enabler of advanced analytics. There are some overall benefits of implementing the IIoT-based solutions, such as improved connectivity among the deployed devices, which helps in improving operational efficiency. In turn, the productivity gets improved, optimized asset utilization, creation of new jobs and business opportunities, reduced time of operation, remote diagnosis, generation of a cost-effective solution, and customer-oriented production.

3.5.1 Industrial Internet System

The term *Industrial Internet* was coined by General Electric (GE), which is considered as one of the leading industrial giants of the world. Although IIoT is not the same as Industrial Internet, they are often used interchangeably (Sisinni et al., 2018). The Industrial Internet Consortium (IIC) is a considerable contributor in shaping the future of the IIoT (Serpanos & Wolf, 2018). According to IIC, the industrial revolution has evolved at three different levels, i.e., the industrial revolution, the Internet revolution, and the industrial Internet. The industrial revolution began during the mid-1700s and ended in the early 1900s. It had two stages. The first stage started when the steam engine was invented, which marked the commercialization and mass production of steam engines during the mid of 18th century. The second stage is considered the more powerful with the invention of the internal combustion engine and electricity, which helped bring about new ways of communication and new forms of transportation systems. There was a significant growth observed in the economy due to the industrial revolution. However, harmful waste products, bad working environment, and inefficiency in the production environment has affected this phase of the revolution to a larger extent.

The Internet revolution started during the 1950s with the gradual need for networking among the computers observed by the researchers. This resulted in the rapid information exchange among computers situated anywhere worldwide, especially with the emergence of the World Wide Web (WWW) in the 1990s, thus improving the computing capacity of these devices. On the other hand, the industrial Internet has focused on the integration of Internet-based technologies and solutions for industrial operations and processes. IIC defines industrial Internet as *the association of the global industrial system with low-cost sensing, interconnectivity through Internet, and high-level computing and analytics* (Serpanos & Wolf, 2018). *Intelligent machines*, *advanced analytics*, and *people-at-work* are the three key elements of industrial Internet. The intelligent machines try to connect and control different devices located at varied places using sensors, actuators, and advanced IT software platforms. Since the number of devices is increasing exponentially during the last decade, a huge amount of data generation is observed. This has led to the need for advanced analytic operations to be performed on these data to generate predictive algorithms to solve the problem-at-hand and in proactive way. Similarly, the people at work are interconnected, and thus, can monitor the machines with more flexibility and quality.

The industrial Internet has observed innovation in terms of the equipment used for production, analytical ability of the software solutions, profound usage of the ubiquitous platform, and improved business processes. Also, infrastructure improvement has helped the industries to grow at a faster rate. In summary, the industrial Internet has many benefits, and it promises to provide a cost-effective solution that can be implemented and used with ease in the industries. However, it needs a little innovation, capital and concrete platform to realize in the current context of industrial operations.

3.5.2 Industrial Sensing and Actuation

With reference to the implementation of IIoT for industries, the sensor serves as the primary or main source of data, whether used for acquisition or communication, at the different levels of operations. These data help develop intelligence using the IoT environment and support the heavy actuators in following the control decision autonomously. The need for sensing in the industries is outlined by the realization of a high degree of automation, the demand for an increase in productivity to cater to the population's needs worldwide, maintaining the quality of production with better safety, and reducing downtime hours during the process production. Since this field is a newer one and its associated technologies are also comparatively more recent, there is a need to standardize and upgrade the industrial standards. The standardization may be related to the communication protocol, hardware, network, data and information usage, and many more, which serves as a fundamental point from where the industries may move towards achieving the acceptability of the technological introduction in ever-changing industrial operations. Some of the benefits of standardization are reliable sensing, low-cost sensing and actuation, and perpetual sensor and actuator network connectivity.

There are two types of sensing required from the viewpoint of industries: *conventional sensing and contemporary sensing*(Kubrusly & Malebranche, 1985). Conventional sensing is involved in the feedback automation of a process in the industrial control systems wherein, based on the sensing or feedback received, further actions are planned by considering the requirements of the applications at different timestamps. On the other hand, contemporary sensing addresses an environment where the sensors are connected with the Internet and participate in sensing product lifetime, loop inefficiency, safety, and reliability. Some examples of the use of industrial sensors are navigation tracking, which uses track sensors with GPS, agriculture industry, healthcare industry, retail industry, milk industry, etc. Some manufacturers of industrial level sensors are MOOG, SKF, KNR, FUYU, SPAT, SIRIUS Electric, Zaber, Eckart, among others.

For instance, consider the example of sensing in the milk packaging unit. The milk packaging unit needs some initial modifications, such as installing sensors in line with the outlet tap. The sensors contain impellers that spins when the milk moves and sends the electrical signals to the control unit. It is the responsibility of the control unit to interpret the amount of liquid flow and stops when a certain threshold (initially set) is reached. To provide such a mechanism, the supporting operating system must be lightweight, such as zephyr, ubuntu, openSUSE, ubilinux, arch Linux, android things. The programming languages which can be utilized to realize this application may be selected from, but not limited to, C, C++, Java, Python, Lua, etc. The sensors may use the Intel IoT libraries such as MRAA and UPM. The MRAA supports a better level of abstraction and is not hardware-specific. At the same time, UPM provides high-level APIs for more effortless connectivity to sensors with industrial-grade sensors' support. The innovation and profound usage of these intelligent devices have led towards the fourth industrial revolution in the digital world, as discussed in the following section.

3.6 Industry 4.0

A revolution can be defined as an instantaneous and complete shift. The first such shift occurred when people started moving from foraging to farming, resulting in the growth in food production, better transportation, and population growth. Similarly, the industrial revolution marks the development of newer technologies and approaches, which has helped improve economic models and social architectures for improved living index. The first industrial revolution observed the invention of the steam engine, which resulted in the utilization of machines in production. The second industrial revolution marked the invention of electricity and its implementation on the assembly lines in factories, which resulted in the improvement in mass production. The third industrial revolution is also known as the digital revolution. In this revolution, computers were evolved, and semiconductor devices were involved, reducing the size of personal computers. Currently, the fourth industrial revolution is in progress worldwide.

The fourth industrial revolution started in the 21st century and proposed to be revolving around the extensive use of ubiquitous computing and mobile Internet. During this revolution, the sensor devices became cheaper, the size of computing devices is getting reduced continuously, and computation powers getting improved (Davis et al., 2015). The fourth revolution focuses on the use of AI, machine learning, and CPS to revolutionize the digital world by producing more sophisticated and integrated computers. This has resulted in the radical transformation of societies and global economies. Industry 4.0, used synonymously with the fourth industrial revolution, was coined in Hannover Fair in 2011 by Brynjolfsson and McAfee (Lasi et al., 2014) and is regarded as the *second machine age*. It is considered to change the manufacturing process at large. The scope of this revolution covers intelligent connected machines, smart factories, gene sequencing, nanotechnology, renewables, and quantum computing. The focus is not only to bring the speed of profound change, but the scale of profound change needs to be dealt with as well. To do this, the designers must focus on exploring and combining computational design, additive manufacturing, material engineering, and synthetic biology to produce mutable and adaptable objects with dynamically changing real-life situations.

There are two drivers of the fourth industrial revolution: *megatrends* whose focus is on the current phase and *tippling points* whose focus is on future phases (Dalenogare et al., 2018). These two drivers of revolution depend on scientific inventions and evolving newer technologies. To pervasively utilize the potential of digitization and information technologies, the megatrends can be understood in different categories: *physical*, *digital*, and *biological*. The physical megatrends discuss the applications of autonomous vehicles, 3D printers, advanced robotics, and other new materials such as thermoset plastic and graphene and their utilization to improve productivity. Similarly, the digital megatrend deals with the introduction of IoT and its utilization in industries for real-time package tracking and monitoring systems to improve complex supply chain management. The biological megatrend focuses on research in genetic sequencing, DNA writing, recommender systems, cell modification, and genetic engineering as modeled in the case of CRISPER (Damian & Porteus, 2013), which is developed to be used as the bacterial defense system. The industries such as IBM Watson, Tesla, GE, etc., are working on realizing this vision. Similarly, the tipping points represent the proposed changes to be required in the near future, such as connecting the clothes with Internet, unlimited and free storage options, robotic pharmacist, etc.

3.7 Case Studies

The two of the essential applications of implementing the current trends in Industry 4.0 are the lean production system (Dennis, 2017) and utilization of unmanned vehicles (Motlagh et al., 2017). The following sections present a case study on both these to understand their importance as drivers of automation in improving the industrial processes.

3.7.1 Lean Production System

One way to improve the industrial processes is to look upon customer-oriented production to cater to their needs and services in real-time. Toyota motor corporation developed a lean production system that focuses on finishing good inventories by eliminating wastes from processes involved in the production hierarchy to give more importance to the needs of the customers. While the other approaches look from the perspectives of a set of tasks and production requirements, the lean approach looks from the customers' perspective. Lean production system is established on two principles. First, whenever there is a problem, stop the production so as to stop producing the defectives. Second, each process involved is responsible for producing what is needed by the next process in a continuous flow so that the task outputs can be achieved just in time.

There are seven types of waste identified in the lean production system: transportation, waiting, motion, inventory, over-processing, defects, and over-production (Dennis, 2017). Transportation waste deals with the excessive movement of people for materials or information. The waiting period is the time of inactivity of people for material or information. The waste concerned with motion revolves around the non-value-added movement of people within the factory premises during the operation. Over-processing and over-production are two of the most dangerous wastes which hinder the goal of optimized production. There is a need to continuously monitor the defects produced during production tenure in terms of products and paper works and need to be minimized. The identification of these wastes has helped to reduce these wastes to improve upon the production process.

The lean production in Industry 4.0 is concerned with the integration of humans in plant activities. This helps develop an automated system whose knowledge base is better with the evolving experiences of the employees involved in the process. Thus, it results in continuous improvement in the industrial processes. It provides a further chance to focus more on the value-added activities and less on the basic production module. The identification of wastes in these processes further eliminates the risks in production. The goal of the lean production system is to help in the production of the best quality products at lower cost and in the shortest lead time possible. Thus, the implementation of the lean production system mainly focuses on four main areas: *business requirements*, *operational movement*, *people management*, and *performance governance*(Dennis, 2017). For improving efficiency, the companies must implement the lean system by concerning the cost, time, and quality constraints. This will help to support the effectiveness of automation in industrial operations.

3.7.2 Unmanned Aerial Vehicles

An Unmanned Aerial Vehicle (UAV) is a device that supports the process of monitoring and communication of the monitored information while operating in on-the-fly mode (Motlagh et al., 2017). As part of the IoT environment, UAVs can be deployed to various locations. They can convey the adaptable payloads, measure the required data from these different locations, and are inherently programmable. The UAVs gather the measurements using IoT sensors, have an end-to-end wireless connection, communicate directly to an industrial control system, and take aerial images, videos of the factory stations and substations. Supervisory Control and Data Acquisition (SCADA) (Boyer, 2009) is considered as one example of industrial control system.

The technology of UAVs has evolved over a considerable period. There are seven generations of UAVs developed in the last few decades. Table 3.1 summarizes the features of each generation of UAVs (Boyle, 2015). It can be pointed out that the evolution of UAVs

TABLE 3.1

Generations of UAV Technologies (Boyle, 2015)

UAV Generation	Features
1st Generation	Fundamental remote-controlled UAVs of different forms
2nd Generation	Static design, fixed camera mount, still imagery, video recording, manual steering control
3rd Generation	Two-axis gimbals, essential safety models, HD video, assisted guiding
4th Generation	Transformable design, 1080 HD video, three-axis gimbals, improved safety modes, autopilot modes
5th Generation	360-degree gimbals, high-quality videos, improved piloting modes
6th Generation	Improved safety, platform and payload adaptability, automated safety modes, full autonomy, airspace awareness
7th Generation	Full autonomy, full awareness of airspace, automatic takeoff, landing, and execution of missions

started from fundamental remote control-based devices in the first generation to enhanced intelligent piloting models. It has provided full autonomy to these devices in terms of take-off, land, and mission execution by having full airspace awareness through advanced technologies in the current generation (Boyle, 2015).

The UAVs have broad application areas such as agriculture, construction sites, mining, energy management, telecommunication, delivery and healthcare, oil and gas industries, warehousing and inventory management, forestry, and entertainment (Pandey et al., 2018). In all these application areas, either the UAV devices are currently being utilized or in a phase of launch. This will meet the needs of both the customers and production systems. The application of UAVs in such areas is aligned with its significant advantages in terms of real-time input-processing, output functionality, support of low-cost camera platform, effectiveness to monitor progress, work and safety standards and reporting for inspections, safety in surveillance, its feature of on-demand deployment, comprehensive network coverage, efficient data collection without the issue of non-line of sight conditions, and it's potential to save time, manpower and resources.

3.8 Conclusion

Due to the gradual shift of focus of the production system from manual to automation, researchers worldwide are provided an opportunity to introduce the digitalization of the process for improved productivity in the industries. In this regard, there are some potential challenges such as manpower management, resource utilization, bridging the gap between the different generations of industrial processes, and at the same, maintaining the standards of production and product. This chapter discusses the role of the Internet in building an IoT environment that serves as a platform to embed ambient intelligence in the current industrial processes. It requires the modeling of various intelligent devices under the umbrella of CPS. Further, there is a discussion of industrial processes and the role of the Internet in realizing Industry 4.0. Finally, the chapter discusses the case studies of lean production systems and the application of UAVs in the industries. The ambient intelligence is the future of technological progress. The future scope of work in this field is multifold in terms of Industry 4.0. There is a need for in-depth research to build collaborative agents with embedded next-generation sensors and the Internet for collaborative communication, computation, and automation for real-time service delivery to support the intelligent industrial revolution.

References

Boyer, S. A. (2009). *SCADA: Supervisory control and data acquisition*. International Society of Automation.

Boyle, M. J. (2015). The race for drones. *Orbis, 59*(1), 76–94.

Cheng, J., Chen, W., Tao, F., & Lin, C.-L. (2018). Industrial IoT in 5G environment towards smart manufacturing. *Journal of Industrial Information Integration, 10*, 10–19.

Dalenogare, L. S., Benitez, G. B., Ayala, N. F., & Frank, A. G. (2018). The expected contribution of Industry 4.0 technologies for industrial performance. *International Journal of Production Economics, 204*, 383–394.

Damian, M., & Porteus, M. H. (2013). A crisper look at genome editing: RNA-guided genome modification. *Molecular Therapy, 21*(4), 720–722.

Davis, R., Sessions, B.-O., & Check, A. R. (2015). Industry 4.0. *Digitalisation for Productivity and Growth, European Parliament, Members' Research Service.*

Dennis, P. (2017). *Lean Production simplified: A plain-language guide to the world's most powerful production system.* CRC Press.

Dunne, R., Morris, T., & Harper, S. (2021). A Survey of Ambient Intelligence. *ACM Computing Surveys (CSUR), 54*(4), 1–27.

Er, M. C. (1990). The History of the Development of Information Technology and its Organizational and Societal Impact. *Journal of Information and Optimization Sciences, 11*(1), 113–143.

Kubrusly, C. S., & Malebranche, H. (1985). Sensors and controllers location in distributed systems—A survey. *Automatica, 21*(2), 117–128.

Kumar, J. S., Kumar, S., Choksi, M., & Zaveri, M. A. (2020). Collaborative data acquisition and processing for post disaster management and surveillance related tasks using UAV-based IoT cloud. *International Journal of Ad Hoc and Ubiquitous Computing, 34*(4), 216–232.

Lasi, H., Fettke, P., Kemper, H.-G., Feld, T., & Hoffmann, M. (2014). Industry 4.0. *Business & Information Systems Engineering, 6*(4), 239–242.

Le, H. M., Do, T. N., & Phee, S. J. (2016). A survey on actuators-driven surgical robots. *Sensors and Actuators A: Physical, 247*, 323–354.

Lee, K. (2000). IEEE 1451: A standard in support of smart transducer networking. *Proceedings of the 17th IEEE Instrumentation and Measurement Technology Conference [Cat. No. 00CH37066], 2*, 525–528.

Lyytinen, K., & Yoo, Y. (2002). Ubiquitous computing. *Communications of the ACM, 45*(12), 63–96.

Marwedel, P. (2021). *Embedded system design: Embedded systems foundations of cyber-physical systems, and the Internet of Things.* Springer Nature.

Metzger, M., & Polakow, G. (2011). A survey on applications of agent technology in industrial process control. *IEEE Transactions on Industrial Informatics, 7*(4), 570–581.

Motlagh, N. H., Bagaa, M., & Taleb, T. (2017). UAV-based IoT platform: A crowd surveillance use case. *IEEE Communications Magazine, 55*(2), 128–134.

Pandey, S. K., & Zaveri, M. A. (2016). Optimized deployment strategy for efficient utilization of the Internet of Things. *2016 IEEE International Conference on Advances in Electronics, Communication and Computer Technology (ICAECCT)*, 192–197.

Pandey, S. K., & Zaveri, M. A. (2018). Quasi random deployment and localization in layered framework for the Internet of Things. *The Computer Journal, 61*(2), 159–179.

Pandey, S. K., Zaveri, M. A., Choksi, M., & Kumar, J. S. (2018). UAV-based localization for layered framework of the Internet of Things. *Procedia Computer Science, 143*, 728–735.

Perera, C., Zaslavsky, A., Christen, P., & Georgakopoulos, D. (2013). Context aware computing for the Internet of Things: A survey. *IEEE Communications Surveys & Tutorials, 16*(1), 414–454.

Rajkumar, R., Lee, I., Sha, L., & Stankovic, J. (2010). Cyber-physical systems: The next computing revolution. *Design Automation Conference*, 731–736.

Ray, P. P. (2016). A survey of IoT cloud platforms. *Future Computing and Informatics Journal, 1*(1–2), 35–46.

Robinson, D. C., Sanders, D. A., & Mazharsolook, E. (2015). Ambient intelligence for optimal manufacturing and energy efficiency. *Assembly Automation, 35*(3), 234–248.

Russell, S., & Norvig, P. (2002). *Artificial intelligence: A modern approach.* Prentice Hall.

Saha, D., & Mukherjee, A. (2003). Pervasive computing: A paradigm for the 21st century. *Computer, 36*(3), 25–31.

Satapathy, S. C., Bhateja, V., & Das, S. (2018). Smart intelligent computing and applications. *Proceedings of the Second International Conference on SCI*, Vijaywada, India.

Satyanarayanan, M. (2001). Pervasive computing: Vision and challenges. *IEEE Personal Communications, 8*(4), 10–17.

Serpanos, D., & Wolf, M. (2018). Industrial Internet of Things. In *Internet-of-Things (IoT) Systems* (pp. 37–54). Springer.

Sisinni, E., Saifullah, A., Han, S., Jennehag, U., & Gidlund, M. (2018). Industrial Internet of Things: Challenges, opportunities, and directions. *IEEE Transactions on Industrial Informatics, 14*(11), 4724–4734.

Wolf, W. (2009). Cyber-physical systems. *IEEE Annals of the History of Computing, 42*(03), 88–89.

Wooldridge, M. (1999). Intelligent agents. *Multiagent Systems, 6*, 27–77.

Wu, G., Talwar, S., Johnsson, K., Himayat, N., & Johnson, K. D. (2011). M2M: From mobile to embedded Internet. *IEEE Communications Magazine, 49*(4), 36–43.

Yurish, S. Y. (2010). Sensors: Smart vs. intelligent. *Sensors & Transducers, 114*(3), 1.

4

Internet of Things in E-commerce: A Thematic Analysis

Prateek Kalia

Masaryk University, Brno, Czech Republic

CONTENTS

DOI: 10.1201/9781003213888-4

4.1 Introduction

Electronic commerce has transformed with the evolution of digital technologies over the past few decades (Kalia, 2017; Kalia *et al.*, 2017). The transformations present various opportunities and challenges because interaction with technologies requires a different set of resources and skills at the organizational (business) or individual level (consumers) (Kalia and Paul, 2021). User interaction with digital technologies is changing due to technological advancements, especially with the exponential growth of the Internet of Things (IoT). A huge number of embedded devices are capable of collecting, analyzing, communicating data through the Internet (van Deursen and Mossberger, 2018) and bridging the gap between the virtual and physical world. The IoT in e-commerce can resolve issues like logistics, asymmetric information, and counter fit products and aids enhanced security, smarter analytics, smart inventory, increased productivity, real-time demand visibility, product quality supervision (Chin *et al.*, 2021), etc.

Understanding the importance of new technology like IoT in e-commerce, this chapter aims to find out important themes emerging out of the research over time to see the current and future directions and importance of IoT implementation in e-commerce.

4.2 Internet of Things (IoT): Origin, Development, and Definition

4.2.1 Origin

In 1999, Mark Weiser described ubiquitous computing stating that the future will have an indefinite number of computers woven into the fabric of everyday life (Weiser, 1999). After few years in 1999, Kevin Ashton while recommending Proctor & Gamble to integrate Radio Frequency Identification (RFID) tags in their supply chain to make computers 'hear', 'smell', and gather information on their own, proposed the term Internet-of-Things (IoT). In the late '90s, while working on the concept of Artificial Intelligence (AI), researchers found that small 'embedded agents' can be designed to create Ambient Intelligence. Different phases of IoT origin are briefly discussed below (Chin *et al.*, 2019).

4.2.2 Development

4.2.2.1 Phase I The Devices and Connectivity Period (2005–2008)

The focus during this phase was to transform objects into embedded computers, give them identity, and connect them to the Internet.

4.2.2.2 Phase II The Machine-to-Machine Period (2009–2011)

During this phase development and application of IoT was the main focus. This included improvement in technological platforms, creation of networks and standards, and adoption of Machine-to-Machine (M2M) communication. Data, software, services, information, remote control, and processing power became focal areas.

4.2.2.3 Phase III The HCI Period (2012–2014)

Commercial adoption of the IoT was accelerated during this phase. There were developments concerning object identification, network connectivity, and empowering users.

4.2.2.4 Phase IV The Smart Period (2015–2017)

Global technology players started commercializing IoT, leading to a high number of devices connected through the Internet generating a huge amount of data and business opportunities. This period also saw the emergence of the System of Systems concept and the use of AI for information processing and decision making, with an impact on the daily life of people.

4.2.3 Definition

The IoT system comprises a network of omnipresent common smart devices connected through the Internet, having sensing, storing, processing, identifying, and networking capabilities to make autonomous decisions during person to person, object to person and object to object communication (van Deursen *et al.*, 2021; van Deursen and Mossberger, 2018). This novel paradigm of pervasive presence has a visible impact on domestic and business users. Domestic use examples include wearables (fitness trackers), smart home appliances (digital assistants, Televisions, fridges), etc. In business, visible consequences can be seen in logistics, intelligent transportation, manufacturing, automation, business process management, etc. (Atzori *et al.*, 2010).

4.3 E-commerce: Origin, Development, and Definition

The origin and development of e-commerce are briefly summarized under three phases discussed below.

4.3.1 Origin and Development

4.3.1.1 Phase I Electronic Data Interchange (EDI) based E-commerce (the 1960s)

EDI came into existence in the 1960s, but it was used in the developed countries by large-scale business enterprises in the 1980s as 'trade without paper'. The EDI included hardware (Value-Added Network) and software (EDI standard) to transfer business documents from one computer to other.

4.3.1.2 Phase II Internet-Based E-commerce (the early 1990s)

Due to the high cost of EDI communication, medium- and small-scale enterprises were devoid of high-speed information sharing. The Internet became main medium for e-commerce after the creation of the World Wide Web (1991) and the first browser (1993).

4.3.1.3 Phase III E-concept E-commerce (the early 2000s)

By the early 2000s, e-commerce developed into a higher e-concept e-commerce as a combination of commerce applications and information technology, i.e., it is not just limited to businesses but applicable to various other fields such as education, medicine, administration, banking, etc.

4.3.2 Definition

There are several e-commerce definitions available, as it is still a novel concept, and a uniform standard definition can limit its development. However, it refers to various commercial activities involving the selling and buying of services, information, and products by consumers or companies electronically via telecommunication or computer networks, especially the Internet (Qin, 2009).

4.4 Methodology

This chapter focuses on the thematic analysis of the Internet of Things in E-commerce. The methodology is depicted in Figure 4.1. The first step was deciding on keywords. Considering Internet of things and electronic commerce as primary keywords, ('Internet of things' OR IOT) AND (e-commerce OR 'electronic commerce') was used as a search string to find relevant articles (in English language only) indexed in high-quality Web of Science database (Durán-Sánchez *et al.*, 2018). After screening, 111 articles were finalized for further analysis. For thematic analysis, R-Studio and the 'biblioshiny' app were used (Aria and Cuccurullo, 2017).

4.5 Data Description

The description includes the main information of the data extracted, annual scientific production, most relevant sources, and country-specific production. Table 4.1 shows the main information of the 111 articles extracted from the Web of Science (WoS) database. It indicates that research on IoT in e-commerce is very recent (2010–2021) and most of the publications are from the last three years (2019–2021) (Figure 4.2).

The total number of keywords is almost five times the number of articles searched. It can be seen that the number of single-authored documents is very less (16 only), and the collaboration index is quite high (3.6). It indicates the multidisciplinary nature of the field. Three journals with the highest number of articles were Sustainability (5), IEEE Access (4),

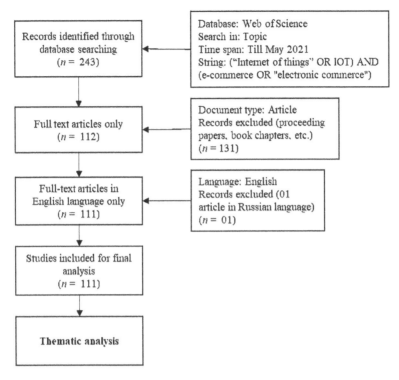

FIGURE 4.1
Methodology.

(Source: Authors' elaboration.)

and Complexity (3). The remaining articles were dispersed among several journals. In terms of scientific production, China is leading the pack, followed by United States, India, Australia, and Germany (Table 4.2).

4.6 Thematic Analysis of Internet of Things in E-commerce

For thematic analysis, the approach advised by Cobo *et al.* (2011) was adopted. The key-word clusters obtained during analysis were grouped into four themes grounded on 'centrality' and 'density'. The analysis identified innovation adoption, e-commerce, and behavior as motor themes, information as emerging themes, and Internet and modeling as underdeveloped themes. Niche themes such as opportunities, challenges, and quality-related to IoT were also identified. These themes had co-occurring keywords, which were identified through the thematic clusters. Each theme is described below (Figure 4.3).

4.6.1 Motor Themes

Important and well-developed themes on the upper-right quadrant with strong centrality and high density reflect motor themes. They are externally related to concepts that may be applied to other themes that are conceptually related.

TABLE 4.1

Data Information

Description	Results
Timespan	2010:2021
Sources (Journals only)	85
Documents	111
Average citations per documents	8.721
References	5437
Document types	
article	104
article; early access	7
Document contents	
Keywords Plus (ID)	271
Author's Keywords (DE)	477
Authors	
Authors	358
Authors of single-authored documents	16
Authors of multi-authored documents	342
Authors collaboration	
Single-authored documents	16
Authors per Document	3.23
Co-Authors per Documents	3.33
Collaboration Index	3.6

Source: Author's elaboration.

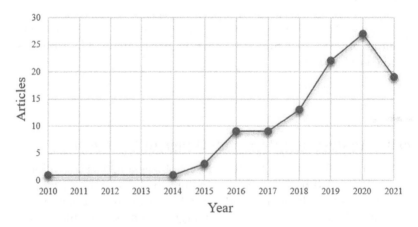

FIGURE 4.2
Annual scientific production.

(Source: Authors' elaboration.)

4.6.1.1 Subtheme 1 Innovation Adoption

This cluster included subthemes related to innovation adoption, integration, and RFID technology, where authors discussed the *adoption* of the Industrial Internet of Things (IIOT) by manufacturing companies or its *integration* in agricultural e-commerce (Li and Huang, 2020), cyber-physical systems, website design, smart e-commerce systems (Song *et al.*, 2019),

TABLE 4.2

Country Scientific Production

Country	Frequency
China	119
USA	25
India	16
Australia	11
Germany	10
UK	9
Japan	7
South Korea	6
Spain	6
Canada	5

Source: Author's analysis.

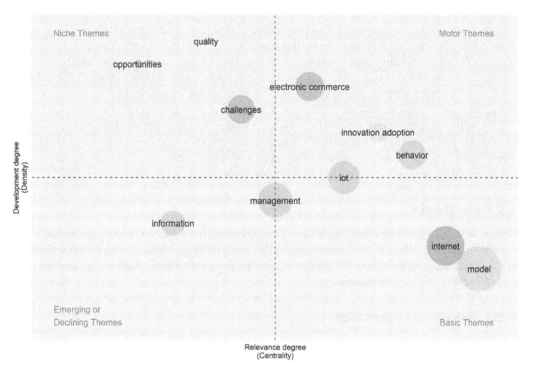

FIGURE 4.3
Thematic map.

(Source: Authors' elaboration.)

production scheduling and logistics, and rural modernization. *RIFD technology* was discussed mostly in the context of logistics and supply chain.

4.6.1.2 Subtheme 2 E-commerce

Since e-commerce was one of the keywords, preference was given to other keywords such as access-control, big data analytics, evolution, information technology, knowledge, social commerce under this subtheme. Authors believe that *access control* is an important aspect of IoT in e-commerce to maintain integrity and confidentiality while devices make authorization decisions to communicate with each other. Further, the implementation of IoT has led to a high amount of device-generated data. In this scenario, *big data analytics* will help in clustering (marketing segmentation) or data mining (predictive behavior). Empowered by the spread of the Internet and smart devices, IoT has led to the rapid *evolution* of e-commerce (Bayer *et al.*, 2021). As *information technology* progresses, researchers suggest management (Polyakov and Kovshun, 2021) and mapping of theoretical (Kuru, 2021) and technological *knowledge* Cheng, Deng et al. (2021), so that IoT can be used to turn information into knowledge. The authors also talked about the customer buying process via IoT-enabled *social commerce* (Bayer *et al.*, 2021).

4.6.1.3 Subtheme 3 Behavior

Keywords like behavior, cloud, services, authentication scheme, information privacy, and security were clustered together under this subtheme. The authors have mentioned IoT as one of the strong tools for predicting customer buying *behavior*. Many authors acknowledged that *cloud* computing is a strong influencer (Zhang and Yue, 2020) and enabler (Song *et al.*, 2019) of IoT and considered them from the same family of the connected world. However, due to the unpredictability and complexity of the data, clouds, and Internet, users will feel *information privacy* (Pal *et al.*, 2021) and *security risks* (Aldossari and Sidorova, 2020) related to IoT device, aggregation, storage and use of their data, affecting IoT adoption. Other researchers have emphasized *authentication schemes* and device integrity for the sustenance of IoT. On the brighter side, researchers believe that IoT can improve data-driven *services* (Aaronson, 2019) related to logistics (Tsang *et al.*, 2021), recommendation, e-commerce transactions, information processing, business collaborations, etc. through optimization (Gao *et al.*, 2019) and personalization to gain consumer confidence (Khan *et al.*, 2021).

4.6.2 Niche Themes

Themes with superior internal linkages but insignificant exterior linkages, having just minor relevance to the domain appearing in the upper-left quadrant are the Niche themes. They are specific and ancillary. Three keywords, i.e., opportunities, challenges, and quality, were observed under this theme.

4.6.2.1 Subtheme 1 Opportunities

In terms of opportunities, researchers believe that the use of IoT in e-commerce can transform the customer experience (Hoyer *et al.*, 2020). IoT can be used to develop affordable (Bayer *et al.*, 2021) smart e-commerce systems (Song *et al.*, 2019), which can collect and integrate object or human-generated data from various resources in real-time to understand and optimize customer preferences and experiences, leading to improved business processes (Zhang and Yue, 2020). Moreover, there is great scope to develop better recommender systems, relationship marketing strategies, supply chain management (SCM), etc. with the help of IoT.

4.6.2.2 Subtheme 2 Challenges

Experts believe that security is one of the major impediments to the adoption of IoT in e-commerce. There are some other issues related to privacy, competitiveness, future viability, and sustainability.

4.6.2.3 Subtheme 3 Quality

IoT is a great tool to improve the quality of the product (Zhang *et al.*, 2021) or service, supply chain or logistics (Dong, 2021), agricultural e-commerce (Li and Huang, 2020), recommendation (Zhang, Zhang et al. 2020), real-time data analytics, etc.

4.6.3 Emerging or Disappearing Theme

Marginal and poorly developed themes with low density and centrality in the lower-left quadrant represent emerging or disappearing themes. The major keyword in this theme was information, which included terms like innovation, and system.

4.6.3.1 Subtheme 1 Information

Under this subtheme, authors have discussed opportunity and issues related to the effect of IoT on information privacy, processing, security, sharing, adoption intention (Xie *et al.*, 2020), automated flow, sensitivity (Pal *et al.*, 2021), management (Shao, 2021), etc. Researchers believe that by implementing IoT in e-commerce, businesses can extract real-time (İzmirli *et al.*, 2021), reliable (Zhang *et al.*, 2021), relevant (Dong, 2021), and strategic information. Moreover, a large amount of data can be turned into information and knowledge, which can be used to empower customers, suppliers, supply chain (Chen *et al.*, 2021), etc. Authors have also linked IoT with themes related to adoption, stimulations, and diffusion of *innovation* (Polyakov and Kovshun, 2021). Large number of studies also mentioned about *systems* related to anti-counterfeiting (Chin *et al.*, 2021), logistics distribution (Ekren *et al.*, 2021), logistics monitoring (Chang *et al.*, 2020), traceability (Zhang *et al.*, 2021), cyber-physical (Polyakov and Kovshun, 2021), Internet (Chen *et al.*, 2021), recommendation (Zhang, Zhang *et al.*, 2020), third-party aggregation (Bhatnagar and Kumra, 2020), manufacturing, information, social e-commerce users (Xie *et al.*, 2020), SCM, warehouse, multimedia (Gao *et al.*, 2019), business, cloud-based mobile gateway operation, autonomous transaction management, smart e-commerce (Song *et al.*, 2019), production-delivery supply chain, enterprise, payment, fraud detection and reputation (Luo and Wan, 2019), multi-agent, and indoor positioning.

4.6.4 Basic Themes

Important but underdeveloped research areas present in the lower-right quadrant are the basic themes. Two major keywords, i.e., Internet and model emerged out of the analysis.

4.6.4.1 Subtheme 1 Internet

Under this subtheme, prominent keywords like the Internet, framework, things, lightweight, privacy, risk, and secure emerged. Since the Internet was one of the search keywords, other keywords under the subtheme are discussed. Most authors based their research on *framework* related to asset-process-performance, technology-organization-environment, fog computing quality of service (QoS), Internet of things, unified probabilistic factor, personalized recommendation (Wang and Zhang, 2021), mobile edge computing (Gao *et al.*, 2019), etc. or they talked about the scalable (Kuru, 2021), theoretical (Pal *et al.*, 2021), technical (Shao, 2021), trade-oriented (AlAshery *et al.*, 2021), application-based, legal, integrated, or security-related framework. Authors have also highlighted that e-commerce based on IoT needs to be *lightweight*, autonomous, and legitimate. However, they mentioned the *risks* related to aphishing attack (Naaz, 2021), data leakage, privacy, perceived privacy (Aldossari and Sidorova, 2020), information asymmetry, physical compromise of devices, infrastructure, technology, deficiency of skills, competencies and decision-maker skepticism. Studies also express concern for the *privacy* of personal data (Pal *et al.*, 2021) and recommend to *secure* personal data control and flow and business transactions.

4.6.4.2 Subtheme 2 Model

Under this subtheme, keywords like the model, e-commerce, technology, adoption, performance, trust, impact, intention, perceptions, loyalty, online, satisfaction are discussed.

One of the most prominent keywords was *model*, under which the majority of authors talked about model related to logistics (Dong, 2021), supply chain (Aldossari and Sidorova, 2020), technology acceptance (Xie *et al.*, 2020), and business process (Ekren *et al.*, 2021). This theme also included data analysis techniques like structural equation modeling (Bhatnagar and Kumra, 2020). The next keyword was majorly linked with *technology* adoption (Polyakov and Kovshun, 2021). Authors also discussed *performance* related to tracing technology (Zhang *et al.*, 2021), algorithm (Wang and Zhang, 2021), value creation (Chen *et al.*, 2021), platform (Shao, 2021), consumers (Fu *et al.*, 2020) and business or improving the performance (Zhang *et al.*, 2020). Studies emphasized that issues related to *trust* should be resolved (Chen *et al.*, 2021) because trust can significantly affect smart home acceptance (Aldossari and Sidorova, 2020), consumers' purchase intentions (Zhao *et al.*, 2020), and user's attitudes for IoT. Similarly, the *impact* of IoT on logistics (Dong, 2021), firm value creation (Chen *et al.*, 2021), customer satisfaction (Tsang *et al.*, 2021), human development (Khrais, 2020), businesses, industrial value creation, etc. was acknowledged by different authors. Researchers confirmed the effect of IoT on e-commerce reflected in terms of electronic word of thing (ewot) *intention* (Bhatnagar and Kumra, 2020), consumers' purchase intentions (Zhao *et al.*, 2020), users' *perceptions* of risk (Alraja *et al.*, 2019), customer loyalty and customer satisfaction (Tsang *et al.*, 2021).

4.6.5 Axial Themes

Two themes appeared on-axis, i.e., management (in between basic and emerging themes) and Internet of Things (in between basic and motor themes). Both these themes are discussed below.

4.6.5.1 Subtheme 1 Management

Under this theme, researchers suggested how the implementation of IoT in e-commerce helps in the management of product traceability (Zhang *et al.*, 2021), knowledge (Polyakov and Kovshun, 2021), communication privacy (Pal *et al.*, 2021), user information (Shao, 2021), process optimization, intelligent logistics, supply chain (Makhdoom *et al.*, 2020), technology, industrial wearables, autonomous transaction, privacy, and identity in cyberspace and data (Zhang *et al.*, 2019).

4.6.5.2 Subtheme 2 Internet of Things

Under this theme keywords like the Internet of Things, time, supply chain, genetic algorithm, location, and transportation were found. Since the Internet of Things was the search keyword, other keywords are discussed below.

Authors discussed how IoT in e-commerce can assist in real-*time* predictions (Kuru, 2021), logistics services, information (İzmirli *et al.*, 2021), monitoring, data insight, etc. They suggest that IoT is a big boon to time-critical deliveries (Tsang *et al.*, 2021) as it helps in timely distribution. It can further help in *supply chain* management (Mohammed *et al.*, 2021), making it flexible, profitable (İzmirli *et al.*, 2021), and low cost. The IoT based applications, such as lateral inventory share applications (İzmirli *et al.*, 2021), will result in smart *transportation* which is low cost, smooth and operates on the best transportation path. Further, the customer can ascertain the *location* (through a global positioning system) and information regarding the package such as humidity and the temperature, any time, through IoT-based intelligence (Chen *et al.*, 2021), hence improving their shopping experience. In this context, authors have used *genetic algorithms* to test customer satisfaction, logistics cost, and order picking operations from the warehouse (Tu *et al.*, 2020).

4.7 Topic Trend Analysis and Thematic Evolution

Based on topic trend analysis the origin of the topic related to the performance of the system is relatively old (Figure 4.4). Similarly, big data, which is considered a member of the IoT family, has less frequency. However, topics related to adoption, challenges, and technology are quite recent. Especially, topics related to e-commerce, IoT, modeling, and management are quite recent. From thematic evolution, it is quite evident that the introduction of IoT in e-commerce is a recent phenomenon and researchers are focusing more on the issues related to its adoption and management (Figure 4.5).

FIGURE 4.4
Topic trend.

(Source: Authors' elaboration.)

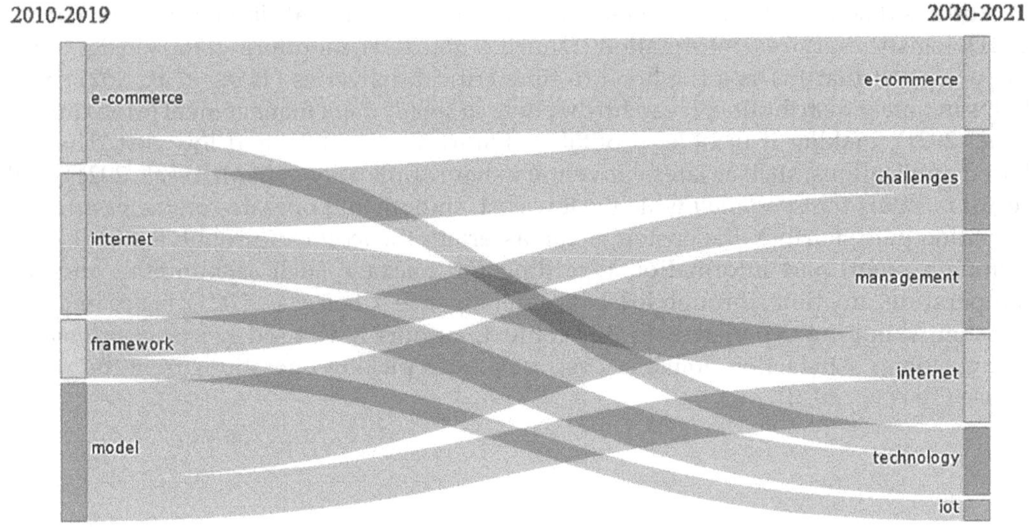

2010-2019   2020-2021

FIGURE 4.5
Thematic evolution.

(Source: Authors' elaboration.)

4.8 Co-occurrence Network

The thematic distance and relations between the significant topics related to IoT in e-commerce are graphically visible through the co-occurrence network (Figure 4.6). Topics with the same color indicate a strong bond between them. One of the networks indicates concern regarding adoption, performance, and impact of e-commerce and technology. Another prominent network hints towards management and optimizations of the framework, smart systems, and big data. One network suggested perceptions, trust, and risk as important concerns for modeling electronic commerce and information technology. Substantial connections were also observed between IoT, genetic algorithm and transportation; big data analytics and social commerce; and security and information privacy.

4.9 Implications

This chapter has highlighted important themes related to research concerning IoT in e-commerce followed by their evolution and interrelation. This chapter presents various future directions and implications which are discussed in this section. First, the motor theme confirmed that innovation adoption in e-commerce is dependent on consumer or organizational behavior. One of the strong implications of this finding is that researchers must make IoT technology available, usable, and affordable for the end-user for wider acceptance and adoption. Secondly, niche themes corroborate that IoT can enhance the competitiveness, future viability, and sustainability of e-commerce businesses but

FIGURE 4.6
Co-occurrence network.

(Source: Authors' elaboration)

challenges like security, privacy, etc. needs attention from future researchers. Thirdly, these concerns are even more visible in the emerging theme (i.e., information) and call for investigations related to privacy, processing, security, sharing, flow, sensitivity, and management of information. Fourthly, the basic themes suggest that with suitable modeling techniques and algorithms, the Internet can be a great source for the management of various e-commerce processes.

4.10 Conclusion

Both e-commerce and IoT are novel concepts and individually they have a great impact on business and society. Now the implementation of IoT in e-commerce has taken this evolution to next level. The purpose of this chapter was to understand this evolution through thematic analysis of the scientific literature to date. Articles related to e-commerce and IoT were extracted from the WOS database and analyzed using R. The application of IoT in e-commerce has become popular in last one decade. Countries like China, the USA and India are leading the research in this field. The thematic analysis identified innovation adoption, e-commerce, and behavior as motor themes; information as emerging themes, and Internet and modeling as underdeveloped themes. Niche themes such as opportunities, challenges, and quality related to IoT were also identified. These themes were elaborated based on thematic clusters. Topic trend analysis indicated that the challenges, adoption, and management of IoT implementation in e-commerce are the focal area for researchers.

References

Aaronson, S.A. (2019), "Data is different, and that's why the world needs a new approach to governing cross-border data flows", *Digital Policy, Regulation and Governance*, Vol. 21 No. 5, pp. 441–460.

AlAshery, M.K., Yi, Z., Shi, D., Lu, X., Xu, C., Wang, Z. and Qiao, W. (2021), "A blockchain-enabled multi-settlement quasi-ideal peer-to-peer trading framework", *IEEE Transactions on Smart Grid*, Vol. 12 No.1, pp. 885–896.

Aldossari, M.Q. and Sidorova, A. (2020), "Consumer acceptance of Internet of Things (IoT): Smart home context", *Journal of Computer Information Systems*, Vol. 60 No. 6, pp. 507–517.

Alraja, M.N., Farooque, M.M.J. and Khashab, B. (2019), "The effect of security, privacy, familiarity, and trust on users' attitudes toward the use of the IoT-based healthcare: The mediation role of risk perception", *IEEE Access*, Vol. 7, pp. 111341–111354.

Aria, M. and Cuccurullo, C. (2017), "Bibliometrix: An R-tool for comprehensive science mapping analysis", *Journal of Informetrics*, Elsevier Ltd, Vol. 11 No. 4, pp. 959–975.

Atzori, L., Iera, A. and Morabito, G. (2010), "The Internet of Things: A survey", *Computer Networks*, Elsevier B.V., Vol. 54 No. 15, pp. 2787–2805.

Bayer, S., Gimpel, H. and Rau, D. (2021), "IoT-commerce - opportunities for customers through an affordance lens", *Electronic Markets*, Springer, Vol. 31 No.1, pp. 27–50.

Bhatnagar, S. and Kumra, R. (2020), "Understanding consumer motivation to share IoT products data", *Journal of Indian Business Research*, Vol. 12 No.1, pp. 5–22.

Chang, W.-J., Chen, L.-B.andSu, J.-P.(2020), "Design and implementation of intelligent tape for monitoring high-price and fragile cargo shipments during transport procedures", *IEEE Sensors Journal*, Vol. 20 No.23, pp. 14521–14533.

Chen, C.-L., Deng, Y.-Y., Weng, W., Zhou, M. and Sun, H. (2021), "A blockchain-based intelligent anti-switch package in tracing logistics system", *The Journal of Supercomputing*, https://doi. org/10.1007/s11227-020-03558-7

Chen, J., Wu, H., Zhou, X., Wu, M., Zhao, C. and Xu, S. (2021), "Optimization of Internet of Things E-commerce logistics cloud service platform based on mobile communication", edited by Wang, W. *Complexity*, Wiley, Handawi, pp. 1–11.

Chin, J., Callaghan, V. and Ben Allouch, S. (2019), "The Internet-of-Things: Reflections on the past, present and future from a user-centered and smart environment perspective", *Journal of Ambient Intelligence and Smart Environments*, Vol. 11No. 1, pp. 45–69.

Chin, S., Lu, C., Ho, P., Shiao, Y. and Wu, T. (2021), "Commodity anti-counterfeiting decision in e-commerce trade based on machine learning and Internet of Things", *Computer Standards & Interfaces*, Elsevier B.V., Vol. 76, p. 103504.

Cobo, M.J., López-Herrera, A.G., Herrera-Viedma, E. and Herrera, F. (2011), "An approach for detecting, quantifying, and visualizing the evolution of a research field: A practical application to the Fuzzy Sets Theory field", *Journal of Informetrics*, Elsevier Ltd, Vol. 5 No. 1, pp. 146–166.

van Deursen, A.J.A.M. and Mossberger, K. (2018), "Any thing for anyone? A new digital divide in Internet-of-things skills", *Policy &Internet*, Vol. 10 No.2, pp. 122–140.

van Deursen, A.J.A.M., van der Zeeuw, A., de Boer, P., Jansen, G. and van Rompay, T. (2021), "Development and validation of the Internet of Things Skills Scale (IoTSS)", edited by Brian D. Loader, *Information, Communication & Society*, Taylor & Francis, University of York, UK, pp. 1–17, https://www.tandfonline.com/action/journalInformation?show=editorialBoard&journal Code=rics20 and https://www.tandfonline.com/doi/full/10.1080/1369118X.2021.1900320" for details.

Dong, Z. (2021), "Construction of mobile E-commerce platform and analysis of its impact on E-commerce logistics customer satisfaction", edited by Lv, Z., *Complexity*, Vol. 2021, Hindawi Complexity, UK, pp. 1–13, https://downloads.hindawi.com/journals/complexity/2021/6636415.pdf.

Durán-Sánchez, A., Álvarez-García, J., del Río-Rama, M. and Oliveira, C. (2018), "Religious tourism and pilgrimage: Bibliometric overview", *Religions*, Vol. 9 No. 9, p. 249.

Ekren, B.Y., Mangla, S.K., Turhanlar, E.E., Kazancoglu, Y. and Li, G. (2021), "Lateral inventory share-based models for IoT-enabled E-commerce sustainable food supply networks", *Computers & Operations Research*, Vol. 130, p. 105237.

Fu, H., Manogaran, G., Wu, K., Cao, M., Jiang, S. and Yang, A. (2020), "Intelligent decision-making of online shopping behavior based on Internet of things", *International Journal of Information Management*, Vol. 50, pp. 515–525.

Gao, H., Duan, Y., Shao, L. and Sun, X. (2019), "Transformation-based processing of typed resources for multimedia sources in the IoT environment", *Wireless Networks*. https://doi.org/10.1007/s11276-019-02200-6

Hoyer, W.D., Kroschke, M., Schmitt, B., Kraume, K. and Shankar, V. (2020), "Transforming the customer experience through new technologies", *Journal of Interactive Marketing*, Elsevier Inc., Vol. 51, pp. 57–71.

İzmirli, D., Ekren, B.Y., Kumar, V. and Pongsakornrungsilp, S. (2021), "Omni-chanel network design towards circular economy under inventory share policies", *Sustainability*, Vol. 13 No.5, p. 2875.

Kalia, P. (2017), "Service quality scales in online retail: Methodological issues", *International Journal of Operations & Production Management*, Vol. 37 No. 5, pp. 630–663.

Kalia, P., Kaur, N. and Singh, T. (2017), "E-Commerce in India: Evolution and revolution of online retail", edited by Khosrow-Pour, M. *Mobile Commerce: Concepts, Methodologies, Tools, and Applications*, IGI Global, Hershey, Pennsylvania, USA, pp. 736–758.

Kalia, P. and Paul, J. (2021), "E-service quality and e-retailers: Attribute-based multi-dimensional scaling", *Computers in Human Behavior*, Elsevier Ltd, Vol. 115, p. 106608.

Khan, S.A., Ahmad, S. and Jamshed, M. (2021), "IoT-enabled services in online food retailing", *Journal of Public Affairs*, Vol. 21 No. 1, p. e2150.

Khrais, L.T. (2020), "IoT and blockchain in the development of smart cities", *International Journal of Advanced Computer Science and Applications*, Vol. 11 No.2, pp. 153–159.

Kuru, K. (2021), "Management of geo-distributed intelligence: Deep Insight as a Service (DINSaaS) on Forged Cloud Platforms (FCP)", *Journal of Parallel and Distributed Computing*, Vol. 149, pp. 103–118.

Li, X. and Huang, D. (2020), "Research on value integration mode of agricultural e-commerce industry chain based on Internet of Things and blockchain technology", edited by Cheng, H. *Wireless Communications and Mobile Computing*, Vol. 2020, pp. 1–11.

Luo, S. and Wan, S. (2019), "Leveraging product characteristics for online collusive detection in big data transactions", *IEEE Access*, Vol. 7, pp. 40154–40164.

Makhdoom, I., Zhou, I., Abolhasan, M., Lipman, J. and Ni, W. (2020), "PrivySharing: A blockchain-based framework for privacy-preserving and secure data sharing in smart cities", *Computers & Security*, Vol. 88, p. 101653.

Mohammed, S., Fiaidhi, J., Ramos, C., Kim, T.-H., Fang, W.C. and Abdelzaher, T. (2021), "Blockchain in eCommerce", *ACM Transactions on Internet Technology*, Vol. 21 No.1, pp. 11–55.

Naaz, S. (2021), "Detection of phishing in Internet of Things using machine learning approach", *International Journal of Digital Crime and Forensics*, Vol. 13 No. 2, pp. 1–15.

Pal, D., Funilkul, S. and Zhang, X. (2021), "Should I disclose my personal data?Perspectives from Internet of Things services", *IEEE Access*, Vol. 9, pp. 4141–4157.

Polyakov, M. and Kovshun, N. (2021), "Diffusion of innovations as a key driver of the digital economy development", *Baltic Journal of Economic Studies*, Vol. 7 No.1, pp. 84–92.

Qin, Z. (2009), *Introduction to E-Commerce*, Springer-Verlag GmbH Berlin Heidelberg, New York.

Shao, X. (2021), "The design of medical IoT operation information platform using reactive algorithm and e-commerce O2O mode", *Network Modeling Analysis in Health Informatics and Bioinformatics*, Vol. 10 No.1, p. 4.

Song, Z., Sun, Y., Wan, J., Huang, L. and Zhu, J. (2019), "Smart e-commerce systems: Current status and research challenges", *Electronic Markets*, Vol. 29 No. 2, pp. 221–238.

Tsang, Y.P., Wu, C.H., Lam, H.Y., Choy, K.L. and Ho, G.T.S. (2021), "Integrating Internet of Things and multi-temperature delivery planning for perishable food E-commerce logistics: A model and application", *International Journal of Production Research*, Vol. 59 No. 5, pp. 1534–1556.

Tu, M., Yang, M.-F., Kao, S.-L., Lin, F.-C., Wu, M.-H. and Lin, C.-K. (2020), "Using a heuristic multi-objective genetic algorithm to solve the storage assignment problem for CPS-based pick-and-pass system", *Enterprise Information Systems*, pp. 1–22.

Wang, J. and Zhang, Y. (2021), "Using cloud computing platform of 6G IoT in e-commerce personalized recommendation", *International Journal of System Assurance Engineering and Management*, https://doi.org/10.1007/s13198-021-01059-1

Weiser, M. (1999), "The computer for the 21 st century", *ACM SIGMOBILE Mobile Computing and Communications Review*, Association for Computing Machinery (ACM), Vol. 3 No.3, pp. 3–11.

Xie, C., Xiao, X. and Hassan, D.K. (2020), "Data mining and application of social e-commerce users based on big data of Internet of Things", edited by Maseleno, A., Yuan, X. and Balas, V.E. *Journal of Intelligent & Fuzzy Systems*, Vol. 39 No.4, pp. 5171–5181.

Zhang, H., Zhang, H. and Guo, X. (2020), "Research on the future development prospects of sports products industry under the mode of e - commerce and Internet of things", *Information Systems and E-Business Management*, Springer Berlin Heidelberg, Vol. 18 No. 4, pp. 511–525.

Zhang, J., Huang, T., Wang, S. and Liu, Y. Jie. (2019), "Future Internet: Trends and challenges", edited by Yunhe Pan, Computer Graphics, CAD, and Industrial Design Zhejiang University, China and Xicheng Lu, High Performance Computing, Computer Network Commission of Science and Technology, China, *Frontiers of Information Technology and Electronic Engineering*, Zhejiang University, China, 1 September, http://www.jzus.zju.edu.cn/article.php?doi=10.1631/FITEE.1800445 and http://www.jzus.zju.edu.cn/editorial_c.php.

Zhang, X. and Yue, W.T. (2020), "A 2020 perspective on 'Transformative value of the Internet of Things and pricing decisions'", *Electronic Commerce Research and Applications*, Elsevier B.V., Vol. 41, p. 100967.

Zhang, Y., Liu, Y., Jiong, Z., Zhang, X., Li, B. and Chen, E. (2021), "Development and assessment of blockchain-IoT-based traceability system for frozen aquatic product", *Journal of Food Process Engineering*, Vol. 44 No.5, https://doi.org/10.1111/jfpe.13669

Zhao, S., Fang, Y., Zhang, W. and Jiang, H. (2020), "Trust, perceived benefit, and purchase intention in C2C E-commerce", *Journal of Global Information Management*, Vol. 28 No.1, pp. 121–141.

5

Data Security and Privacy in Fog Computing Applications

Nazeer Haider and Chandrashekhar Azad

National Institute of Technology, Jamshedpur, India

CONTENTS

5.1 Introduction

CISCO recently announced its Fog computing vision, which allows applications to run on billions of linked devices at the network's edge (Somayya Madakam, 2018). Customers may use the Cisco system of networked devices, including switches and robust routers (Somayya Madakam, 2018), to design, manage, and operate software applications. Cisco combines the Linux operating system (OS) and the network OS into a single networked unit.

As seen in Figure 5.1, there is a basic three-level hierarchy. Every smart device is linked to one of the Fog nodes (PeiYun Zhang, 2018) in this system. Fog nodes can be connected, and (Mithun Mukherjee, 2017) each one is connected to the Cloud.

Fog computing is a type of distributed computing model (Mamata Rath, 2018) in which data is recorded and processed in a cloud platform between the origin of the source and the cloud platforms. As a result, data processing overheads are reduced, and computational capacity in Cloud systems is improved due to the reduced need to store and process vast quantities of unnecessary information and data. The concept of the Fog system is inspired by the increasing number of devices that collect data (in terms of variety, volume, and velocity (Sagiroglu & Sinanc, 2013)) from an ever-increasing number of IoT devices.

DOI: 10.1201/9781003213888-5

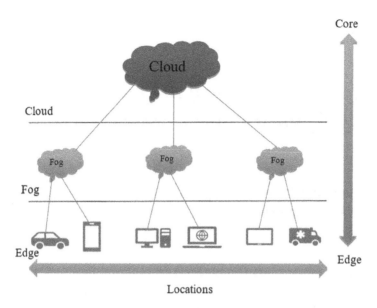

FIGURE 5.1
A basic three-level hierarchy. It shows that Fog computing is the intermediate layer of Edge and Cloud computing.

5.2 Review Procedure

Cisco's Fog model can be interpreted as a (Sagiroglu & Sinanc, 2013) catalyst for a wide range of emerging technologies when analyzed effectively and integratively. It may involve, distribute, and affect many additional features and functionalities such as real-time detection, system interoperability, improved reaction time, low bandwidth usage, centralized or machine-to-machine management, system abstraction, adequate energy consumption, and so on. Fog computing and other similar techniques are now being used to improve Cloud systems' usability and potential. The Fog and related systems as Micro-data centers, Edge computing, and Cloud computing are vulnerable to cyber-attacks that jeopardize 'confidentiality, integrity, and availability (CIA)' (Dimitrios Zissis, 2012) because of their broad applicability. Other researchers, such as (Stojmenovic, 2014), have listed twelve critical security problems, according to the Cloud Security Alliance. These problems have a significant effect on cloud computing's distributed, cooperative, and on-demand nature. The fog system can be affected by the same risks as Cloud because it is a virtualized environment (see Figure 5.2).

Our research considers the 12 security categories listed below to form a systematic analysis:

1 **Issues with Access Control (IAC)** may lead to poor management results, which allows (Mahmood, 2018) any unauthorized person to obtain data, as well as computer software installation permissions and settings.

2 **APTs (Advanced Persistent Threats)** are cyber-attacks that attempt to compromise a business's infrastructure to steal intellectual property and data (Mahmood, 2018).

3 **Denial of Service (DoS)** is discouraged from using a device (applications and data) by overloading the finite resources of the device (Mahmood, 2018).

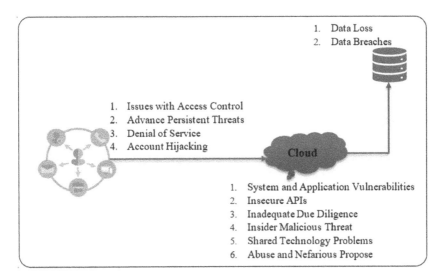

FIGURE 5.2
Cloud computing has brought with it several security concerns, which the Fog Platform may have inherited. This diagram illustrates how virtualization and other Cloud platform issues can have an impact on the Fog platform as well.

4 **Account Hijacking (AH)** is a form of cyberattack that attempts to control a user's account to harm others.

5 **Data Loss (DL)** always does not occur by a cyber-attack. It may result from a natural disaster.

6 **Data Breaches (DB)** is an intruder release or steals sensitive, secure or confidential data.

7 **Application and System Vulnerabilities (ASV)** are vulnerabilities that can be exploited that arise from software or configuration (Mahmood, 2018) failures that an intruder can use to enter and jeopardize the system.

8 **Insecure APIs (IA)** are provided by several Fog/Cloud providers. The stability of these APIs is a key in the security of some programs or other software applications (Mahmood, 2018) that we are using them.

9 **Inadequate Due Diligence (IDD)** When a company rushes through the planning, adoption, and execution of a system.

10 **Insider Malicious Threat (IMT)** is such a type of user who has been granted permission to access the device and network but has chosen to behave maliciously.

11 **Shared Technology Problems (STPs)** arise when infrastructures, platforms, or software are shared. The components of the underlying hardware, for example, may not have been configured to provide strong isolation.

12 **Abuse and Nefarious Propose (ANP)** occurs when tools are freely accessible and malicious users use them to carry out the negative operation.

5.2.1 Security-Related Issues

Table 5.1 displays the connection between the measured Fog applications and the security problem categories. The segment 'Review technique' contains an overview of each group.

TABLE 5.1

Application-specific Knowledge Gaps Based on an Analysis of Existing Fog Installations Against all the 12 Security-related Problem Categories Are as Follows

Areas of Applications	IAC	APTs	DoS	AH	DL	DB	ASV	IA	IDD	IMT	STPs	ANP
Search engine optimization				Yes	Yes			Yes				
Radio access through virtualization	Yes	Yes		Yes		Yes	Yes			Yes	Yes	Yes
5G cellular networks					Yes	Yes				Yes	Yes	Yes
Response to disasters and a hostile climate	Yes		Yes						Yes			
Smart Meters	Yes				Yes				Yes			
Reduction of energy					Yes	Yes						
Systems of healthcare	Yes		Yes	Yes		Yes	Yes	Yes	Yes			
Computerized Brain Augmentation	Yes	Yes				Yes			Yes			
Video processing for surveillance		Yes				Yes			Yes			
Road safety and Networks of vehicles			Yes			Yes					Yes	
Traceability of foods				Yes	Yes		Yes					
Data on speech					Yes				Yes			
Resources management	Yes		Yes	Yes						Yes	Yes	Yes

While the table was created by analyzing published literature, it should be noted that the writers are not even allowed to have shared details about their application that reduce the risk of a security breach in some instances. According to the table, no one of the studied application fields that have been taken the requisite measures to reduce the possible effects and risk of every security threat category (Mahmood, 2018).

Table 5.2 summarizes the security controls relevant to each application region. This table illustrates the possible effect of the CIA model on Fog platforms. Security procedures in fog platforms are rapidly evolving, and some existing publications lack adequate information to provide a detailed assessment. Consequently, some of the blank spots are theoretical and futuristic and focused on existing studies. It is worth mentioning that, due to the ever-increasing number of vectors of attack, this is not an extensive list, and some security problems might have been overlooked. New protection problems will need to be identified and accepted as Fog infrastructure growth progresses.

5.2.2 Existing Fog Computing Security Solutions

As mentioned in the preceding parts, the implementation of Fog system features between Cloud mode and end-users introduces a new type of vulnerability that can theoretically be used for malicious purposes. In contrast to cloud computing, there are no industry-wide protection certifications or measures specified for the Fog model. Furthermore, a Fog platform could be listed:

- Their existence has limited computational resources, making it tough to implement a comprehensive set of security solutions capable of detecting and preventing advanced, targeted, and distributed attacks.

TABLE 5.2

A List of Possible Security Vulnerabilities Discovered in Fog Computing Applications

Class of Attack	Threats that Could Exist	Possible Solutions	Their Impact
Issues with web security	• Injection of SQL • Site-to-site scripting • Forgery of cross-site requests • Hijacking of a session or an account • Direct object references that are insecure • Redirections of malicious intent • Drive-by killings	• Safe code • Find and repair security bugs • Update the apps daily • Auditing regularly • A firewall is a system that protects an Intrusion Prevention Scheme (IPS) with anti-virus security.	As a result of revealing confidential information, an intruder will become a legitimate member of the network, allowing malicious applications to be enabled.
Issues with virtualization	• Attacks on hypervisors • Attacks on virtual machines • Logical Segregation is either lacking or non-existent • Attacks on the side channels • Escalation of Rights Abuse of the service • Attacks on privilege escalation • Ineffective resource policies	• Intrusion Detection with Multi-factor Authentication • Isolation of device usage data • Encryption based on attributes or identities • Permissions depending on the user • Process isolation model	All Fog facilities, data, and users are run in a virtual environment, and any agreement will be detrimental.
Issues with internal or external communication	• Assault by a MITM attack • Laws and procedures that are unsuccessful • Inadequate access protection • Hijacking of a session or an account APIs and facilities that are not safe • Vulnerabilities in software Failure at a single stage	• Encrypted communication • Authentication of several factors (mutual/multi-factor) • Encryption that is just partially encrypted Isolating infected nodes pinning the certificate • The number of Transport Layer Security (TLS) connections is limited	Eavesdropping helps an intruder to obtain confidential information and gain access to unauthorized Fog services.
Issues with wireless security	• Impersonation that is involved • Replay assaults on messages • Issues with message distortion • Loss of data • Breach of confidential details • Attacks by sniffing • Illegal exploitation of natural resources	• Encrypted verification Communication • Service for key management • Routes that are safe for a personal network • Protocols for wireless authentication	Wireless access points that are vulnerable can cause many problems like continuity, availability, precision, and trustworthiness.
Issues with data security	• Replication and exchange of data • Attacks on data tampering and erasure • Unauthorized data access • Problems with data ownership • Attack tolerance is poor • Insiders with a vengeance issue with multi-tenancy • Attacks that cause a denial of service	• Enforcing policies • Protection is integrated into the architecture • The use of encryption Key management that is secure • Difficulty Masking of data • Classification of data • Monitoring of the network	A fair chance that an intruder could gain unauthorized access to files and databases compromises both the user's and the Fog system's data.

(Continued)

TABLE 5.2 (*Continued*)

A List of Possible Security Vulnerabilities Discovered in Fog Computing Applications

Class of Attack	Threats that Could Exist	Possible Solutions	Their Impact
Protection with Malware	• Virus • Ransom-ware • Trojans • Root-kits • Worms • Spyware • Performance reduction	• Anti-malware software • Data backups that are meticulous • Intrusion Detection System (IDS) • Vulnerabilities must be tackled • Restore points for the system	Malware-infected nodes can slow down the entire Fog network, allow backdoors into the system, permanently corrupt or damage data (Afroj Alam, 2020), and allow the system to have backdoors.

- Due to a huge amount of data throughput and the possibility of obtaining confidential data (Qiu et al., 2020) from the Cloud and IoT computers, it is an enticing aim for cybercriminals.
- In contrast to Cloud systems, it is more available, based on the exact location and the configuration of the network and precise place, which raises the possibility of an attack (Mahmood, 2018).

Fog computing and related technologies have real-world applications, such as analyzed in the section 'Related work - current fog applications' primarily driven by features. Even so, it has been discovered that in the vast majority of situations, future security checks that could be introduced to prevent threats are overlooked. One explanation for this may be that the security problems that Fog systems face are still in the early stages of study, with only a few bit options to detect and avoid malicious activity on Fog computing. A summary of such systems can be found in the above tables.

5.2.3 Privacy-Preserving in Fog Computing

Privacy problems in smart grids revolve around concealing data, such as which appliance was used to allow detailed overview information for accurate charging.

The following steps summarize the (Jain, 2020) research in sensor-fog networks to maintain privacy (Jing Liu, 2020) to stable data from sensors transmission between the end-user and the fog network (Afroj Alam, 2020) system:

- They gather data from features and sensors to be extracted
- Data fuzzing is the method of injecting data with Gaussian noise at a specific number of variances to decrease the probability of sniffing attacks and eavesdropping
- Data is broken down into blocks and shuffled to avoid MITM attacks (see Figure 5.3)
- Putting in place Public Key System to encrypt and data block
- Send separated data to the Fog server, where it is decoded and reordered.

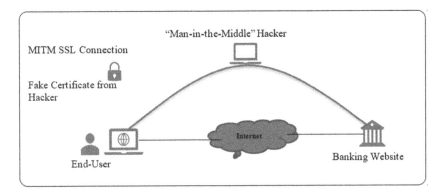

FIGURE 5.3
MITM Insecure SSL Connection which shows that a hacker in the middle of the end-user and bank website.

To further minimize risk, the device requires a functionality reduction and capability for reducing data contact with Fog nodes. This work is essential because it focuses on the preservation of personal and sensitive data during transmission. By choosing an algorithm for encrypting and managing keys, the methodology can be enhanced, focusing on those who play a crucial role in data privacy. Furthermore, a few discussions of the computation overheads needed to perform comprehensive data manipulation (fuzzing, decryption, encryption, reordering, ordering, and Segregation) before and after contact. This may be significant when manufacturing and designing a Fog computing model because the required calculations have a chance that overheads will not be available. A different vital point to note here is that sensors continuously transmit data (Mahmood, 2018), potentially for extended periods. The privacy mechanism might cause the underlying Fog system model to become overloaded or even crash.

5.3 Conclusion

This article has explained the (Jain, 2020) privacy and security problems in the term of fog platform, a modern computing model for (Afroj Alam, 2020) providing flexible services to nearby end-users at the network's edge. The article concludes with a discussion of (Jain, 2020) how recommended security solutions might avoid, track, and protect from the threats mentioned in Table 5.2 summarized in Table 5.3. These security technologies are designed to safeguard the CIA of the whole Fog computing users and their systems. According to the literature, various applications are using fog computing, all of which require a high degree of protection to protect user data for the CIA.

Fog computing could supplant conventional cloud computing as much as possible in the future. Research can be done to reduce latency and bandwidth requirements much more without jeopardizing the system's protection. After setting up the system with all of the specifications, it should operate on its own. This article is meant to serve as a starting point for creating safe data services in fog computing and assisting developers and readers in anticipating security challenges and measures when designing new Fog systems.

TABLE 5.3

Security Solutions that Are Recommended and Their Impacts Based on the CIA Model

Category	Solutions	Impacts based on CIA model
Protecting against cache attacks	• Vulnerabilities in services and applications • Insecure API • Sniffing attacks • Sensitive data leakage	When a Fog system acts as a cache server, the most requested (sensitive and relevant) information and data by users or other devices through Fog remains private (Mahmood, 2018).
Data Encryption	• Data Breach • Malicious insiders • Due Diligence is Insufficient • Data Loss • Malicious processes or Spyware	Encryption can maintain the original secret data from unauthorized recipients if (Mahmood, 2018) data is compromised at processing, rest, or motion.
Malware protection	• Vulnerabilities in API services and applications • Account Hijacking • Shared Technology Issues • Damage risks or Data corruption • Performance degradation	Static analysis allows for real-time testing and detection. It removes suspected malicious applications, while dynamic analysis protects from zero-day vulnerabilities through intelligent behavior/event monitoring and ensures that the Fog system consistently performs.
Network monitoring	• Access control issues • Advance Persistent Threats • Insufficient Due Diligence • DoS attack • Malicious Insiders • Data Breaches • Misuse of resources and nefarious activities • Attack detection	Can alert users to a log of malicious incidents for review, a persistent attack, block suspected network traffic inbound and outbound, and indicate or determine the system's overall performance.
Wireless security	• Access control issues • Advance Persistent Threats • Eavesdropping attacks • Data breach • Unauthorized use of bandwidth	Fog nodes will improve their flexibility safely, allowing to raise the number of IoT devices that can communicate from anywhere while also lowering the Fog network's cost.
Secure multi-tenancy	• Account Hijacking • Issues with access control • Insecure APIs • Segregation Issues • Misuse of resources and nefarious activities • Malicious Insiders • Data Breaches	Safe collaboration on data among authorized users improved Fog resource use and allocation and shielded each user's room from memory hopping or escaping attacks.
Securing vehicular networks	• Access control issues • Persistent Threats in Advance • DoS attacks • Session or Account Hijacking • Identity theft protection for users	Maintains the communication of data confidentiality while protecting the location of users and identity data confidential, which increases road safety.
Recovery and backup	• Data unavailability issues • Data Loss • Due Diligence is Insufficient • Problems of data integrity • Malware infection	The data and its integrity will be accessible to users and the system in the event of a natural disaster, Denial of Service attack, or malware infection.

5.4 Future Scope

The Fog computing paradigm in the smart grid will be developed further in future research. Using this scenario, it is possible to develop two different models of fog-generating devices. When it comes to price and demand updates, Fog devices that are self-contained consult with the Cloud regularly, whereas interconnected Fog devices may consult with one another and form coalitions to provide even greater benefits to users.

Fog-as-a-service (also known as FaaS) is an interesting new field of development in which a Fog service provider constructs a network of interconnected fog nodes that will cover a large service area, which is a promising new development. Developing innovative apps and services that are difficult to develop on cloud-based and current host-based platforms will, as a result, become possible. Fog-based security services, for example, would alleviate many (Mahmood, 2018) of the present difficulties in the IoT environment.

In terms of security concerns, there is some potential future work that should be investigated further. For example, avoiding and defending against MITM attacks can be difficult. The incorporation of an anti-tampering mechanism into the Fog device would be a promising solution.

References

Afroj Alam, S. Q. (2020). *Fog, Edge and Pervasive Computing in Intelligent Internet of Things Driven Applications.* (A. K. Deepak Gupta, Ed.) https://doi.org/10.1002/9781119670087.ch1

Dimitrios Zissis, D. L. (2012). Addressing cloud computing security issues. *Future Generation Computer Systems, 28*(3), 583–592. https://doi.org/10.1016/j.future.2010.12.006

Jain, R., Gupta, M., Nayyar, A., and Sharma, N. (2020). Adoption of fog computing in healthcare 4.0. In S. Tanwar (Ed.), *Fog Computing for Healthcare 4.0 Environments* (pp. 3–36). Springer, Cham. https://doi.org/10.1007/978-3-030-46197-3_1

Liu, J., Yuan, C., Lai, Y., and Qin, H. (2020). Protection of sensitive data in industrial internet based on three-layer local/fog/cloud storage. *Security and Communication Networks, 2020.* https://doi.org/10.1155/2020/2017930

Mahmood, Z., and Ramachandran, M. (2018). Fog computing: Concepts, principles and related paradigms. In Z. Mahmood (Ed.), *Fog Computing* (pp. 3–21). Springer, Cham. https://doi.org/10.1007/978-3-319-94890-4_1

Mamata Rath, R. M. (2018). An exhaustive study and analysis of assorted application and challenges in fog computing and emerging ubiquitous computing technology. In *Applied Evolutionary Computation* (Vol. 9, p. 16). *International Journal of Applied Evolutionary Computation (IJAEC).* https://doi.org/10.4018/IJAEC.2018040102

Mithun Mukherjee, R. M. (2017, September 6). Security and privacy in fog computing: Challenges. *IEEE Access, 5,* 19293–19304. https://doi.org/10.1109/ACCESS.2017.2749422

PeiYun Zhang, M. Z. (2018). Security and trust issues in Fog computing: A survey. *Future Generation Computer Systems, 88,* 16–27. https://doi.org/10.1016/j.future.2018.05.008

Qiu, T., Chi, J., Zhou, X., Ning, Z., Atiquzzaman, M., and Wu, D. O. (2020). Edge computing in industrial Internet of Things: Architecture, advances and challenges. *IEEE, 22*(4), 2462–2488. https://doi.org/10.1109/COMST.2020.3009103

Sagiroglu, S., and Sinanc, D. (2013). Big data: A review. *International Conference on Collaboration Technologies and Systems (CTS),* (pp. 42–47). San Diego, CA, USA. https://doi.org/10.1109/CTS.2013.6567202

Somayya Madakam, P. B. (2018). Fog computing in the IoT environment: Principles, features, and models. In Z. Mahmood (Ed.), *Fog Computing* (1 ed., pp. 23–43). Springer, Cham. https://doi.org/10.1007/978-3-319-94890-4_2

Stojmenovic, I. W. (2014). The fog computing paradigm: scenarios and security issues. *FedCSIS 2014: Proceedings of the Federated Conference on Computer Science and Information Systems* (pp. 1–8). IEEE, Warsaw, Poland. https://doi.org/10.15439/2014F503

6

Energy-Efficient Cloud and Fog Computing in Internet of Things: Techniques and Challenges

Avita Katal and Vitesh Sethi

University of Petroleum and Energy Studies, Dehradun, India

CONTENTS

6.1 Introduction

Cloud infrastructure has disrupted the Information and Communications Technology (ICT) market by providing cost-effective data-sharing solutions. Image processing, digital analytics, and augmented and virtual reality are examples of big data and artificial intelligence technologies. According to Cisco, cloud storage traffic accounted for 56% of all Internet traffic in 2017. Global cloud storage traffic is anticipated to exceed 72% of all

DOI: 10.1201/9781003213888-6

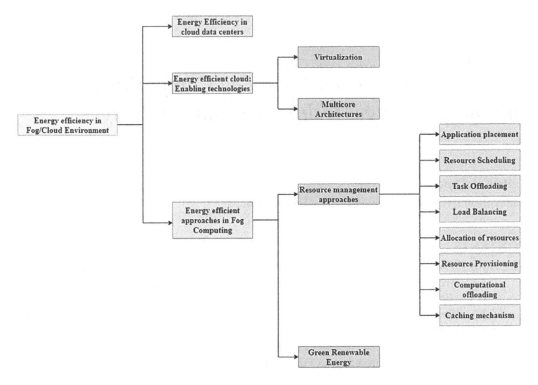

FIGURE 6.1
Taxonomy of energy-efficient approaches in the fog cloud environment.

Internet traffic in 2022 (Cisco Systems, 2019), showing further growth. Due to the rise in data volume and processing needs, a new generation of on-demand processing placement and administration is required. Academia and business have suggested fog computing (FC) as a way to get cloud services closer to customers.

Energy conservation has recently been recognized as one of the key criteria required to build a sustainable ICT system that leads to the rapid increase in demand for ICT services. The ICT market is expected to absorb 20% of global energy demand by 2025 ('Tsunami of Data' Could Consume One-Fifth of Global Electricity by 2025, *The Guardian*, 2017). Virtualization has been suggested as a resource consolidation technique that allows energy-efficient services of the fog cloud. Figure 6.1 shows the taxonomy of energy-efficient approaches in the fog cloud environment.

The remainder of the chapter is organized as follows: Sections 6.2 and 6.3 discusses energy efficiency in cloud data centers and its enabling technologies, respectively. Section 6.4 focuses on energy-efficient approaches in FC followed by discussion of research challenges in Section 6.5. The chapter concludes with the discussion of case studies in Section 6.6.

6.1.1 Architecture of Fog Computing

FC is a network that enables end-user computers to do local computation, distribution, and storage instead of relying on centralized data centers (Katal et al., 2021). This framework is increasingly being utilized and even required for a wide range of applications, including geodistributed, web-based, and real-time particularly in the Internet of Things (IoT). The following three levels make up the hierarchical architecture:

- Terminal Layer. It is close to the user. Sensors, cell phones, smart cars, smart cards, readers, and other IoT products are among the components. Even though cell phones and smart vehicles have computing resources but are used as smart sensing instruments in this application. In general, these instruments are commonly spread around the globe. They are in charge of sensing physical object or event attribute data and transferring it to the fog layer for computation and storage.

- Fog Layer. This layer is found at the network's edge. It comprises fog nodes that include routers, gateways, and switches. Fog layer can be used for latency-sensitive applications and real-time calculation. Additionally, the nodes are connected to the data center by an IP core network and are in charge of interacting and cooperating with the cloud in order to gain more efficient processing and storage capability.

- Cloud Layer. This layer is made up of a number of storage devices. It has strong computational and storage facilities to enable extensive computation and analysis, as well as the long-term storage of vast amounts of data. Unlike standard Cloud Computing architecture, however, not all computing and retrieval operations are performed in the cloud. The cloud core modules are effectively handled and scheduled according to demand-load by certain management strategies to increase cloud resource usage.

6.2 Energy-Efficient Cloud: Enabling Technologies

Besides depending only on hardware-oriented technologies such as high-capacity computers, energy-efficient servers, and operating fans, as well as a range of power-saving gadgets, some software-oriented energy management methods can also be employed. CC is a preferred paradigm for achieving energy savings due to a number of software-oriented innovations. The following section discusses CC viewpoints that allow energy efficiency. The section further identifies the main factors that make those projections credible in terms of lowering energy consumption.

6.2.1 Virtualization

Virtualization abstracts programs from the operating environment's inherent hardware and device nuances. Virtualization protects applications from networks, allowing many, geographically dispersed applications to share a single server. This aids in increasing resource use. The amount of energy used is reduced when underutilized services are more used. This is due to the fact that underutilized commodities use far more electricity than those that are fully used. Virtualization also improves protection and stability by allowing programs to operate securely and independently inside sandboxes.

Virtual Machine (VM) migration and consolidation techniques are two main aspects of virtualization that allow energy efficiency via VM migrations; the virtualized cloud environment reduces the number of operating physical devices. Furthermore, VM migrations allow workload balancing across all machines and avoid overuse of specific machines.

In addition to VM migrations, CC also conducts VM restructuring depending on the VMs' existing resource requirements. Consolidation is known as the method of incorporating into an integral whole that helps in reducing energy demand by assigning tasks between less loaded machinery and switching off idle devices.

Apart from VM consolidation, CC also conducts task and server consolidation. In practice, server consolidation entails the consolidation of several servers' resources onto a smaller number of more efficient servers. Server restructuring tends to increase resource usage while lowering energy consumption. Virtualization, which allows multiple tasks to operate on a single resource at the same time, greatly aids task consolidation. Tasks with identical specifications are mapped to the same servers to reduce unmatched computation and energy waste while allowing servers to perform similar types of tasks to avoid the complexity of add-on tasks.

6.2.2 Multicore Architectures

The use of multicore architecture is becoming more popular in today's computing technologies. Multicore processors also tend to mitigate the disadvantages of single-core processors by increasing data transfer speeds and lowering power consumption.

Modern multicore processors were reported to be more power efficient than previous generation multicore processors. Although modern multicore processors are designed to consume less power and generate less heat, their implementation is fraught with technical problems such as cache and memory contention. To get the most out of the multicore architecture, both the networking middleware and the programs must be multicore to avoid cache and memory contention.

Regardless of design issues, tests have shown that multicore processors have a significant environmental effect. As a result, it's critical to investigate the role of multicore processors in achieving energy efficiency, especially in CC.

6.3 Energy Efficiency in Cloud Data Centers

Energy performance simply refers to how easily virtualized datacenters providing cloud administrations can use or consume energy. Energy management aims to reduce the amount of energy used to deliver a range of goods and services while maintaining Quality of Services (QoS) standards. The increase in the number and size of cloud server farms has necessitated the need for energy management. To reduce the number of physical servers, server consolidation is used, and the problem of VM placement is to get the correct strategy for the placement for the least amount of resource waste and power use.

In Kliazovich et al. (2015), the authors discussed the energy usage of communication and computing equipment, stressing how energy efficiency can be accomplished. It tackles routing, load balancing, storage duplication, VM placement, and networking challenges which are used to minimize data center energy consumption.

6.4 Energy-Efficient Approaches in Fog Computing

In FC, energy efficiency can be achieved by resource management approaches and green renewable energy. The resource management approaches comprise application placement, resource scheduling, resource allocation, load balancing, resource provisioning, caching mechanism, and computational offloading. The detailed information for these approaches is mentioned in the subsequent sections.

6.4.1 Resource Management Techniques

FC, as previously said, is a distributed computing infrastructure that delivers data storage and computation resources locally rather than moving them to the cloud. It offers storage, processing, and networking services in the same way as CC does.

6.4.1.1 Placement of Application

An IoT service-oriented framework is made up of many IoT services that run on virtualized fog nodes and work together to provide perfect functions. In the fog landscape, the fog service placement decides an optimum placement strategy among fog nodes and IoT to optimize fog resource usage while satisfying IoT service Quality of Service (QoS) specifications. The three subcategories of application placement methods focused on broker management are centralized, decentralized, and hierarchical. The centralized broker requires data from all fog landscape agencies in order to make global optimization decisions, while the clustered broker only has a portion of the data and is more suited to ecosystems with fewer elements. Decentralized methods are inefficient as opposed to centralized ones due to the coordination overhead across management cores. Furthermore, hierarchical strategies create some semi-global, and a large number of local administrators and all managers collaborate to offer the benefits of both centralized and decentralized approaches. Figure 6.2 shows the application placement in the fog environment.

Table 6.1 shows the work done in the area of application placement.

6.4.1.2 Resource Scheduling

In FC, resource scheduling determines the best allocation of different tasks applied to be executed on nodes at the network's edge to satisfy QoS constraints agreed upon with the owner of an IoT device thereby reducing task execution time.

There are three major types of resource scheduling (or job scheduling) approaches: static, dynamic, and hybrid.

Tasks arrive at the fog nodes at the same time in static scheduling methods, and scheduling choices are taken before tasks are sent. It implies that justification of scheduling can be done if all required details about obtained demands and available resources are available prior to scheduling. However, in dynamic scheduling methods, task arrival dates are unknown prior to request, and assignments are scheduled as soon as they enter the system. Many scheduling criteria are combined in hybrid scheduling approaches to fit a multitude of program types, including workflows and batch jobs. Because no one solution/criterion can meet all sorts of requests in a fog situation, this function is very important in fog resource scheduling. Figure 6.3 illustrates the distribution of resources in a fog system.

Table 6.2 shows the work done in the domain of resource scheduling in a fog environment.

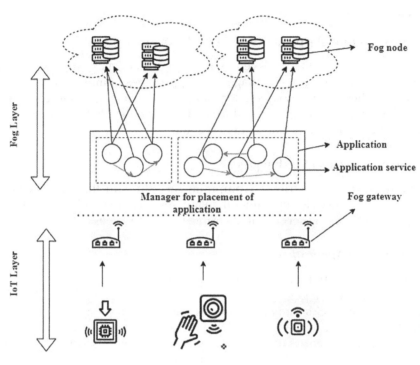

FIGURE 6.2
Application placement in the fog environment.

TABLE 6.1

Works in the Area of Application Placement

Work	Technique Used	Procedure Followed	Advantage	Disadvantage
Selimi et al. (2018)	Heuristic based	Using a quick heuristic algorithm, state knowledge about the network will be used to guide service placement decisions.	Considers the change in conditions of network topology.	Less scalable
Mahmud et al. (2019)	Heuristic based	Deploying clustered fog nodes to satisfy a variety of data delivery latency for various IoT applications.	Reduces the time for deployment	Users' preferences and versatility have not been taken into account.
Mahmud et al. (2019)	Fuzzy logic	To improve application implementation on fog resources and to categorize them, fuzzy logic models are used to prioritize numerous application placement requests.	Reduces the processing time	The approach's overhead has not been investigated.

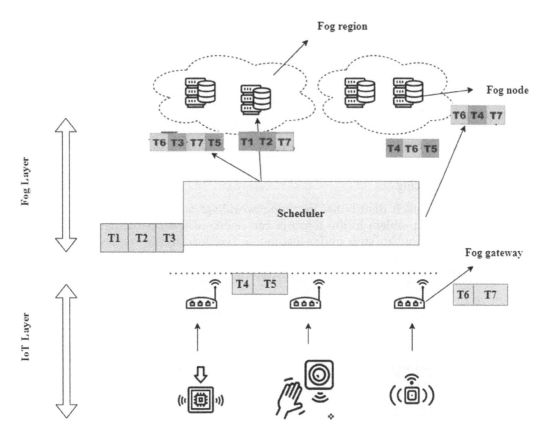

FIGURE 6.3
Resource scheduling in a fog environment.

TABLE 6.2

Work Done in the Domain of Resource Scheduling in a Fog Environment

Work	Technique Used	Procedure Followed	Advantage	Disadvantage
Sun et al. (2018)	NSGA II	The resource scheduling algorithm is divided into two sections: scheduling of resources within the same fog cluster, fog clusters, and resource scheduling between fog nodes.	Low execution time.	High cost.
Sun and Zhang (2017)	Game theory	Replicated game theory and a crowdfunding algorithm.	Low latency rate.	High energy consumption.
Chen and Wang (2017)	Heuristic based	Two hierarchical scheduling algorithms for data scheduling on vehicular networks based on variations in length of queue and response time in fog infrastructure.	High dynamic efficiency.	Not mentioned.
Ahmad et al. (2020)	Software Defined Networking (SDN)	In fog-assisted CC, use the Fog Node (FN) scheduling scheme to save resources.	Energy savings in fog-assisted CC.	Not mentioned.

6.4.1.3 Task Offloading

The task offloading approaches can be split into two groups depending on the number of offloading destinations: single and multiple. Multiple-type offloading approaches have multiple destinations for offloading computation activities, i.e., multiple fog nodes for transaction execution, in order to follow QoS requirements. Single-type offloading approaches offload computational loads to a single fog node for concurrent processing. Figure 6.4 shows the task of offloading in a fog environment.

Table 6.3 shows the work done in the area of task offloading in the fog environment.

6.4.1.4 Load Balancing

Load balancing, which distributes incoming workload across available fog nodes, is another important problem in the resource management area, particularly for latency-sensitive applications. To stop under-loading or overloading fog nodes, activities are spread across several fog nodes according to one technique for balancing of load over the fog nodes with different capacities. Different types of load balancing approaches are used.

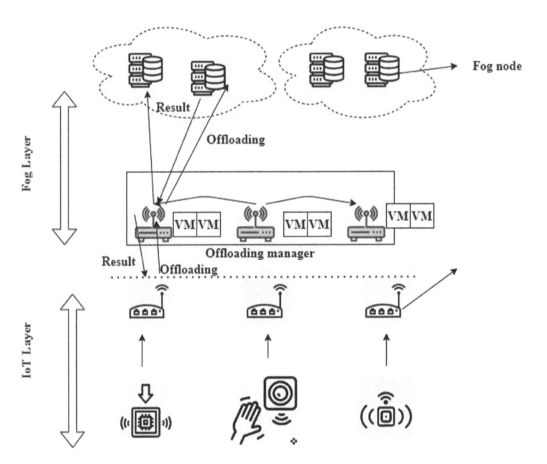

FIGURE 6.4
Task offloading in fog environment.

TABLE 6.3

Work Done in the Area of Task Offloading in the Fog Environment

Work	Technique Used	Procedure Followed	Advantage	Disadvantage
Liu et al. (2018a)	Queuing theory+ IPM based algorithm	Researchers employed queuing models and offloading payment expenditure processes as a multi-objective issue to investigate the trade-off between delay and energy usage.	Reducing energy consumption.	High computational complexity.
Wang et al. (2018)	Queuing theory+ Approximate based	Offloading approach based on queuing theory for reducing the reaction time for events registered by vehicles as fog nodes.	On the Internet of Vehicles (IoV) applications, real-time traffic is supported.	Not evaluated energy consumption.

Centralized approach makes use of central node whereas in the decentralized approach all the nodes are divided into clusters and each of the cluster uses the central node to balance it. Both fog facilities and IoT demands must be considered by the global controller of a single load balancer. Centralized architecture is not robust or flexible because of the centralized single control node. Since there is no overarching point of influence, decentralized options seem to be more promising for fog resource management. Figure 6.5 shows the load balancing mechanism in the fog environment.

Table 6.4 depicts the literature in the domain of load balancing of the fog environment.

6.4.1.5 Allocation of Resources

The problems associated with resource allocation in FC systems are characterized as a double matching problem, with cloud providers and fog nodes matched for IoT users and fog nodes and IoT users matched for cloud servers. There are two methods for allocating resources: auction-based and optimization-based. The auction-based resource allocation mechanisms are a market-based pricing technique for expanding and leveraging demand and supply fog nodes by bidding on them and then selling them to the highest bidder. With resource allocation being modeled in the optimization methods as a double-matching problem, cloud servers and fog nodes are interconnected for IoT users. Figure 6.6 shows the allocation of resources in the fog environment.

Table 6.5 shows the literature in the domain resource allocation in the fog environment.

6.4.1.6 Resource Provisioning Approaches

Since the workload of IoT services varies with time, there may be variations in workload. Over-provisioning or under-provisioning issues can arise as a result of the fluctuating workloads. As a result, dynamically providing a sufficient number of fog nodes needed to accommodate the submitted IoT workload is critical for reducing device costs while maintaining QoS constraints. The resource provisioning methods can be categorized into three categories based on the provisioning time: reactive, proactive, and hybrid policies. The reactive policy makes no forecasts and instead reacts to the actual state of the environment, while the pragmatic policy uses modeling techniques to estimate future IoT

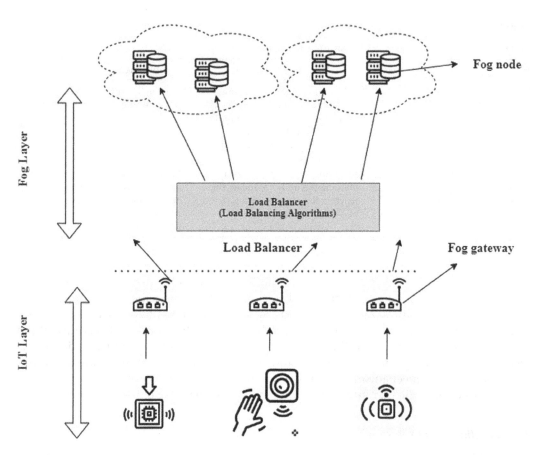

FIGURE 6.5
Load balancing mechanism in the fog environment.

TABLE 6.4

Literature Survey in the Load Balancing of Fog Environment

Work	Technique Used	Procedure Followed	Advantage	Disadvantage
Li et al. (2018)	Threshold approach	Load balancing for self-similarity-based large-scale applications.	Low overhead and high scalability.	Energy consumption and throughput not considered.
Manasrah et al. (2017)	Differential evolution algorithm	Enhanced utility broker solution using differential evolution optimization and throttled load balancing technique.	Reducing response time and cost.	Lack of data privacy mechanism.

application demand and adjust resource provisioning accordingly. The reactive policies scale the IoT deployment only after a workload transformation has occurred, while the pragmatic policies predict incoming IoT workload shifts in real time using modeling techniques are typically handled by the reactive policy while scaling in is handled by the proactive policy. Figure 6.7 shows the resource provisioning in the fog environment. Table 6.6 shows the literature in the domain of resource provisioning in FC.

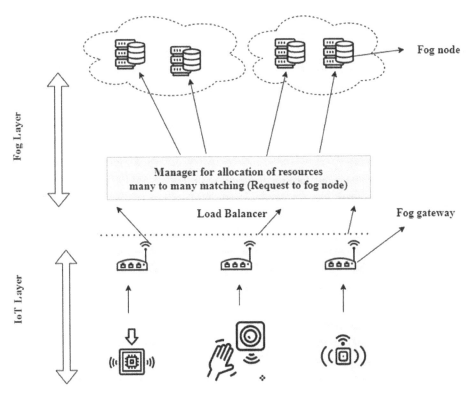

FIGURE 6.6
Allocation of resources in FC environment.

TABLE 6.5

Literature Survey in the Domain of Resource Allocation in the Fog Environment

Work	Technique Used	Procedure Followed	Advantage	Disadvantage
Zhang et al. (2017)	Game theory	Included a range of network services, data service customers as consumers, and small processing capacity as fog nodes.	Low delay.	Less scalable and high cost.
Naranjo et al. (2017)	Heuristic based	Dynamically schedules incoming traffic through fog nodes to provide high availability operations to smartphone devices in a vehicular FC environment.	Low delay.	Not evaluating time.
Jia et al. (2018)	Double matching	Following an examination of utility and cost in FC networks, a cost-efficient double-matching approach for the resource allocation problem in FC networks was proposed.	Low-cost.	Less scalable.

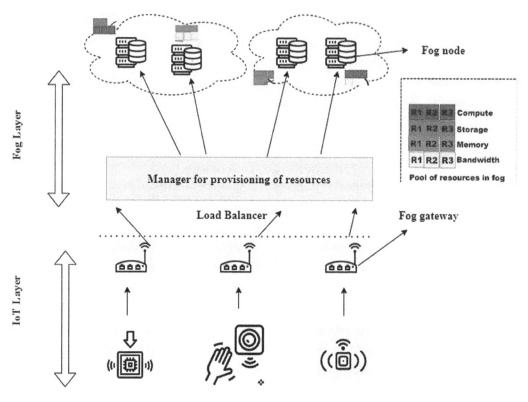

FIGURE 6.7
Resource provisioning in the fog environment.

TABLE 6.6

Literature in the Domain of Resource Provisioning in Fog Computing

Work	Technique Used	Procedure Followed	Advantage	Disadvantage
Tseng et al. (2018)	Fuzzy theory	For resource provisioning, a lightweight fuzzy-based auto-scaling approach is used.	Low cost.	Live migration not considered.
Vinueza Naranjo et al. (2018)	Heuristic based	A penalty aware bin packing style heuristic architecture was developed for complicated resources planning of virtualized services shared from each fog node.	Support container based virtualization.	Workload not considered.
Russo Russo et al. (2018)	Reinforcement learning	For managing elastic Data Stream Processing (DSP) systems and frameworks, an autonomous approach is used.	Avoid resource wastage.	Resource estimation not considered.
Pereira dos Santos et al. (2021)	Mixed Integer Linear Programming	Incorporates SFC principles, various LPWAN technology, and several optimization goals.	Full end-to-end (E2E) resource provisioning.	Not mentioned.

6.4.1.7 Computational Offloading

The transition of resource-intensive computing functions to a different processor, such as a hardware accelerator, or an external network is known as computation offloading. End users will offload computationally intensive tasks to a fog node nearby in FC. Furthermore, fog nodes offload these functions to the cloud and nearby fog nodes in order to find additional computing tools.

The developers of (Liu, Chang et al., 2018b) use queuing theory to conduct a detailed investigation into the energy usage and offloading phase execution delay. An energy-efficient optimization problem is formulated based on the theoretical analysis, with the goal of minimizing energy consumption. In (Zhao et al., 2019), the authors looked at how to design computation offloading in Fog Radio Access Networks (F-RANs) in reducing the entire expense. A combined optimization problem is designed in order to optimize the offloading decision, processing, and radio resource distribution. In (Liu et al., 2018a), the authors suggested an optimized FC and CC solution, in which users would cooperatively offload a collection of applications to fog nodes in the surrounding area (FNs). This reduces offloading transmission latency and frees up finite radio resource.

6.4.1.8 Caching Mechanism

The core of FC is efficient data caching. Furthermore, in the case of a high miss ratio, less efficiency caching mechanism can place an additional strain on network resources. FC, as an emerging concept, increases the need for reliable caching methods, which must be consistent with IoT and its broad range of applications.

A popularity-based caching framework is proposed in (Shahid et al., 2020) for content distribution fog networks. In this regard, two energy-conscious techniques, namely material filtering and load balancing, have been employed. Common contents are discovered using random distribution in the suggested method, and these contents are divided into three groups. Following the determination of file popularity, an active fog node is selected based on the number of neighbors, energy level, and operating capacity. This approach suffers from high latency. A filtration function is often used to cache common content on the active node. CachinMobile is a caching network suggested by the authors in (S. Wang et al., 2016) in the FC model. End users in the CachinMobile network request content from edge nodes through D2D communication. End users can query eNodeB for the requested content if it is not available in adjacent edge nodes. The authors of (Assila et al., 2018) suggested a green approach for improving energy quality in an FC system and Internet of All (IoE) devices by using caching technologies combined with fog functionality.

6.4.2 Green Renewable Energy in Fog Environment

In a machine with a large number of processing nodes, energy consumption is an issue. Renewable energy sources can be utilized to offset carbon emissions by lowering demand on the main power system; but, owing to unpredictability, careful resource management is necessary.

The authors of Gougeon et al. (2020) provide an energy-efficient fog architecture that integrates renewable energy. They investigate three distinct resource allocation algorithms and three distinct consolidation strategies. Based on real traces, their simulation findings show that the nodes' intrinsic limited computational capability makes it more difficult to harvest renewable energy in a fog sense. The authors of (Karimiafshar et al., 2020) proposed an effective component for progressively dispatching demands among figuring hubs and scaling recurrence and adjustment level dependent on the current responsibility and accessibility of sustainable power sources to lessen administration time while keeping up satisfactory environmentally friendly power use and steadiness.

6.5 Research Challenges

- Scalability – The topic of scalability is a significant obstacle in the application placement strategy for mobile institutions like healthcare and transportation apps. The use of a vehicular ad hoc network (VANET) architecture in FC may have an effect on platform mobility.

- Scheduling – Fog nodes typically have the minimal capacity and computational saving control, despite the massive workload they are expected to handle. In the FC world, fog node scheduling and efficient usage are critical. The difficult part is scheduling fog nodes with unpredictably high relinquish odds and then making the best use of the tools available. Utilizing CPU operations, optimum task assignment, and concurrent scheduling are some of the latest challenges to this open topic.

- Offloading – The act of choosing how to split an application and allocating each assignment to one of three layers is known as computational offloading. It's especially beneficial for time-consuming computations and conserves battery life. The offloading platform can take into consideration, the fog nodes' heterogeneity and functionality. The static design of certain stream and data processing contexts makes them unsuitable for fog and IoT environments. Functional partitioning, system heterogeneity, and complex data configuration are some of the recent obstacles to this accessible problem.

- Privacy and Security – Because fog nodes deal with lot of sensitive data, data privacy is critical. Since FC is easy to set up but difficult to maintain, trust is a possible threat, and solving it is still a work in progress. Authentication at different layers of the fog remains a critical issue for which no ideal solution identified. Detecting fake or unqualified fog nodes may even lower the cost of authentication. Trust accessing, and complex authentication are some of the latest obstacles to this transparent topic.

- Interoperability – The ability of fog nodes and IoT artifacts to exchange resources and data is one of the most important factors in fog node interconnections. Resource interoperability comprises a management controller that communicates with the virtual apps for each request. Some of the new challenges confronting this open issue include dynamic on-the-fly communications, optimum data exchange, and information distribution.

- Energy consumption – In FC, there are several new problems, such as data transfer, energy waste, and possible battery drain. Every fog node's energy is conserved by controlling bandwidth in data transmission. The utilization of 5G in fog infrastructure will also increase energy usage for IoT smart devices with poor battery life.

6.6 Case Studies

'A Green Adaptive FC and Networking Architecture (GAUChO)', the title of the PRIN2015 initiative seeks to create a new heterogeneous and distributed architecture capable of functionally integrating and optimizing FC and network functionality on the same platform. Furthermore, the ubiquity, decentralized control, cooperation, proximity to consumers, dense geographical delivery, and effective mobility support of the GAUChO platform are possible by the development of relevant analytic techniques and the specification of appropriate mechanisms (Description | Project | Progetto Di Ricerca PRIN 'GAUCHO' - UniFI, 2017). Low-latency and energy efficiency will be prioritized in the proposed FC+FN architecture, as well as security, self-adaptation, and spectrum efficiency. End-devices and processing units of the integrated FC+FN architecture can work closely together to achieve these properties.

The Sapienza University of Rome-led 'Vehicular Fog energy-efficient QoS mining and distribution of multimedia Big Data streams (V-Fog)' project aims to identify, design, and verify advanced data mining and management of resource decentralized adaptive algorithms for V-Fog. V-ultimate Fog's goal is to provide power-efficient aid for practical applications, such as data transmission (Vehicular Fog for Energy-Efficient QoS Mining and Dissemination of Multimedia Big Data Streams (VFog), n.d.). The ultimate aim is to enable real-time Big-Data streaming-type future Internet applications, such as multimedia human behavior detection and immersive infotainment platforms, with minimal energy consumption (e.g., VTube).

6.7 Conclusion

CC offers a variety of resources, such as storage and retrieval that can be accessed as needed. Despite its many advantages, it still has several drawbacks that hinder the cloud's complete adoption. The main problem encountered during CC adaptability is high latency and lack of knowledge of location. To address these problems, the idea of FC was developed to minimize cloud load and optimize resource utilization. The fog is similar to the cloud in that it offers the same resources. The increasing popularity of CC and FC has resulted in an increase in energy consumption. FC is gaining popularity as a result of its many benefits, and the rise of IoT devices is increasing the load on FC. Because of the increased production of the IoT devices, power and energy usage in the cloud fog network has become a challenge for environmental and economic reasons. In this chapter, the energy efficiency in cloud data centers has been discussed. The chapter also covers the detailed information about the enabling technologies that allow energy efficiency in CC and FC and concludes with the research challenges in saving energy in the fog and cloud environment.

References

'Tsunami of data' could consume one fifth of global electricity by 2025, *The Guardian*. (2017). Retrieved August 2, 2021, from https://www.theguardian.com/environment/2017/dec/11/tsunami-of-data-could-consume-fifth-global-electricity-by-2025

Ahmad, M., Patra, S. S., & Barik, R. K. (2020). Energy-efficient resource scheduling in fog computing using SDN Framework. *Advances in Intelligent Systems and Computing, 1119*, 567–578. doi:10.1007/978-981-15-2414-1_57.

Assila, B., Kobbane, A., Walid, A., & El Koutbi, M. (2018). Achieving low-energy consumption in fog computing environment: A matching game approach. *19th IEEE Mediterranean Eletrotechnical Conference, MELECON 2018 - Proceedings*, 213–218. doi:10.1109/MELCON.2018.8379096.

Chen, X., & Wang, L. (2017). Exploring fog computing-based adaptive vehicular data scheduling policies through a compositional formal method - PEPA. *IEEE Communications Letters, 21*(4), 745–748. doi:10.1109/LCOMM.2016.2647595.

Cisco Systems, Inc. (2019). Cisco Visual Networking Index: Forecast and Trends, 2017–2022 White Paper. *Cisco Forecast and Methodology, 2017–2022*. Retrieved August 2, 2021. http://www.cisco.com/en/US/solutions/collateral/ns341/ns525/ns537/ns705/ns827/white_paper_c11-481360_ns827_Networking_Solutions_White_Paper.html

Description | Project | Progetto di ricerca PRIN "GAUCHO" - UniFI. (2017). Retrieved August 2, 2021, from https://www.gaucho.unifi.it/vp-93-description.html

Gougeon, A., Camus, B., & Orgerie, A. C. (2020). Optimizing green energy consumption of fog computing architectures. *Proceedings - Symposium on Computer Architecture and High Performance Computing, 2020-September*, 75–82. doi:10.1109/SBAC-PAD49847.2020.00021.

Jia, B., Hu, H., Zeng, Y., Xu, T., & Yang, Y. (2018). Double-matching resource allocation strategy in fog computing networks based on cost efficiency. *Journal of Communications and Networks, 20*(3), 237–246. doi:10.1109/JCN.2018.000036.

Karimiafshar, A., Hashemi, M. R., Heidarpour, M. R., & Toosi, A. N. (2020). Effective utilization of renewable energy sources in fog computing environment via frequency and modulation level scaling. *IEEE Internet of Things Journal, 7*(11), 10912–10921. doi:10.1109/JIOT.2020.2993276.

Katal, A., Sethi, V., Lamba, S., & Choudhury, T. (2021). Fog Computing: Issues, Challenges and Tools. In Ajith Abraham, Paramartha Dutta, Jyotsna Kumar Mandal, Abhishek Bhattacharya, & Soumi Dutta (Eds.), *Emerging Technologies in Data Mining and Information Security*, 971–982. Springer. doi:10.1007/978-981-15-9927-9_92.

Kliazovich, D., Bouvry, P., Granelli, F., & da Fonseca, N. L. S. (2015). Energy Consumption Optimization in Cloud Data Centers. *Cloud Services, Networking, and Management*, 191–215. doi:10.1002/9781119042655.CH8.

Li, C., Zhuang, H., Wang, Q., & Zhou, X. (2018). SSLB: Self-similarity-based load balancing for large-scale fog computing. *Arabian Journal for Science and Engineering, 43*(12), 7487–7498. doi:10.1007/S13369-018-3169-3.

Liu, L., Chang, Z., Guo, X., Mao, S., & Ristaniemi, T. (2018b). Multiobjectiveoptimization for computation offloading in fog computing. *IEEE Internet of Things Journal, 5*(1), 283–294. doi:10.1109/JIOT.2017.2780236.

Liu, Y., Richard Yu, F., Li, X., Ji, H., & Leung, V. C. M. (2018a). Distributed resource allocation and computation offloading in fog and cloud networks with non-orthogonal multiple access. *IEEE Transactions on Vehicular Technology, 67*(12), 12137–12151. doi:10.1109/TVT.2018.2872912.

Mahmud, R., Srirama, S. N., Ramamohanarao, K., & Buyya, R. (2019). Quality of Experience (QoE)-aware placement of applications in Fog computing environments. *Journal of Parallel and Distributed Computing, 132*, 190–203. doi:10.1016/J.JPDC.2018.03.004.

Manasrah, A. M., Aldomi, A., & Gupta, B. B. (2017). An optimized service broker routing policy based on differential evolution algorithm in fog/cloud environment. *Cluster Computing, 22*(1), 1639–1653. doi:10.1007/S10586-017-1559-Z.

Naranjo, P. G. V., Baccarelli, E., & Scarpiniti, M. (2018). Design and energy-efficient resource management of virtualized networked Fog architectures for the real-time support of IoT applications. *The Journal of Supercomputing, 6*(74), 2470–2507. doi:10.1007/S11227-018-2274-0.

Naranjo, P. G. V., Pooranian, Z., Shamshirband, S., Abawajy, J. H., & Conti, M. (2017). Fog over virtualized IoT: New opportunity for context-aware networked applications and a case study. *Applied Sciences, 7*(12), 1325. doi:10.3390/APP7121325.

Russo Russo, G., Nardelli, M., Cardellini, V., & Lo Presti, F. (2018). Multi-level elasticity for wide-area data streaming systems: A reinforcement learning approach. *Algorithms*, 11(9), 134. doi:10.3390/A11090134.

Santos, J., Wauters, T., Volckaert, B., & de Turck, F. (2021). Towards end-to-end resource provisioning in fog computing over low power wide area networks. *Journal of Network and Computer Applications*, 175, 102915. doi:10.1016/J.JNCA.2020.102915.

Selimi, M., Cerdà-Alabern, L., Freitag, F., Veiga, L., Sathiaseelan, A., & Crowcroft, J. (2018). A lightweight service placement approach for community network micro-clouds. *Journal of Grid Computing*, 17(1), 169–189. doi:10.1007/S10723-018-9437-3.

Shahid, M. H., Hameed, A. R., ul Islam, S., Khattak, H. A., Din, I. U., & Rodrigues, J. J. P. C. (2020). Energy and delay efficient fog computing using caching mechanism. *Computer Communications*, 154, 534–541. doi:10.1016/J.COMCOM.2020.03.001.

Sun, Y., Lin, F., & Xu, H. (2018). Multi-objective optimization of resource scheduling in fog computing using an improved NSGA-II. *Wireless Personal Communications*, 102(2), 1369–1385. doi:10.1007/S11277-017-5200-5.

Sun, Y., & Zhang, N. (2017). A resource-sharing model based on a repeated game in fog computing. *Saudi Journal of Biological Sciences*, 24(3), 687–694. doi:10.1016/J.SJBS.2017.01.043.

Tseng, F. H., Tsai, M. S., Tseng, C. W., Yang, Y. T., Liu, C. C., & der Chou, L. (2018). A lightweight autoscaling mechanism for fog computing in industrial applications. *IEEE Transactions on Industrial Informatics*, 14(10), 4529–4537. doi:10.1109/TII.2018.2799230.

Vehicular Fog for energy-efficient QoS mining and dissemination of multimedia Big Data streams (VFog). (n.d.). Retrieved August 2, 2021, from https://sites.google.com/a/uniroma1.it/enzobaccarelli-eng/pubblicazioni/main-ongoing-reseach-project

Wang, S., Huang, X., Liu, Y., & Yu, R. (2016). CachinMobile: An energy-efficient users caching scheme for fog computing. *2016 IEEE/CIC International Conference on Communications in China, ICCC 2016.* doi:10.1109/ICCCHINA.2016.7636852.

Wang, X., Ning, Z., & Wang, L. (2018). Offloading in Internet of vehicles: A fog-enabled real-time traffic management system. *IEEE Transactions on Industrial Informatics*, 14(10), 4568–4578. doi:10.1109/TII.2018.2816590.

Zhang, H., Xiao, Y., Bu, S., Niyato, D., Yu, F. R., & Han, Z. (2017). Computing resource allocation in three-tier iot fog networks: a joint optimization approach combining stackelberg game and matching. *IEEE Internet of Things Journal*, 4(5), 1204–1215. doi:10.1109/JIOT.2017.2688925.

Zhao, Z., Bu, S., Zhao, T., Yin, Z., Peng, M., Ding, Z., & Quek, T. Q. S. (2019). On the design of computation offloading in fog radio access networks. *IEEE Transactions on Vehicular Technology*, 68(7), 7136–7149. doi:10.1109/TVT.2019.2919915.

7

Deployment of Distributed Clustering Approach in WSNs and IoTs

Rachna
CT University, Ludhiana, India

Pankaj Bhambri
CT University, Ludhiana, India

Yogesh Chhabra
Guru Nanak Dev Engineering College, Ludhiana, India

CONTENTS

7.1 Introduction

WSNs are made of low-energy sensor devices outfitted with sensation board, processing, and wireless transmission resources. Sensor devices work together to gather and dispatch sensed data to a sink device using multi-hop transmission. These networks are used in diverse applications such as medical management, armed forces, manufacturing, observing, tracking depending on the multimedia sensor and several other areas. In recent times, IP-dependent sensor networks are fascinating extra awareness. These networks enable the expansion of the IoT. Still, today power consumption is the main obstacle in several sensor network applications which need always long life (Otayf, 2021) (Figures 7.1–7.3).

WSNs give many kinds of applications that are secure and intelligent-profitable existence. Many applications of WSNs help to minimize the infrequent supply of energy, to control the noise and impressive observing the reduction of contamination, and medical

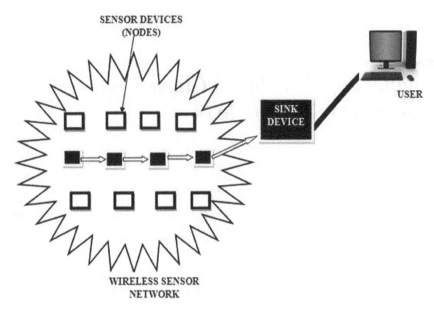

FIGURE 7.1
Structural design of WSNs.

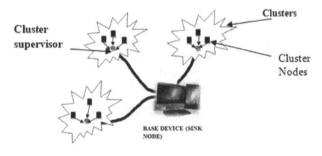

FIGURE 7.2
Low energy distributed clustering architecture.

management which is helping the health. Transmission between the sensors and the diverse types of servers is required for any application. These transmissions can be done through the three main retrieve tools structural design. These structural designs gain from significant wireless transmission tools such as IEEE 802.15.3 and IEEE 802.15.4 for WPAN, IEEE 802.11g and 802.11n for WLAN, and HSDPA and LTE for WWAN (Abdelkareem, 2018).

Increasing application accomplishments, the routing approaches are used for finding out the most excellent way to the goal, the power-saving approaches which are used for increasing the time of sensors, and safety rules are used for own confidentiality in WSN(Minh Nguyen, 2019) (Shokat Ali, 2020)

System (SOSUS), built by the United States Armed forces in the 1950s to expose and follow Soviet submarines. Rumbling the savings is prepared in the 1960s. DARPA organized the Disseminated projection Nets Workshop, which focuses on arranged transmitter systems investigating experiments such as set of connections tools, indicator dealing out tools, and disseminated approaches. The military developed wireless sensor networks for monitoring

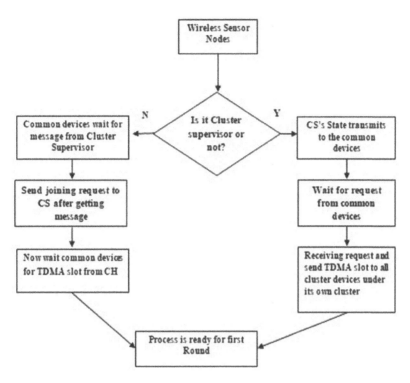

FIGURE 7.3
Flow chart of cluster supervisor selection.

the enemies' tasks (Harwood, 2019). In 1980, DARPA also organized the disseminated projection Nets (DPN) program; the Sensor Information Technology program followed these networks. They also gave the current sensor networks new potentials such as active inquiry and tasking, ad hoc networking, reprogramming, and multitasking. Bult et al. showed a result of the WINS project and LWIM formed in 1996. This stylish importance scheme is based on a CMOS microprocessor, incorporating manifold sensors, crossing point paths, digital signs dealing with a way, wireless data lines, and a small controller against a solitary microprocessor. In 1999, the University of California at Berkeley paid attention to the blueprint of hugely tiny projection devices called particle in the Smart Dust Development. The main motive of this development was to exhibit that a whole intelligent scheme obtainable built into little devices, maybe the amount of a particle of sandpaper or still a soil particle. In 2000, BWRC focused on the built-up of less-energy transmitter nodes in the PicoRadio project. In 2005, Mini-Robust Multi- field Energy-attentive Instruments urbanized (Harwood, 2019).

In 1832, an ultraviolet transmit was established by Baron Schilling in Russia, and in 1833, Carl Friedrich Gauss and Wilhelm Weber made-up own peculiar cipher to converse concluded an extension of 1200 m in the interior of Gottingen, Germany. In 1844, Samuel Morse transmits the paramount peculiar cipher unclosed transmit idea 'What has Almighty produced?' from Washington, D.C. to Baltimore. In 1926, Nikola Tesla in an interlocution alongside haulers publication

> As long as cordless is entirely realistic the entire floor might be transformed right into a widespread mind, what contained by validity it has miles, each and everyone matter existent subdivision of an actual and musical general, in addition to that equipment

attributable to what type of one and all should be successful to execute the aforementioned may stay exceedingly easy in comparison with belonging to us gift smart phone. A gentleman will be capable of bring one in his hand bag.

In 1950, Alan Turing in its artifact Computing equipment as well as understanding within the Oxford thoughts journal,

> it is able to as well as be enriched that it has miles great to offer the equipment with the exceptional sensation body parts that currency can purchase, after which train it to apprehend and speak English. This method may want to comply with the ordinary coaching of a toddler.

In 1964, In knowledge Media Marshall McLuhan said by powered broadcasting, They launch flexible approaches through which each and every prior tools can be converted into records methods. (Labs, 2013)

In 1966, Karl Steinbuch a German processor hi-tech explorer stated, 'In a minimal year instance, broadcast computer systems could be amalgamated into approximately every business manufactured goods' in 1969, Arpanet. In 1974, the Initial stages of TCP/IP. In 1984, region depict domestic device is added. In 1989, Tim Berners-Lee recommended the arena enormous mesh. In 1990, contemplating the primary IoT piece of equipment, John Romkey formed a microwave oven that would be turn out to be on as well as stale above the net for the October '89 INTEROP conference. Dan Lynch, Head of INTEROP gave guarantee Romkey that, if Romkey become competent of 'carry up his microwave oven at the internet', the tools might get large designation put in the ground –extensive displayer on the conference. The microwave oven became associated with a processor with Transmission Control Protocol/ Internet Protocol set of connections. It later used a truth base (SNMP MIB) to convert the power on. In 1991, the most important position sheet was made by Tim Berners-Lee. In 1991, Mark Weiser's Scientific American critique on top of persistent catalog labeled 'The processor designed for the 21st Century' is compiled'. The mainly significant advances are individuals with the intention of vanishing. It meshes itself into the texture of regular day-to-day existence till it is unclear from it. In 1993, the Strong Room Coffee container was developed by Quentin Stafford-Fraser and Paul Jardetzky. It was situated in the Strong Room in the Processing labs of the University of Cambridge. It was exploited to supervise the container layers by way of a print being invigorated as regards 3x per instant as well as transported off the company employee. It was consequently kept online for study one time plans could demonstrate prints. In 1994, Steve Mann builds Wear Cam. In 1995, The Net starts trade with Amazon and Echobay (EBay) (Labs, 2013). In 1997, Paul Saffo's perceptive critique 'Sensory: The Next Wave of InfoTech Innovation'. In 1998, Google is combined and connected a mission at the Massachusetts Institute of Technology. It was created by Scott Brave, Andrew Dahley, and Professor Hiroshi Ishii. After that, they contemporary connected at that point, which utilizes Corresponding Disseminated Substantial Things to assemble a 'definite receiver' for substantial space haptic communication. Before one year of losing of fight with his disease, Mark Weiser built a drinking fountain outside his office whose length touched the volume and pattern of financial exchange. 'Universal indexing is normally incredible opposing to improved realism', Weiser articulated, 'Wherever improved realism sets personnel in a PC formed sphere, persistent shaping powers the PC to live in the region of now on the world with persons' (Nguyen, 2019).

The most significant year for the Internet of Things and Massachusetts Institute of Technology was 1999. The Internet of Things were introduced by Kevin Ashton, who was center head of the Auto-Identification Hub: 'It cannot be correct; however it's authentically sure the expression' Web of Effects

> start life as the label of a show it prepared at Procter and Gamble (P&G) in 1999. Connecting the groundbreaking thought of Radio Frequency Identification in P&G's store network to the there, super enthusiastic theme of the Internet was somewhat beyond a decent method to stand out enough to be noticed. It's anything but an important acquaintance which is still consistently misunderstood.

Neil Gershenfeld was chatting about proportional effects from the Massachusetts Institute of Technology Media Lab in his volume whilst Special effects start to imagine and at the same time as locating up the Midpoint for Bits and Atoms in 2001

> as a rule it comes into view as however the fast growth of the Information superhighway may have been reasonably lately the activate cost that is currently conditioning off the indisputable explosion, as effects start to use the Net.
>
> **(Labs, 2013)**

Auto-Identification Labs unclose which is the searching sited substitution to the Massachusetts Institute of Technology Auto-Identification hub, formerly determined by Kevin Ashton, David Brock and Sanjay Sharma. They cultivated the Electronic Product Code, a global Radio Frequency Identification –support effect Identification agenda projected to succeed the UPC scanner tag. Neil Gross in Trade Week

> In the following century, the globe will wear an electronic outside. It will use the net as a display place to aid as well as exchange a few words its sensations. This outside is as of now being basted together. It encompasses of millions of set of connections electronic guessing tools: interior managers, force events, contagion qualifiers, and camcorder, and representative, blood starch sensors, Electrocardiography, electroencephalographs. These will test as well as observe built-up region and put at risk variety, the surroundings, belonging to us vessel, superhighway and flotilla of trucks, belonging to us debates, belonging to us bodies – even belonging to us illusions.

In 2000, beginning off the effect is at this time rotating into a picture, LG announces it has original net cooler tactics. In 2002, The climate sphere built by David Rose as well as others in a side project from the Massachusetts Institute of Technology Medium Lab is distributed into the undomesticated with NY Period Periodical identification which is one of the opinion of the Year. The sphere checks by Dow Jones, personal choice, typical climate as well as other data resource and revolutionize its gloominess reliant on the influential limitations (Labs, 2013). The term is referenced in standard distributions such as The Protector, technological American and the Boston Globe conditions are intimated by accepted propagation in 2003–2004. Projects such as Chill city, Internet, and the Vanishing Computer steer gaze to take out a piece of the opinion, and the Internet of Things expression starts to display up in volume label entertainingly. Radio Frequency Identification is transmitted for an outrageous scale by the US Department of Defense in their Rescue plan and Wal-Mart in the trade globe. 2005: The Internet of things beat a further stage when the UN's International Telecommunications Union ITU circulated its primary details on the subject matter.

> A further capability has been added to the universe of records and association progression (ICTs): from at whatever time, any stain accessibility for everyone, they will presently have set of connections for everything. Links will enlarge and build an totally novel sole association of corporation—an Internet of Things.

2005 year was the right time for the Nabaztag to initially create a piece of Aldebaran Robotics by the corporation Mauve and built by Rafi Haladjian and Olivier Mével. The small Wi-Fi un-build here had the choice to care as well as concentrate on you about monetary substitute summary, news features, daybreak control, RSS –provides for, and so smooths now as crossing point with one an extra. The affirmation was 'in the occurrence that you can constant border bunnies, you can connect everything'. In 2006–2008, classification by the EU and the novel European IOT meeting is seized. A meeting of establishment sends off the IPSO Association to improve the consumption of Internet Protocol (IP) in companies of 'know-how bits and pieces' and to sanction the Internet of Things. The IPSO coalition presently brag further than 50 part business, containing Bosch, Cisco, Ericsson, Intel, SAP, Sun, Google and Fujitsu. The FCC introduced a secret ballot 5–0 to carry unlocking the consumption of the 'empty space region' scope. In 2008–2009, The Internet of Things was 'Instinctive' As pointed to by Cisco Internet Business Solutions Group (IBSG), the Internet of Things was transported into the globe in the center 2008 and 2009 at immediately time as more 'effects or critiques' were related with the net than personal. In 2010 the cell phones, tablet PCs and so many new gadgets were developed near about 12.5 billion, at the same time as the globe's population increased to 6.8 billion, and it was building the number of connected gadgets per person multiple not including pattern for the past. In 2008, U.S. Public Intelligence Council evidenced that IoTs as one of the six 'Problematic Polite equipment' with probable things on U.S. interests out to 2025.

19xx-Current: The whole scope of IoT steps, standard equipment and programming have full-grown conversely the course of procedures delicacy of each is exterior the level of the piece of writing. (Labs, 2013)

In 2010, Chinese Leader Wen Jiabao imagines the IoTs a serious manufacturing for China and has procedure to create remarkable wellbeing in it. 2011: IPV6 unrestricted send off– The novel practice gets into thoughtfulness 2,128 concentrates on or as Steven Leibson place it, 'They could granted out an IPV6 concentrate to each particle on the external of the Globe, and still have sufficient be inclined to left to do another 100+ earths' (Labs, 2013).

- Cisco, IBM, Ericsson create huge instructive as well as advertising drives on the borderline.
- Arduino as well as additional equipment stages develop and build the IoTs available to check out the subject.
- Attainment and WC interest in the gap comprising the IoTs stage you tube being obtained.
- IoT security organization Mocano increasing a series of subsidizing and additional WC's paying attention to the business.
- Gartner Hype Cycle added the term to the 2011 yearly which paths innovation living - sequence from 'innovation activate' to 'level of efficiency' and has bitten the Hype Cycle's 'Summit of Overstated Outlook' in 2014
- Gartner discharges their 2012 Top 10 Strategic Technologies list at their 2011 Symposium.

They characterize an essential innovation as one with the potential for a critical effect on the endeavor in the following three years. Variables that mean critical effect incorporate a far above the ground possible for the interruption to IT or the trade, the requirement for a significant money venture, or the danger of being belatedly to squeeze. The IoTs arrive in as #4 on the rundown and they reference: "The IoTs is an idea that depicts how the net will extend as sensors and wisdom are added to actual things like buyer gadgets or actual resources and these articles are associated with the Internet". The vision and idea have survived for quite a long-time, nevertheless, there has been a speed increase in the number and sorts of things that are being associated and in the advances for distinguishing, detecting, and imparting. These advancements are coming to minimum amount and a financial spilling point the following not many days. Input components of the IoT comprise Entrenched sensation: Sensation that recognizes as well as convey modify are being incorporated, in cell phones, however in an expanding number of spots and items. Picture Detection: Picture recognition advances endeavor to recognize matter, individuals, structures, spaces symbols, and whatever as well that has worth to shoppers as well as undertaking. Cell phones and tablets furnished with camcorder have pressed this innovation from chiefly modern appliances to expansive shopper as well as undertaking appliances (Nguyen, 2019). Near Field Communication (NFC) repayment: NFC permits customers to create reimbursement by signal their cell handset before a practical per user. When NFC is inserted in a minimum amount of handset for installment, businesses such as public transportation, aircraft, retail, and medical care can investigate different regions in which NFC innovation can further develop effectiveness and client care. Dissimilar developments referenced on the recapitulation contain: Media Tablets and Further than, Mobile phone – Centric appliances and boundary, comparative and freely available Client Understanding, App Supplies and Marketplaces, Subsequently –Production Analytics, Enormous Data (Labs, 2013).

7.2 Relevant Work

TABLE 7.1

Table of Relevant Work

Year	Author's Name	Technology	Scrutiny
2021	(Otayf, 2021)	WSN	• Reduces the gap sorting out the cluster heads and portable sinks; • Increases the total effective devices; • Reduces the total of lifeless devices; • Keeping the force contribution; • Reduces the gap between the sensation.
2021	WalidOsamy (2021)	IOT, two algorithms i.e. 1) DCCS 2) RSMP	• Uses two algorithms DCCS and RSMP • Resolves the problem of battery constraints of sensor • Deals with large amount of data acquirement • Introduces new CS scheme for IT • Reduces the overall data traffic by compression method by network • DCCS approach changes the set of connections into many clusters(groups) as well as manages every group into a sequence for starting the group supervisor information collection • RSMP utilizes in cloud side for reconstructing the original data fruitfully • RSMP checks the correctness in each round whether it is modify or not • Increases the network life of IOT • Improves the reconstruction results and decreases the power expenditure in networks

(Continued)

Year	Author's Name	Technology	Scrutiny
2020	Shokat Ali (2020)	Wireless Medical Sensor Network	• Reduces the counting of daily visits of paramedic look • Reduces the counting of observing of patients • Reduces the chances of spreading of any type of pandemics • Increases the remedy preparation • Increases the satisfaction level of patients in the time of COVID-19. • Shows the future of medical science through Wireless Communication
2019	Bello, Xiaoping, Nordin, and Xin (2019)	Cross-layer; PHY and MAC approaches on passive wake-up radio based on previous work, IOT applications	• Listening carefully on intersect - level; substantial as well as intermediate entrée organize (PHY and MAC) advances on inactive awaken means of communication established on the past labor from the journalism. • An elucidation of the track blueprint as well as system construction of an inactive awakens means of communication is obtainable. • The past acts on RF power cropping techniques and the presented an inactive awakens means of communication hardware construction presented in the relative worked as well as arranged. • An appraisal of the many MAC protocols used for the new an inactive awakens means of communication tools presented. • Finally, the paper decorated the prospective investigate occasions as well as workable confronts connected to the workable accomplishment of awaken tools for prospect IoTs appliances.
2019	Chen, Zhang, and Xu (2019)	Multiplicative Replica based on physical mechanism of NLOS and non- curved model	• It presented a novel multiplicative replica supported on the substantial machinery of the NLOS proliferation as well as comfortable the projected non- curved replica into its curved wrapper. • This replica has an influential ability to moderate the NLOS influence as well as outstanding toughness in modifying surroundings. • Secondly, this designs a superfluous conceptualization to putrefy the curved difficulties into plentiful subordinate -difficulties, as well as after that create an well-organized disseminated algorithm, which facilitates each sensation device closely to solve each subordinate-difficulty in a similar way, to cut the calculational intricacy. • The theoretical scrutiny and reproduction demonstrate that the projected algorithm is better to obtainable approaches in both dispensation hurry as well as localization correctness.
2018	Mouradian, Naboulsi, Yangui, Glitho, Morrow, and Polakos, First Quarter (2018)	Fog Computing	• It projected an inclusive study on fog calculating. • It dangerously worked the modern in the light of a brief set of appraisal norm. • They wrapped both the constructions as well as the methods that build fog techniques. • Confronts and investigates guidelines also commenced. • In addition, the lessons studied are worked as well as the diagnosis are conversed in conditions of the important job smog is probable to compete in promising tools such as the perceptible net.
2017	El Khamlichi (2017)	WSN	• employs an development replica for elucidating the problems of WSN • Resolve the region treatment issue as well as obstacle treatment issue • Supply the explanation of K- treatment and K-connectivity problems. • Decreases the set of connections expense as well as increases the set of connections living.

7.3 Modern Research and Deployment

There are many applications in which WSNs are used. These applications are Cultivation, medical management, Protection, Uncultivated Life Habitation supervising, Below Water supervising, Calamity Organization (Security), and Manufacturing (supervising, managing, industrial unit computerization) applications. The research institutes are set up for all these applications and it shows those products which include wireless sensor networks. The present research concentrates on application- an obliged organization with the intention of addressing more specific matters. Beginning consequences achieved from these deployments are promoting and extensive work is extremely achievable. WSNs technologies are gradually arranged from the investigator 'bazaar' to the new adopters in the trade. The armed force remains to finance investigate in this province, at the present extra so in the situation of helping mobile units (Bukhari, Rehmani, & Siraj, 2015) (Kyoungsoo Bok, 2016) (Rao, 2016).

As per Freedonia Group report on sensors, 2002, the sensation bazaar in 2001 was just about $11 Billion at the same time as the Electric wiring fitting expenses were greater than $100Billion. With novel developments as well as the convenience of wireless sensation devices which can be outing motorized the rate of electrics would be the majority imperative lessening. Additional over-the-air coding and solar force sensation devices assist in dropping the consumption and continuation expense to a great amount (Charan, Usmani, Paulus, & Saeed, 2019) (Chen, Zhang, & Xu, 2019).

7.4 Why Need WSNs and IoT in Daily Life

Wireless sensation set of connections play a most significant job in our daily inhabits through increasing technologies for habitat computerization, health protection, warmth organize, liveliness expenditure supervising, and so on. WSNs are competent to proficiently since numerous considerations with excessive exactness and low liveliness expenditure. The promotion of sensors as well as networks dependent on sensor devices has influenced and manipulated our daily existence. Connecting WSNs in habitat and industrialized supervising organization, remedy and health protection organization, activity, edification, and so on, has open-minded and superior the thought of contemporary existing. In WSNs there are three main fundamentals: sensor device (utilize to obtain dimensions), calculating device (utilize to procedure information), and exchange of ideas device (utilize to facilitate the exchange of ideas among the wireless devices). Dissimilar broadcasting know-how can be utilized for the exchange of ideas, such as ZigBee, Wi-Fi, Bluetooth, GSM, and OFDMA. ZigBee is promising know-how that has been established to generate WSN auto-configuration and auto-medicinal as working at low liveliness expenditure, a characteristic specifically extremely significant for wireless sensors. Intellectual elegant habitat structures have been projected in recent times by a research group of people. Example: - an organization for temperature supervising in an academic college grounds. The reason for this organization is to give the most favorable organization of the calming organization due to lessening the liveliness expenditure. The organization includes the customer element with network-dependent boundary and MySQL database and two types of devices: controller device that is accountable for the information collecting and finishing devices that determine warmth, moisture, and illumination concentration. This sample app is executed on a nationalized network (using a star topology). The greatest distance between the manager and the terminal devices utilizes the same microcontroller. This has many limitations. The central set of connections could not wrap university grounds obtaining into account the disadvantages of the greatest distance between the terminal devices and the manager. The organization is dependent on Mica motes that are in communication with distant users (Dehghania, Pourzaferanib, & Barekatain, 2015)(El Khamlichi, 2017) (Koriem & Bayoumi, 2018) (Shuai Gao, 2016).

Some certifiable instances of IoT are wearable wellness and trackers (like Fitbits) and IoT medical care applications, voice colleagues (Siri and Alexa), savvy vehicles (Tesla), and keen machines (iRobot). With IoTs quick organization coming into contact with various IoT gadgets consistently will be unavoidable soon. The web of things, otherwise called IoT, similar to it or not – get it or not – has, as of late, effectively upset our everyday lives to the point that even the non-innovatively slanted have begun to get tied up with the accom-modation, the solace, and the significant bits of knowledge that it offers. From associated home center points, keen indoor regulators, distant entryway locks, and all the different application-controlled machines, odds are, you definitely know how accommodating IoT is in your regular day-to-day existence.

IoT infiltration in our everyday lives is on the expansion, as well. The worldwide mar-ket for IoT is on target to reach $520 billion by 2021, addressing a development of around 50% in each progressive year since 2017 (Bello, Xiaoping, Nordin, & Xin, 2019) (Harwood, 2019).

7.5 Deployment of Low Energy Distributed Clustering Approach

This approach LEDCA is a proposed approach used to decrease the power utilization as well as improve the living time of WSNs. This approach will also achieve the QoS objective of the proposed research work. For Implementation of this approach, MATLAB 2020b, Intel CORE i3, and Windows10 (64-bit Operating System is used). First of all, for the deployment of low energy distributed clustering approach in MATLAB2020b, deploy a virtual Wireless Sensor Networks with 200 × 200 m² wireless sensor network, 60 devices intensity, 1 cluster supervisor (cluster head), 59 Base devices(Sink Nodes), and 10% of Base Devices are nasty devices taken. Now next step is to deploy the cluster supervisor (Head), cluster devices (nodes), and base device. Here, this approach will be an extension of LEACH algorithm.

7.6 Methods of Selection of Cluster Supervisor (Head)

The choice of cluster supervisors will be made by the following equation:

$$\text{Thr}(n) = \frac{\text{Prob}}{1} - \text{Prob} * \left(\text{Rounds mod} \left(\frac{1}{\text{Prob}} \right) \right) \text{if n } \varepsilon \text{ ON} \qquad (7.1)$$

$$\text{Thr}(n) = 1 \qquad \qquad \text{otherwise 0}$$

Here, Prob is used for probability of a raised cluster supervisor (head) or expected number of cluster heads, Rounds is used for number of rounds passed, mod is used as modulo operator, and ON is used for collection of number of ordinary nodes, and Thr is used for Threshold value of the choice of cluster heads in each round. Cluster heads are created according to this equation but wireless sensor nodes are created when arbitrary amount between 0 and 1 if number is less than Thr (n) then it will create a cluster head otherwise not. And when energy of one node is greater than other node then it will become cluster head from cluster node. After that Cluster head send request to all other cluster nodes for joining if common nodes agree then joined otherwise not. After receiving acceptance from common devices CH will allocate TDMA technique to all devices.

Because Cluster supervisor (head) first assembles the data from all other cluster devices and then sends it to Base Device (Sink Device), it's true that cluster head requires more energy as compared to other cluster devices. And cluster head also selected from those clusters which having more energy as compared to others. When cluster supervisors are fixed then it takes higher energy and it will die early. This is the reason the complete cluster becomes out of reach after the cluster supervisor's fail. While in LEDCA approach the cluster supervisors are rotated among all the cluster devices of WSNs. And the energy consumed by each cluster device also distributed equally. But for this reason the lifetime of WSNs is enhanced significantly. Once the clusters are created then TDMA scheme is also created. All devices will send their data to cluster supervisor and cluster supervisor will combine that data (Pathak, 2020).

(1) Unit stage: cluster-supervisor choice and cluster configuration. (2) Fixed -state-stage: data gathering, accumulation, distribution to the sink device.

Low Energy Adaptive Clustering Hierarchy (LEACH) is the initial low-power professional direction-finding tool. Significantly reduce energy. LEACH forms groups in the sensation set of connections and arbitrarily chooses group heads for each group. Devices without a group head recognize the information and broadcast it to the group head, summative the standard information, and then send it to the receiver. This procedure generates it easier for devices with further outstanding power to be chosen to guide the group. In order to expand the living time of the whole sensation set of connections, the power weight must be consistently disseminated on all sensation devices so that the power in a sensation device or a tiny group of sensation devices will not be tired in the close to potential. The major rule is to assign the entirety energy utilization of the set of connections uniformly to each sensation device by frequently choosing different devices as group heads so that the continued existence period of the device is closer to the life of the set of connections. The diminution can enhance the repair life of the whole set of connections. There are two stages in the LEACH procedure, called the design stage as well as the fixed stage. In the design stage, groups are shaped and group heads are preferred. In the fixed stage, information is sent from the non-group head to the receiver. The sensation device converses with the group head through the TDMA plan. In the place reserved for them elude conflict. Arbitrarily choose the initial group in each round [(Alisa & Nassrullah, 2016)].

Although LEACH prolongs the life of the network compared to multi-step direction-finding and not dynamic direction-finding, there are still issues. The heads in the group are arbitrarily chosen, so the quantity and disseminated of heads in the group may not be the best possible. Devices with low outstanding capability and devices with high outstanding capability have the same precedence, so devices with low outstanding capability can be chosen as group heads, reasoning these devices to die first. However, the exchange of ideas between the group supervisor and the center station adopts a private –step way, which makes LEACH not suitable for great – level wireless sensor networks, thus limiting the efficient exchange of ideas range of sensor devices (Rao, 2016). For these reasons, we use a genetic algorithm (Kyoungsoo Bok, 2016) and fuzzy clustering algorithm (Charan, Usmani, Paulus, & Saeed, 2019) in this work to improve the selection of cluster heads and the clustering of Sensor. LEACH approach has been adapted to enhance lifetime of WSNs. This adapted approach decreases the use of power at each stage in WSNs. Moderately; the adapted LEACH approach creates steadiness of the power in the network and reduces power expenditure by 10% when compared with other protocols (Mancilla, Mellado, & Siller, 2016).

7.7 Implementation

A geographical area of 200 × 200 is developed in the MATLAB R2020b. The sensor devices are arbitrarily positioned in that region. The implementation steps are described below Initialize the parameters of LEACH protocol such as Initial Energy, Number of Nodes, rounds in LEACH, energy for transferring/receiving of each bit, transmit amplifier free space/multipath energy, aggregation energy, and the packet length. Using these network parameters a network with randomly placed nodes is created as shown in Figure 7.2: placed the nodes into the developed geographical area. Consider 5% of the total nodes as the clusters. So, among 200 nodes 5 cluster are formed using LEACH protocol. The algorithm for Distributed Clustering is

Step1: All active devices will broadcast their device Identity numbers.

Step2: Count the number of devices' Identity numbers.

Step3: Suppose num_d number of devices (d).

Step4: Implement function f (num_d, e_d) $num_d e^4{}_d$.

Step5: Now devices that broadcast in step2 will cluster supervisors and others will become non-cluster supervisors.

7.8 Conclusions and Future Scope

Clearly, Wireless Sensor Networks are incredibly significant headways used in every office such as the military, prosperity workplaces, tutoring divisions, plant workplaces, mechanical workplaces, banking regions, free dares to colossal degree associations, etc. Without Wireless Sensor Networks, life is nothing. Nowadays, each field is working simply through this is a result of COVID-19. In case Wireless Sensor Networks don't present in our lives, how should arrive at one another in this period of COVID-19? That is the explanation it is expected to pass on of appropriated gathering approach in Wireless Sensor Networks. This chapter shows how the proposed coursed batching approach is most useful stood out from other gathering approaches used in it. This chapter moreover shows approaches in Wireless Sensor Networks for checking the capability, usage, and QoS of WSNs on different association test frameworks such as MATLAB, NS, OPNet, TetCos, NetSim, etc. There are various reasons why this chapter proposes the scattered gathering approach in

Wireless Sensor Networks, for instance, sensor contraptions are in danger of deficiency, to make available devices with support in case of insufficiency of the basic device and for the overhauled amassing of data. WSNs related to IoT address obliging associations in supporting, controlling, following, and distinguishing unique natural direct. Sensors' features expect the primary part in plotting and impacting WSNs.

References

Abdelkareem, M. A. (2018). Vibration Energy Harvesting in Automotive Suspension System: A Detailed Review. *Applied Energy*, Elsevier, 229(C), 672–699. doi:10.1016/j.apenergy.2018.08.030.

Alisa, Z. T., and Nassrullah, H. A. (2016, May9–10). Minimizing energy consumption in wireless sensor networks using modified genetic algorithm and an energy balance filter. *Published in: 2016 Al-Sadeq International Conference on Multidisciplinary in IT and Communication Science and Applications (AIC-MITCSA)*. Baghdad, Ira. doi:10.1109/AIC-MITCSA.2016.7759947.

Bello, H., Xiaoping, Z., Nordin, R., and Xin, J. (2019, July12). Advances and opportunities in Passive Wake-Up Radios With Wireless Energy Harvesting for the Internet of Things Applications. *MDPI*. https://www.mdpi.com/1424-8220/19/14/3078.

Bukhari, S. H., Rehmani, M. H., and Siraj, S. (2015, November30). A Survey of Channel Bonding for Wireless Networks and Guidelines of Channel Bonding for Futuristic Cognitive Radio Sensor Networks. *IEEE Communications Surveys Tutorials*, 18 (ISSN1553-877X), 924–948. doi:10.1109/COMST.2015.2504408.

Charan, P., Usmani, T., Paulus, R., and Saeed, H. S. (2019). Performance of Distributed Energy Aware Routing(DEAR) Protocol Cooperative Caching for Wireless Sensor Networks. *Wireless Sensor Network*, 11, 35–45. Http://Www.Scirp.Org/Journal/Wsn

Chen, S., Zhang, J., and Xu, C. (2019). Robust Distributed Cooperative Localization With NLOS Mitigation Based on Multiplicative Convex Model. *IEEE Access*. doi: 10.1109/ACCESS.2019.2915512.

Dehghania, S., Pourzaferanib, M., and Barekatain, B. (2015). Comparison on energy-efficient cluster based routing algorithms in wireless sensor network. *The Third Information Systems International Conference Comparison, Procedia Computer Science*, 72, 535–542. Science Direct, Elsevier. doi: 10.1016/j.procs.2015.12.161.

El Khamlichi, A. T.-B.-L. (2017, July 18). A Hybrid Algorithm for Optimal Wireless Sensor Network Deployment with the Minimum Number of Sensor Nodes. *Algorithm*, 10(3), 80. doi:10.3390/a10030080.

Harwood, T. (2019, December 11). *Internet of Things (IoT) History*. Retrieved from www.postscapes.com: https://www.postscapes.com/iot-history/

Koriem, M. S., and Bayoumi, A. M. (2018, August1). Detecting and Measuring Holes in Wireless Sensor Network. *Journal of King Saud University—Computer and Information Sciences 30*, 1–8.

Kyoungsoo Bok, Y. L. (2016, May 10). An Energy-Efficient Secure Scheme in Wireless Sensor Networks. *Hindawi Publishing Corporation Journal of Sensors*, 2016, 11.

Labs, S. (2013). *Evolution-of-Wireless-Sensor-Networks*. (Silicon Labs) Retrieved from Silicon Laboratories, Inc. Rev 1.0 1: https://www.silabs.com/documents/public/white-papers/evolution-of-wireless-sensor-networks.pdf

Mancilla, C. M., Mellado, L. E., and Siller, M. (2016). Review Article Wireless Sensor Networks Formation: Approaches and Techniques. (E. Llobet, Ed.) *Journal of Sensors*, 2016, 18. doi:10.1155/2016/2081902.

Minh Nguyen, H. T. (2019, April30). Wireless Communication Technologies and Applications for Wireless Sensor Networks: ASurvey. *ICSES Transactions on Computer Networks and Communications*, 5(1), 1–15.

Mouradian, C., Naboulsi, D., Yangui, S., Glitho, H. R., Morrow, M. J., and Polakos, A. P. (First Quarter 2018). A Comprehensive Survey on Fog Computing: State-of-the-Art And Research Challenges. *IEEE Communications Surveys & Tutorials*, 20(1), 1–8.

Nguyen, M. T. (2019, June13). An Energy-Efficient Framework for Multimedia Data Routing in Internet of Things (IoTs). *EAI Endorsed Transactions on Industrial Networks and Intelligent Systems*, 6(19). doi:10.4108/eai.13-6-2019.159120.

Otayf, M. A. (2021, April30). A Novel Methodology for Optimum Energy Consumption in Wireless Sensor Networks. *The Creative Commons Attribution (CC BY 4.0) Licence*, 1(1). doi:10.1108/FEBE-02-2021-0011.

Pathak, A. (2020, January23). A Proficient Bee Colony-Clustering Protocol to Prolong Lifetime of Wireless Sensor Networks. *Hindawi Journal of Computer Networks and Communications*, 9. doi:10.1155/2020/1236187.

Rao, S. B. (2016). Improving the Network Life Time of a Wireless Sensor Network Using the Integration of Progressive Sleep Scheduling Algorithm with Opportunistic Routing Protocol. *Indian Journal of Science and Technology*, 9(17), 1–16. doi:10.17485/ijst/2016/v9i17/93011.

Shokat Ali, R. P. (2020). A Review of the Role of Smart Wireless Medical Sensor Network in COVID-19. *Journal of Industrial Integration and Management*, 05(04), 413–425. doi:10.1142/S2424862220300069.

Shuai Gao, H. Z. (2016). Energy Efficient Interest Forwarding in NDN-Based Wireless Sensor Networks. *Mobile Information Systems / 2016 / Article*, 2016. doi:10.1155/2016/3127029.

WalidOsamy, A. A. (2021, April 7). Deterministic Clustering Based Compressive Sensing Scheme for Fog-Supported Heterogeneous Wireless Sensor Networks. *PeerJ Computer Science*, 7, e463. doi:10.7717/peerj-cs.463.

8

Long-Range IoT for Agricultural Acquisition through Cloud Computing

Kalpana Murugan and R. Jenitha

Kalasalingam Academy of Research and Education, Virudhunagar (Dt), India

CONTENTS

8.1 Introduction

The main factor which is essential for every living being is food that is obtained from agriculture. It is predicted that by 2050 (Elijah et al., 2018), the country's population will become 970 crores. Agricultural holding practice is carried out with farming in various modes such as food crop farming, poultry farming, fruit farming, vegetable farming, dairy farming, and many more depending upon the climatic condition, fertility of the land, and economy of the farmer as well. Agriculture is directly linked with the environment. Unless proper climatic conditions are met, one cannot do farming successfully. It is like a give and takes policy between nature and farming because when nature is well, agriculture is well and when agriculture goes on well, we are protecting our nature. The farmer is the one who stands still between nature and agriculture. Depending upon the environmental condition of the farm, the farmer has to choose the crop or vegetation. Above all, due to the mismatch in the climatic conditions, lack of manpower, commercialization, and agriculture is unnoticed. Apart from agriculture, all the technologies are growing day by day tremendously. Ultimately, everyone gets into a surge of food commodities soon, but it is already in a phase of depletion. So, early measures should be taken with the available and forthcoming technology to rectify the problem faced by the farmers. The main thought to be kept in mind while designing any system are the following,

(1) the technology mode of operation should be user-friendly for farmers and
(2) a cost-effective method for implementation

Considering the above, the Internet of Things (IoT) comes into play to support farming. Looking into the IoT, various techniques are available to give a helping hand to farmers such as Bluetooth, Zigbee, Wi-Fi, LoRa WAN, NB-IoT, Sigfox, and many more. Due to the flexibility, easy installation, long-range, and low power consumption feature, LoRa-based controlling and monitoring of farms is considered. It can be operated at an unlicensed spectrum with lesser bandwidth. Specifically, it is designed for sensor integrated applications that help send data for long distances with minimum power consumption and cover long-range.

8.2 Related Work

IoT is an emerging trend that plays a vital role in various applications due to its vast advantages. Some of the applications are discussed in this section as follows. One of the foremost applications includes the health of every living creature. Under the health monitoring of the human being, the medical field helps a lot to improve the condition. A medical IoT architecture (Cao et al., 2020) has been developed which is readily available on the cloud to monitor conditions then and there as and when required. Integration of multiple clouds involves the installation of IoT-enabled devices at various cities and every device information is being scrutinized with cloud and when there is an emergency, that particular node can be identified. This gave the idea of IoT integration through various nodes. At the same time, it is also widely used in remote bill monitoring and payment such as biogas monitoring (Mabrouki et al., 2021). Where a model is developed to monitor and measure biogas production at various sites. In which the system is developed with Arduino UNO to monitor the gas usage level and sends the notification via GSM messages to the user. In case the user has not paid the bill it will be notified via SMS at the same time the gas connection is blocked for that particular user. Similar to biogas monitoring, smart city monitoring with IoT for municipal assets was developed (Nelson et al., 2019). In this case, a project was developed for the city of Rockville, where every house has been integrated with the safety measuring sensors and during an emergency or any fire accident immediately the message will be conveyed to the municipal office for help. So everywhere the city is being monitored carefully. IoT not only plays a role in land system monitoring, but it also plays a major role in coastal monitoring as well (Girau et al., 2020). An IoT module was developed to monitor the crowd with object detection, air temperature monitoring, humidity monitoring, average wind speed, and direction of wind using a mobile application. At the same time, a sea unit and beach unit hardware were developed and deployed. Likewise, the IoT is used in various monitoring applications. Coming to our subject it is widely applicable in agricultural monitoring applications. Sanjeevi et al. (2020) and Ahmed et al. (2018) structured smart farming agriculture using IoT in rural areas. It is mainly applied to utilize water resources for irrigation effectively, which was applied to fertilize the plants and monitor the soil water level for irrigation. The developed system also monitors the features of the farm from remote using fog computing. Also, the module gave maximum throughput and SNR as well as minimum latency and MSE with improved coverage area. Another review by Ayaz et al. (2019) mentions all the possible things which can be applied to the farm for smarter monitoring purposes. It infers the major applications that can be applied on the farm, advanced agricultural practices, the sensors available for farm monitoring, and the communication modes of the monitored data. The wireless sensors used for monitoring purpose include acoustic sensors, FPGA-based sensors, an optoelectronic sensor which helps to differentiate plant type, and electromechanical and chemical sensor that can be applied for monitoring the nutrient level of the plant. Similarly, for communication purposes, it addresses various communication modes such as cellular communication mode, Zigbee, Bluetooth, LoRa, Sigfox, smartphones, and drones. From this review, it is clear that LoRa-based monitoring system is cost-effective and achieves a perfect data transmission rate of 90%. Under wireless communication (Ramezani et al., 2019), various wireless sensors were utilized for IoT networks where energy for the sensors has been obtained by radiofrequency. It is clear that with IoT not only one source of energy is combined but numerous energy sources are combined and harvested (Akan et al., 2018). A module of the wireless agricultural monitoring system is developed and compared three communication technologies like Wi-Fi, Zigbee, and LoRa WAN (Sadowski & Spachos, 2020). The comparison results reveal that LoRa WAN consumes less power with more lifetime. The module is powered by a solar panel. So, it is much clear to go with LoRa-based IoT for efficient and cost-effective communication. Under the IoT, the basic principles which employ private Internet for various technologies were summarized in Li and Palanisamy(2018). At the data center, the IoT plays a major role while machine learning is the tool to interface and make a decision in IoT (Samie et al., 2019). DNN, security, health care, and edge computing are an increasing trend in recent years. The architecture of the IoT-based design approach which was used for the farm information management system is employed (Köksal & Tekinerdogan, 2019). It gives information about various farms such as paddy fields, grain fields, etc., using single information system. A survey on LoRa WAN technology, architecture, and the protocol was detailed (Ertürk et al., 2019). The LoRa-based model, Edge-based model, and fog-based computing were explored in the traffic-based monitoring system (Nguyen Gia et al., 2020). From the recent trending works, it is concluded that LoRa-based IoT system works well for sensor-level data harvesting as well as for data transmission purposes.

8.3 System Design Architecture

The proposed system design architecture mainly focuses on the agricultural acquisition system using Raspberry Pi with LoRa-based module for remote monitoring of the farm with the handheld device. A prototype has been developed for the model of the agricultural acquisition system. Figure 8.1 shows a diagram of the system architecture. The system architecture is developed with an application that helps to control and to monitor the farm.

The proposed system architecture consists of four modules to acquire the status of the agricultural farm. The sensor module is considered as the input of the system which is acquired from the agricultural farm. The acquired input is fed to the controller module which consists of the LoRa transmitter module. It is powered by a power supply unit. The collected input at the controller module is transmitted to the receiver module with the

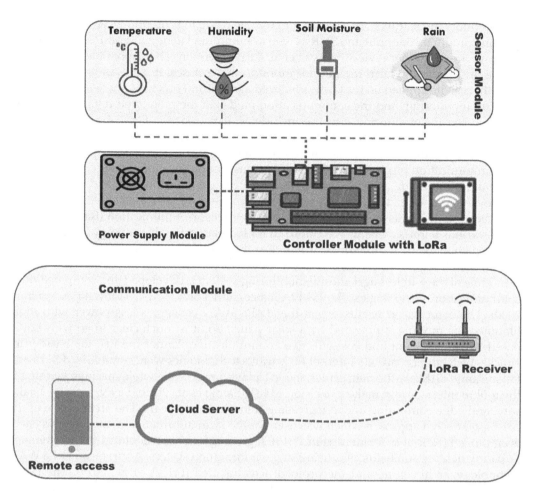

FIGURE 8.1
System architecture for agricultural acquisition system.

LoRa transmitter. The communication module helps the farmer to access the environmental condition of the farm remotely using the mobile application. The detailed view of each module is detailed as follows.

8.3.1 Sensor Module/Input Module

The sensor module is considered as the input of the acquisition system. For a prototype module, the parameters considered for monitoring are as follows:

- Temperature sensor,
- Humidity level sensor,
- Moisture sensor of soil, and
- Rainfall monitoring sensor.

The temperature measure helps to monitor the temperature condition of the farm ranges from 0°C to 50°C. The humidity sensor helps to monitor the environmental humidity of

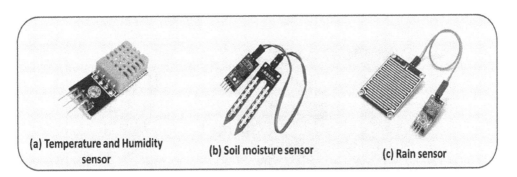

(a) Temperature and Humidity sensor   (b) Soil moisture sensor   (c) Rain sensor

FIGURE 8.2
Hardware components used for the sensor module.

the farm ranging from 20% to 90%. The temperature and humidity integrated sensors are available as shown in Figure 8.2(a). It has an accuracy range of ±1°C and ±1%. The moisture sensor of soil senses the moisture condition of the farm which is much useful in the irrigation process. It will be in PCB size 3.2cm × 1.4cm as shown in Figure 8.2(b). Similarly, a rainfall monitoring sensor is shown in Figure 8.2(c), which helps to find the rainfall status of the farm. If the farmer is at a remote location, then the rain status is found by the farmer through the rainfall monitoring sensor and the irrigation process is carried out. All these sensors are integrated with the raspberry controller for acquisition purposes which operates in 3.3V to 5V and provides a digital output.

8.3.2 Input Power Module

The power module which is shown in Figure 8.3 is applied to step down the incoming supply voltage. The incoming supply capacity is 220V at a 50Hz frequency. All the hardware components in the system architecture operate in the range of 3.3V to 5V DC supply. At

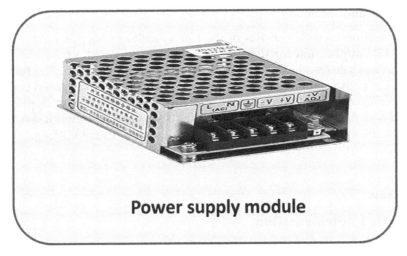

Power supply module

FIGURE 8.3
Hardware power supply module.

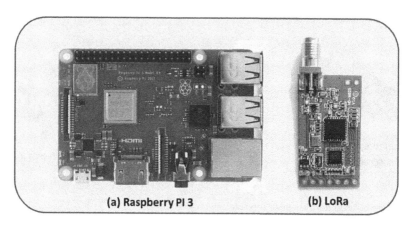

(a) Raspberry PI 3   (b) LoRa

FIGURE 8.4
Hardware of controller module.

first, the AC voltage is stepped down to the lesser voltage ranging between +5V to −5V and rectified to DC using a rectifier circuit. Once the signal is rectified, it is fed to the filter circuit for filtering the unwanted noisy signals. The rectified output is now given to the controller module for the activation of the acquisition process.

8.3.3 Controller Module

The controller module consists of a Raspberry PI controller for the integration of the sensor module and LoRa transmitter. The Raspberry PI controller has a quadcore 1.2-GHz, 64-bit CPU with 1GB worth of RAM. It has BCM43438 for wireless LAN along with Bluetooth for communication. It also has a 40-pin input-output port, through which all the sensors are connected. Figure 8.4 shows the LoRa module for creating the wireless area network on the farm.

8.3.4 Communication Module

The communication module consists of the LoRa receiver which is further interlinked with the mobile application for the user or farmer to access the monitored data. The LoRa receiver module creates the wireless area network on the farm. The LoRa covers a radius of 15 km with a data rate of 0.3 to 40 kbps in a 125-kHz unlicensed band. The IoT architecture consists of four layers: namely network layer, device layer, application layer, and service layer. All the sensor integration takes place and the network layer consists of the LoRa module in the device layer. It is compatible with IEEE 802.15.4g.

8.4 Hardware Implementation

The proposed architecture is implemented by the hardware integration of all the sensor nodes at the end layer which is deployed at various irrigation nodes. The monitored sensor

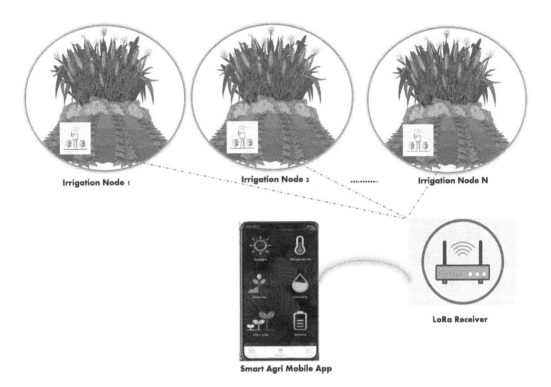

FIGURE 8.5
System implementation.

readings are being acquired at the receiver end with the help of LoRa WAN architecture which creates the gateway with the help of the LoRa device attached with it. The transmitted data are viewed by the farmer at a remote location, using the Smart Agri farm application developed with PHP. The sensor module is connected with the controller module and powered by the power supply module. This prototype consists of wired sensor nodes but it can also be implemented wirelessly for wireless irrigation processing. The detailed architectural design is shown in Figure 8.5.

The developed system module is implemented in the agricultural farm as shown in Figure 8.6. At the farmland, the irrigation methods vary depending upon the type of crop planted. So, the developed module should be deployed at various irrigation nodes. The power module, sensor module, and controller module should be installed at various locations on the farm.

The hardware implementation is carried out on the farm at a GPS location 9°25′33.9″N 77°28′23.9″ E which is located at Virudhunagar district in Tamil Nadu, India is shown in Figure 8.7. This location is considered as the irrigation node where coconut trees, banana trees, and mango trees are planted which rotationally needs irrigation through the drip.

For a prototype hardware module, only one irrigation node is considered. The receiver LoRa is located at the control room of the farm which is located 1 km from the irrigation node. Now the LoRa WAN environment is created on the farm. Every second the sensor measures the temperature, humidity, soil moisture, and rain status of the farm. In the

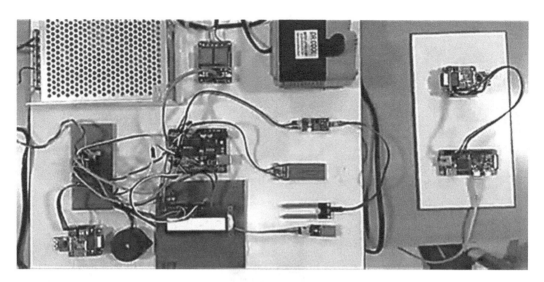

FIGURE 8.6
Implemented hardware module.

FIGURE 8.7
GPS location of the hardware-implemented farm.

FIGURE 8.8
LCD showing status of the farm during a sunny day.

control room, the display displays the current reading. The results are analyzed at various environmental conditions.

8.4.1 Case 1: Sunny Day

This case is considered a sunny day where rainfall has not occurred and the moisture level of the irrigation field is low. During any sunny day, due to higher temperature, the moisture level of the soil is reduced which is shown in Figure 8.8.

Now the data is being captured for the farm acquisition system. The collected data from the transmitter will reach the receiver through a frame structure that is maintained by LoRa (Koon, 2020). An android application called Smart Agri is developed for time-to-time monitoring of the data acquired. If the farmer is located at a remote location, then with the help of the application, the farmer can able to access the status of the farm. The screenshot of the status obtained on the Smart Agri application is shown in Figure 8.9.

8.4.2 Case 2: Rainy Day

Similarly, during a rainy day, the temperature is low and the moisture level of the soil is high. This case is analyzed on the farm and the monitored status of the LCD is shown in Figure 8.10.

From the mentioned cases, it is clear that these IoT-based agriculture monitoring systems can be effectively utilized during any sunny or rainy day. This prototype model is verified on the farm for these conditions which can be further enhanced to apply for the irrigation of the farm by connecting it to the motor pump.

Temperature: 38.00

Humidity: 29.00

Moisture   moisture_Low

Rain: Rain_ok

internet connected

FIGURE 8.9
Smart Agri app output.

FIGURE 8.10
LCD showing status of the farm during a rainy day.

8.5 Conclusion and Scope for Future

Thus, the long-range IoT in the acquisition of agricultural farms is carried out with a hardware module. The hardware module is designed and implemented at a farm for real-time monitoring purposes. The obtained results reveal that the LoRa based monitoring system covers a long-range with less latency and a cost-effective unlicensed mode of communication. This fits well for every farmer who is located in a remote location. By implementing this latest trending technology in the farm, agriculture is being uplifted to the next level where every generation that needs to carry out farming in the future are also benefited. As the next step, by monitoring the status of the farm the farmer can control the irrigation process of various nodes by switching the motor and valve ON and OFF. Thus, the crop yield of the farm is increased to a huge extent to supply the food requirements.

Thus, farming is made easier with the latest trending techniques such as the IoT in integration with cloud computing. In the future, resources are successfully safely guarded with the help of these technologies. Similar to the agriculture monitoring system it can also be extended further by introducing fertilizing robots, LoRa tractors, and unmanned vehicles that can visualize the current situation of the farm. The IoT drones can capture the image of the plants and leaves which is used to find the status of harvesting and fertilizing the crops. These kinds of agricultural applications increase the scope of living in a nature-friendly environment.

References

Ahmed, N., De, D., & Hussain, I. (2018). Internet of Things (IoT) for Smart Precision Agriculture and Farming in Rural Areas. *IEEE Internet of Things Journal*, 5(6), 4890–4899. https://doi.org/10.1109/JIOT.2018.2879579

Akan, O. B., Cetinkaya, O., Koca, C., & Ozger, M. (2018). Internet of Hybrid Energy Harvesting Things. *IEEE Internet of Things Journal*, 5(2), 736–746. https://doi.org/10.1109/JIOT.2017.2742663

Ayaz, M., Ammad-Uddin, M., Sharif, Z., Mansour, A., & Aggoune, E. H. M. (2019). Internet-of-Things (IoT)-based smart agriculture: Toward making the fields talk. *IEEE Access*, 7, 129551–129583. https://doi.org/10.1109/ACCESS.2019.2932609

Cao, R., Tang, Z., Liu, C., & Veeravalli, B. (2020). A Scalable Multicloud Storage Architecture for Cloud-Supported Medical Internet of Things. *IEEE Internet of Things Journal*, 7(3), 1641–1654. https://doi.org/10.1109/JIOT.2019.2946296

Elijah, O., Rahman, T. A., Orikumhi, I., Leow, C. Y., & Hindia, M. N. (2018). An Overview of Internet of Things (IoT) and Data Analytics in Agriculture: Benefits and Challenges. *IEEE Internet of Things Journal*, 5(5), 3758–3773. https://doi.org/10.1109/JIOT.2018.2844296

Ertürk, M. A., Aydın, M. A., Büyükakkaşlar, M. T., & Evirgen, H. (2019). A Survey on LoRaWAN Architecture, Protocol and Technologies. *Future Internet*, 11(10), 216. https://doi.org/10.3390/fi11100216

Girau, R., Anedda, M., Fadda, M., Farina, M., Floris, A., Sole, M., & Giusto, D. (2020). Coastal Monitoring System Based on Social Internet of Things Platform. *IEEE Internet of Things Journal*, 7(2), 1260–1272. https://doi.org/10.1109/JIOT.2019.2954202

Köksal, Ö. & Tekinerdogan, B. (2019). Architecture Design Approach for IoT-based Farm Management Information Systems. *Precision Agriculture*, 20(5), 926–958. https://doi.org/10.1007/s11119-018-09624-8

Koon, J. (2020). LoRaWAN Empowers Very Low-power, Wireless Applications. *Tech Idea Research, 1.0.*

Li, C., & Palanisamy, B. (2018). Privacy in Internet of Things: From Principles to Technologies. *ArXiv*, *6*(1), 488–505.

Mabrouki, J., Azrour, M., Fattah, G., Dhiba, D., & Hajjaji, S. El. (2021). Intelligent Monitoring System for Biogas Detection Based on the Internet of Things: Mohammedia, Morocco City Landfill Case. *Big Data Mining and Analytics*, *4*(1), 10–17. https://doi.org/10.26599/BDMA.2020.9020017

Nelson, A., Toth, G., Linders, D., Nguyen, C., & Rhee, S. (2019). Replication of Smart-City Internet of Things Assets in a Municipal Deployment. *IEEE Internet of Things Journal*, *6*(4), 6715–6724. https://doi.org/10.1109/JIOT.2019.2911010

Nguyen Gia, T., Queralta, J. P., & Westerlund, T. (2020). Exploiting LoRa, edge, and fog computing for traffic monitoring in smart cities. In *LPWAN Technologies for IoT and M2M Applications*. INC. https://doi.org/10.1016/b978-0-12-818880-4.00017-x

Ramezani, P., Zeng, Y., & Jamalipour, A. (2019). Optimal resource allocation for multiuser internet of things network with single wireless-powered relay. *IEEE Internet of Things Journal*, *6*(2), 3132–3142. https://doi.org/10.1109/JIOT.2018.2879373

Sadowski, S., & Spachos, P. (2020). Wireless technologies for smart agricultural monitoring using internet of things devices with energy harvesting capabilities. *Computers and Electronics in Agriculture*, *172*(March), 105338. https://doi.org/10.1016/j.compag.2020.105338

Samie, F., Bauer, L., & Henkel, J. (2019). From Cloud Down to Things: An Overview of Machine Learning in Internet of Things. *IEEE Internet of Things Journal*, *6*(3), 4921–4934. https://doi.org/10.1109/JIOT.2019.2893866

Sanjeevi, P., Prasanna, S., Siva Kumar, B., Gunasekaran, G., Alagiri, I., & Vijay Anand, R. (2020). Precision Agriculture and Farming Using Internet of Things Based on Wireless Sensor Network. *Transactions on Emerging Telecommunications Technologies*, *31*(12), 1–14. https://doi.org/10.1002/ett.3978

9

Resource Allocation with Task Scheduling in Cloud Computing

Ranjan Kumar Mondal, Enakshmi Nandi, Payel Ray, and Debabrata Sarddar
University of Kalyani, Nadia, India

CONTENTS

9.1 Introduction

Resource allocation with task scheduling (Ma et al. 2014) is an imperative research issue in the cloud computing field (Jaeger et al. 2008). Gaining high-quality performance with efficient resource allocation of the job is necessary. Discovering the best possible resource allocation algorithm for the effective utilization of resources is a crucial job (Pham and Le 2017). The basic motivations of resource allocation are resource discovery, collaborating resource data, and job performance (Wang et al. 2011).

Cloud users perform their applications in a decentralized manner in the cloud. After this process, users submit their tasks to the respective cloud resource brokers. The resource broker then wishes to know about the cloud information service and its properties for the accessibility of resources (Kumar and Sharma 2020). Next stage, cloud resources are

DOI: 10.1201/9781003213888-9

registered with more than one information service. After the scheduling process, the resource broker monitors the job execution process and collects the results. At the last stage, it sends back to the users (Mondal et al. 2016).

For minimizing the make-span, there are several resource allocation algorithms available.

All of these algorithms identify the resources that should be allotted to the relevant tasks, reducing the overall job execution time (Şerifoğlu and Ulusoy 2004). Reducing the total execution time of all tasks does not imply that the actual execution time of each task is reduced. Min–Min and Max–Min are two well-known and simple resource allocation algorithms. Two algorithms work by taking into account the time it takes for each task to complete on each cloud computing server (Sinha 2016).

The Min–Min first determines the system's smallest amount completion time from all jobs. The system then selects the task with the shortest implementation time from all present tasks. The algorithm then assigns tasks to the resources that take the least amount of time to finish. Min–Min follows the same procedure until all tasks have been scheduled (Wang et al. 2011).

The drawback of the Min–Min is that it picks up the least jobs foremost, making the usage of resources at higher execution power. But there is a hazard at the time of smaller tasks that exceed the large ones. As a result, the scheduling technique of the Min–Min process is not optimum. To solve this problem, the Max–Min algorithm has come, which allows larger tasks at first. But in some issues, the waiting time of less important jobs has enlarged in the Max–Min algorithm (Ritchie and Levine 2003).

The algorithm proposed in this chapter performs concerning make-span and resource allocation factor with task scheduling. Hence to achieve better resource allocation, we get improved response time across the whole system. Here proposed algorithm applies the Min–Min schedules in the primary case, and then rearranges have been done by taking the most implementation time, which is below the make-span found in the first case (Shivasankaran et al. 2013).

9.2 Related Works

The Hungarian method is an optimization method to solve the assignment problem. It was built up and published by Harold Kuhn, in 1955 (Armstrong et al. 1998).

Min–Min Algorithm: It all initiates with a set of jobs. The resource with the shortest execution time among all jobs is then identified. The job with the smallest size is then chosen and allotted to the appropriate resource (therefore the name is Min–Min). Lastly, the job is to get rid of the set, and Min–Min repeats the process until all jobs are allotted. The technique is effortless, but it does not account for current resource loads before assigning a job. As a result, the proper load balance is not observed (Wang et al. 2011).

Load Balance Min–Min (LBMM): This technique utilizes the Min–Min algorithm, the earlier discussed, as its foundation. It makes use of a three-level hierarchical structure. The second level of LBMM, it's the first part, similar to MM, where it's dependable for receiving the job and allotting it to one service supervisor. The service supervisor divides the demand into jobs after receiving it to expedite the process. The service machine then assigns the job to a server for execution based on modified attributes like remaining CPU (machine obtainability), memory size, and transmission rate. This scheduling progresses Min–Min load balance and reduces each machine's execution time, but it eliminates the need to choose a machine for a complicated job requiring huge-scale computation (Kokilavani and Amalarethinam 2011).

Load Balance Max–Min-Max (LB3M): The following is a summary of LB3M progress: Its purpose is to examine the average job execution time for all systems. The next step is to find the job with the fastest average execution time. The next step is to find the unassigned system with the shortest execution time compared to the job's highest average execution time (Step 2). The job is then sent to the chosen system for processing. Then if no unallocated system can be picked in Step 2, all systems, both unallocated and allocated, should be reevaluated. The total of the smallest execution time of the assigned job on this system and the lowest execution time of the running job is the smallest execution time of the assigned system. The current least execution time for the job is the least execution time of an unallocated system. It's to find the unassigned or assigned system with the shortest completion time compared to the task's highest average execution time in Step 2. The job is then dispatched to the selected node for processing. Steps 2–3 should be repeated until all jobs have been completed. The authors proposed a well-organized scheduling algorithm, LB3M, for the cloud computing network to assign jobs to computer systems based on their resource capability in this algorithm (Hung et al. 2012).

9.3 The Motivation

There is a countless server connected to web computing to deliver the various types of web services to cloud clients. So, inadequate numbers of servers united to the cloud have to execute more than a countless number of tasks at a time (Wagemann et al. 2018). So it is easy to accomplish all available jobs at a specific interval. Therefore, few nodes perform all jobs; hence, there is a necessity to balance all loads at a time. Here load balance reduces the total makespan as well as meticulously executes all jobs (Kumar and Sharma 2020).

There are a few servers to perform the tasks/jobs. Jobs to be executed in cloud computing would be more than sometimes than the attached servers. We propose an algorithm that some nodes carry out the jobs. Here jobs and balance all nodes are to maximize the quality of services in cloud computing.

Example: Suppose an IT company has one thousand servers and they have to perform one thousand tasks or subtasks at any time. So, they want to execute all tasks at a certain period. There are many procedures to solve this problem to complete all tasks. We propose a new technique to execute all tasks in minimum time with resource allocation.

A cloud computing system consists of a number of machines. Specifically, each machine has different capabilities for completing the task; thus, only considering the remaining CPU of the machine when selecting a machine to complete a job is insufficient. As a result, in cloud computing, knowing how to prefer an active machine to run a job is critical. So it is a tough job to execute all different jobs on a different machine at the same time. Now when a user wants to execute his value task to a company server, then he will want to complete his task in minimum time.

All machines have different capabilities to execute a task or tasks that have different completion times or execution times by a particular machine.

9.3.1 System Manager

There are several working machines in the cloud field. Each machine has a variety of skills to execute its task; thus we see that the CPU remaining of the machine is not enough while a machine has picked up to carry a definite task out. Thus, determining a suitable machine to execute a task is a very significant issue in a cloud computing system. Due to the tasks, that has different characteristics for the user to pay execution. So the requirement of some resources of specific, for instance, when designing particles sequence assembly.

In this situation, a service manager collected relevant information of distinct machines involved in this cloud computing system, for example, CPU capability, memory size, and network bandwidth. All data are assembled, then it will be offered to the manager to pertain it in regulating the resource allocation of the system. The features are defined as the following:

V_1 = The existing CPU capability;

V_2 = The existing memory; and

V_3 = Transmission rate

To efficiently match managers with appropriate machines, all of the machines in the system will be formulated by a threshold derived from the user's demand for the resource required to complete the jobs. The service manager who surpasses the 'threshold of service manager' is regarded as effective and will be the manager's candidate for capable machines. The service machines that pass the 'threshold of service machine' are considered effective, and the service manager will consider them as candidates for capable machines.

Cloud computing consists of a collection of machines, each with its own set of capabilities. In other words, the CPU's computing capability, memory size, and transmission rate are all different. Because cloud computing makes use of all of a machine's resources, the state of each machine's resources may vary. As a result, in our research, the average value for estimating service manager values was taken as the CPU capacity, memory size, and bandwidth rate. The following is an example of particular (Table 9.1):

1) The CPU capability of 510 Megabytes

2) The memory capacity 205438 Kilobytes

3) The transmission rate of 8.03 Megabytes

TABLE 9.1

The Threshold for Estimating Service Manager Values

T_i	M_j						
	M_1	M_2	M_3	M_4	M_5	....	M_m
T_1	12	24	32	27	24	...	25
T_2	15	34	23	28	25	...	32
T_3	17	32	23	26	36	...	27
T_4	23	33	33	36	42	...	29
T_5	15	14	23	45	55	...	27
...	...	...	...	...	...	...	...
T_n	17	13	23	42	17	...	26

TABLE 9.2

Tasks to Be Executed by Different Machines Takes Different Time

Machine	M_1	M_2	M_3	M_4	M_5	....	M_m
Task (ms)	10	12	13	13	11		16

TABLE 9.3

The Same Machine Executes Different Tasks at a Different Time

Task	T_1	T_2	T_3	T_4	T_5	....	T_n
Machine (ms)	26	22	18	26	19		21

TABLE 9.4

Some Machines to Execute Some Tasks Take Different Time

T_i	M_j						
	M_1	M_2	M_3	M_4	M_5	....	M_m
T_1	17	24	31	29	34	...	27
T_2	25	34	23	28	25	...	32
T_3	19	32	23	27	36	...	29
T_4	23	34	23	34	42	...	29
T_5	25	14	23	25	35	...	19
...	...	...	...	...	...	...	...
T_n	17	23	23	32	27	...	28

9.3.2 Meta Task About Machines

Suppose a specific task to be executed by different machines takes different times as follows (Table 9.2).

Because the different machines have different capabilities to execute the same task. Similarly, the same machine executes different tasks at a different time as follows (Table 9.3).

Therefore some machines to execute some tasks take different times as follows (Table 9.4).

9.4 Problem Definitions

To assign different natures of tasks to different servers in a cloud system, that the matrix cost is to be least, recognized as the matrix problem.

If the quantity of tasks is equal to the number as the quantity of the servers, then it is recognized as a balanced matrix problem.

Consider a problem consisting of a group of 'm' servers $M = \{M_1, M_2, ..., M_n\}$. And a group of 'n' jobs $\{T = T_1, T_2, ..., T_n\}$ is considered which is to be allocated for implementation on 'm' obtainable servers. In the problem of the order of n, the cost of implementing all tasks on all servers is recognized and stated. The method aims to find the best possible solution. The illustrious Hungarian method is used to solve this problem.

9.4.1 Server Specification

Every cloud server has its meta-task that is given below. The following table signifies the processing speed and bandwidth of M_1 to M_5. Processing speed is represented with the million instructions per second and bandwidth is stated with Megabyte per Second (Table 9.5).

9.4.2 Task Measurement

The following table signifies the instruction size and data size of T_1 to T_5. The size of instruction is indicated by a million instruction and data size as Megabyte (Table 9.6).

9.4.3 The Completion Time of the Tasks of the Server

The following table evaluates the completion time of each task of their related server (Table 9.7).

9.4.4 Required Methods

If the equal number of servers is corresponding to the equal tasks, then we relate our proposed method. In this chapter, we work with some servers and some tasks parallel where some tasks are more significant than the number of servers to catch the smallest

TABLE 9.5

Example of a Table Representing the Processing Speed and Bandwidth

Server	Processing Speed (MIPS)	Bandwidth (MBPS)
M_1	180	60
M_2	156	76
M_3	185	68
M_4	210	56
M_5	160	83

TABLE 9.6

The Table Represents the Instruction Size and Data Size

Task	Instruction Size (MI)	Data Size (MB)
T_1	7845	327
T_2	10564	224
T_3	9285	126
T_4	12010	207
T_5	8960	183

TABLE 9.7

The Size of Instruction and Data Size of Various Tasks

Task/Server	S_1	S_2	S_3	S_4	S_5
T_1	43.58	50.28	42.40	37.35	49.03
T_2	58.69	67.71	57.10	50.30	66.02
T_3	51.58	59.52	50.18	44.21	58.03
T_4	66.72	76.99	64.92	57.19	75.06
T_5	49.78	57.43	48.43	42.67	56.00

TABLE 9.8

The Chart Showing the Completion Time of Each Task of Their Server

T_n/M_m	S_1	S_2	S_3	S_4	S_5
T_1	151	277	185	276	321
T_2	245	286	256	264	402
T_3	246	245	412	423	257
T_4	269	175	145	125	156
T_5	421	178	185	425	235

completion time as well as an optimum value also. In this type of method, we follow a procedure like a matrix as follows (Table 9.8).

9.5 Performance Metrics

A set of parameters are to be considered when building a resource allocation algorithm. These parameters play a dynamic role to rise the entire cloud performance. We can explain these parameters in the following section.

Makespan: This is the sum of all completion times of all tasks of the VM queue. An excellent scheduling algorithm attempts to shrink the makespan, which is defined in Eq. 9.1.

$$Makespan = max\{CTi\} \tag{9.1}$$

where i∈VMs
To estimate the Average Makespan time

$$Average\ makespan = \frac{\sum_{k=1}^{m} Makespane}{m} \tag{9.2}$$

Response Time (RT): It says to the time of the search process, which contains the time to perform the tasks in a cloud computing structure.

$$RTj = FTj - SBj \tag{9.3}$$

Here, FTj is the finish time of the task and SBj is the submission time of the task
To calculate the Mean of Average Response Time of all VMs, defined as

$$M.Av.RT = \frac{\sum_{k=1}^{m} Av.RT_k}{m} \tag{9.4}$$

Av.RT is the average response time of VM represented as

$$M.Av.RT = \frac{\sum_{j=1}^{m} RT_j}{m} \tag{9.5}$$

Execution Time: It is defined as the time difference between the job finishing time and the task starting time within the resource. It is defined as

$$Execution\ Time_j = FTj - STj \tag{9.6}$$

where *STj* is the start time of task.

9.5.1 Matrix Formulation

The problem can be expressed in two ways: as a matrix or as an equation. We are given an n × n matrix in the matrix formulation, while the element in the *i*th row with the *j*th column signifies the cost of assigning the *j*th task to the *i*th machine (Chen et al. 2013). We must assign tasks to the machines in such a way that each task is allotted to each machine, and each machine is allotted by one task, resulting in the lowest total cost of the assignment. The assignment's goal is to find the cheapest solution.

9.5.2 Mathematical Representation

Consider c_{ij} is the cost if the *j*th machine is assigned the *i*th jobs, the problems are to evaluate an assignment so that the total cost to perform each task is lowest. This can be stated in the figure of an **n*n** matrix [*cij*] (Nace and Pióro 2008).
    Mathematically, an assignment problem can be stated as follows (Braun et al. 2001).
    Minimize the total cost

$$Z = \sum_{i=1}^{n}\sum_{j=1}^{n} C_{ij} X_{ij} \tag{9.7}$$

where $x_{ij} = 1$, if the *j*th processor is assigned the *i*th task
    = 0, otherwise

$$\sum_{i=1}^{n} X_{ij} = 1, \left(j = 1,2,3,\ldots\ldots,n \right) \tag{9.8}$$

And

$$\sum_{j=1}^{n} X_{ij} = 1, (i = 1,2,3,\ldots\ldots,n) \tag{9.9}$$

9.6 Proposed Work

To calculate the matrix as well as a combination of tasks versus. For a balanced matrix problem's machine (s), here we would concentrate on a problem that consists of a set of 'm' machines N= {$N_1, N_2, \ldots, N_m$}. A set of 'n' jobs T= {$T_1, T_2, \ldots, T_n$} is considered to be allocated for implementation on the 'm' available machines and the execution cost C_{ij}, while i=1, 2, ..., m and j=1,2, ..., n are referred to in the cost matrix (Kuhn 1955). The algorithm is discussed as follows.

There is a given n*n matrix:

Step 1: To deduct row minima – To deduct the row smallest from each row.

Step 2: To deduct column minima – To deduct the column smallest from all columns.

Step 3: To cover every zero with the lowest number of lines – There are three lines needed to wrap all zeros.

Step 4: To construct additional zeros – The line number is lesser than 4. The least wrapped number is 4. To deduct this number from all wrapped elements and insert it into all elements that are wrapped two times.

Step 5: To cover every zero with the lowest number of lines – There are four lines needed to wrap all zeros.

Step 6: The optimal Solution – Because there are four lines required, the zeros wrap the best possible matrix. This corresponds to the following best possible matrix in the given problem.

Now we discuss the algorithm with an example. The best possible value will be determined, and a clarification of the Hungarian algorithm will be discussed as follows.

The following is the given an arbitrary matrix (Table 9.9).

TABLE 9.9

An Example of a Balanced Matrix Problem

Task	Node			
	N_{11}	N_{12}	N_{13}	N_{14}
T_{11}	18	14	38	26
T_{12}	14	12	24	18
T_{13}	26	18	66	42
T_{14}	19	20	24	36

TABLE 9.10

Requiring the Zeros to Cover an Optimal Assignment Result

Task	Node			
	N_{11}	N_{12}	N_{13}	N_{14}
T_{11}	0	0	15	2
T_{12}	2	4	7	0
T_{13}	4	0	39	14
T_{14}	0	5	0	11

TABLE 9.11

The Optimum Result of the Given Matrix

Task	Node			
	N_{11}	N_{12}	N_{13}	N_{14}
T_{11}	**18**	14	38	26
T_{12}	14	12	24	**18**
T_{13}	26	**18**	66	42
T_{14}	19	20	**24**	36

The best possible matrix cost -

Because there are four lines required, the zeros cover the best possible assignment value (Table 9.10).

This corresponds result in the original matrix is as follows (Table 9.11).

9.7 Result Analysis

In this part, we took various matrixes like 2*2, 4*4, 8*8, and 16*16 to understand the efficiency of our algorithm compared to other existing algorithms. We show execution time of 2*2 matrix while two machines (C_1, C_2) execute tasks differently at a time of different algorithms in Figure 9.1. We also show the execution time of different matrices for the Min–Min algorithm in Figures 9.2–9.4. Next, we show the execution time of different cost matrices for the LBMM algorithm in Figures 9.5–9.10. Next, we show the execution time of different matrices for the LBHM algorithm in Figures 9.11–9.13. Figure 9.14 shows the comparison of individual algorithms with individual sets. Figure 9.15 shows the makespan of an individual matrix with various algorithms. Figure 9.16 shows time complexity in a nanosecond of an individual matrix with various algorithms. And Figure 9.17 shows used memory is bytes.

From the above chart, we compared our proposed algorithm (LBHM) and other presented algorithms for example Min–Min (MM), Load Balanced Min–Min (LBMM), and Load Balance Max–Min–Max (LB3M). All algorithms are showing the same results with two machines, C_1, C_2 as well as our proposed algorithm. The next three charts show the result of the MM algorithm. Then next three charts (12.5, 12.6, and 12.7) show the result of the LBMM algorithm. The next three charts (12.8, 12.9, and 12.10) show the result of the

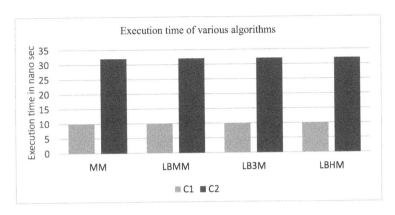

FIGURE 9.1
Execution time of 2 × 2 matrix of various and our proposed algorithms.

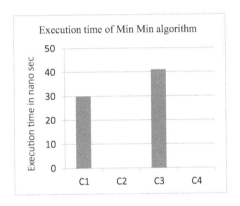

FIGURE 9.2
Execution time of the 4*4 matrix of MM algorithm.

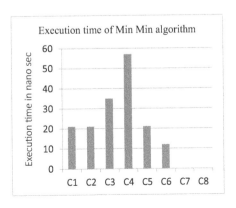

FIGURE 9.3
Execution time of 8*8 matrix of MM algorithm.

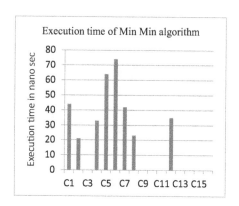

FIGURE 9.4
Execution time of 16*16 matrix of MM algorithm.

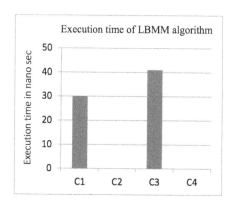

FIGURE 9.5
Execution time of the 4*4 matrix of LBMM algorithm.

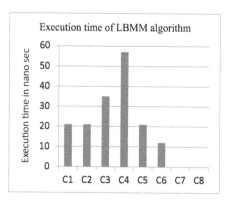

FIGURE 9.6
Execution time of 8*8 matrix of LBMM algorithm.

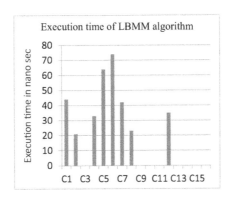

FIGURE 9.7
Execution time of 16*16 matrix of LBMM algorithm.

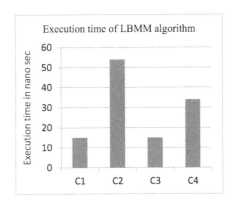

FIGURE 9.8
Execution time of the 4*4 matrix of LBMM algorithm.

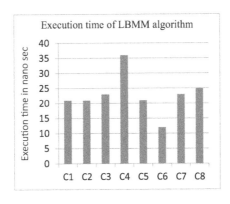

FIGURE 9.9
Execution time of 8*8 matrix of LBMM algorithm.

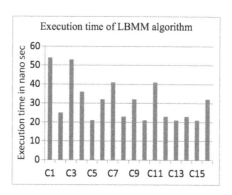

FIGURE 9.10
Execution time of 16*16 matrix of LBMM algorithm.

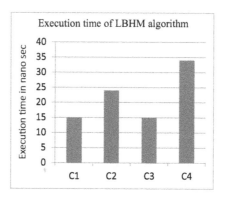

FIGURE 9.11
Execution time of the 4*4 matrix of LBHM algorithm.

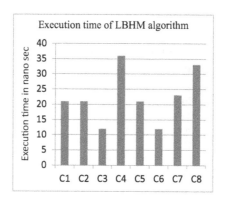

FIGURE 9.12
Execution time of 8*8 matrix of LBHM algorithm.

LB3M algorithm. The next three charts (12.11, 12.12, and 12.13) show the result of the LBHM algorithm.

In the following chart, we merge all results of the 4*4 matrix, that compares different algorithms with different sets.

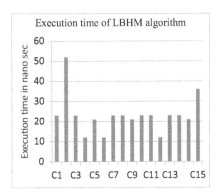

FIGURE 9.13
Execution time of 16*16 matrix of LBHM algorithm.

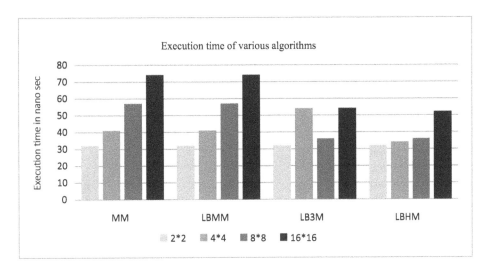

FIGURE 9.14
Comparison of different algorithms with different sets.

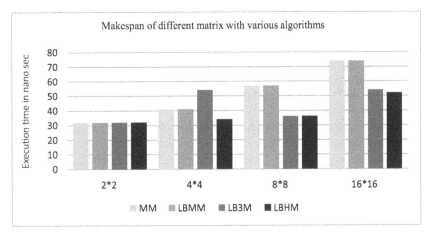

FIGURE 9.15
Makespan of the different matrices with various algorithms.

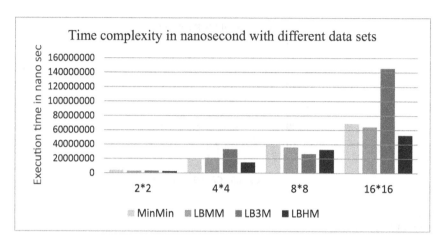

FIGURE 9.16
Execution time of different matrices with various algorithms.

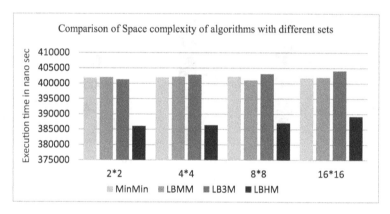

FIGURE 9.17
Memory used of the different matrix with various algorithms in bytes.

In the following chart, we merge all results of Makespan of the different matrix with various algorithms.

In the following chart, we merge all results of the execution time of different matrices with various algorithms

In the following chart, we merge all results of memory used of the different matrix with various algorithms in bytes

In the above all results analysis, we have seen the various cost matrixes like 2*2, 4*4, 8*8, and 16*16 to understand the efficiency of our algorithm compared to other algorithms. We have seen the execution time of 2×2 matrix while two machines (C_1, C_2) execute tasks differently at a time of different algorithms in Figure 9.1. We have shown the execution time of different matrices for the Min–Min algorithm in Figures 9.2–9.4. Next, we show the execution time of different matrices for the LBMM algorithm in Figures 9.5–9.10. Next, we show the execution time of different matrices for the LBHM algorithm in Figures 9.11–9.13. Figure 9.14 shows the comparison of individual algorithms with individual sets. Figure 9.15 shows the makespan of an individual matrix with various algorithms. Figure 9.16

shows time complexity in a nanosecond of an individual matrix with various algorithms, where our proposed algorithm is less than other algorithms. And Figure 9.17 shows used memory is bytes where our proposed algorithm takes minimum memory in bytes which is less than other algorithms.

9.8 Conclusion and Future Work

In this chapter, we propose an efficient resource allocation algorithm for cloud computing networks, which assigns all tasks to computing nodes based on their resource capabilities. We used the Java programming language to run all of the algorithms described in this chapter on a Windows 7 operating system. We used an Intel i3 processor with a clock speed of 3.6 GHz. In this case, our proposed work can achieve improved resource allocation and performance than other algorithms from the case study, such as LBMM, LB3M, and MM. Our proposed algorithm is more efficient than other algorithms currently in use. The time complexity and space complexity of our proposed algorithm is less than other presented algorithms shown above outlines. The present work is defined for n number machine execute n number task. In future, the work can be extended n number machines execute m number tasks, where m >n.

References

Armstrong, R., Hensgen, D., & Kidd, T. (1998, March). The relative performance of various mapping algorithms is independent of sizable variances in run-time predictions. In *Proceedings Seventh Heterogeneous Computing Workshop (HCW'98)* (pp. 79–87). IEEE.

Braun, T. D., Siegel, H. J., Beck, N., Bölöni, L. L., Maheswaran, M., Reuther, A. I., ... & Freund, R. F. (2001). A comparison of eleven static heuristics for mapping a class of independent tasks onto heterogeneous distributed computing systems. *Journal of Parallel and Distributed Computing, 61*(6), 810–837.

Chen, H., Wang, F., Helian, N., & Akanmu, G. (2013, February). User-priority guided Min–Min scheduling algorithm for load balancing in cloud computing. In *2013 National Conference on Parallel Computing Technologies (PARCOMPTECH)* (pp. 1–8). IEEE.

Hung, C. L., Wang, H. H., & Hu, Y. C. (2012, April). Efficient load balancing algorithm for cloud computing network. In *International Conference on Information Science and Technology (IST 2012)*, (pp. 28–30).

Jaeger, P. T., Lin, J., & Grimes, J. M. (2008). Cloud computing and information policy: Computing in a policy cloud? *Journal of Information Technology & Politics, 5*(3), 269–283.

Kokilavani, T., & Amalarethinam, D. G. (2011). Load balanced Min–Min algorithm for static meta-task scheduling in grid computing. *International Journal of Computer Applications, 20*(2), 43–49.

Kuhn, H. W. (1955). The Hungarian method for the assignment problem. *Naval Research Logistics Quarterly, 2*(1–2), 83–97.

Kumar, M., & Sharma, S. C. (2020). Dynamic load balancing algorithm to minimize the makespan time and utilize the resources effectively in cloud environment. *International Journal of Computers and Applications, 42*(1), 108–117.

Ma, T., Chu, Y., Zhao, L., & Ankhbayar, O. (2014). Resource allocation and scheduling in cloud computing: policy and algorithm. *IETE Technical Review, 31*(1), 4–16.

Mondal, R. K. Ray, P., & Sarddar, D.(2016). Load balancing. *International Journal of Research in Computer Applications & Information Technology*, 4(1), 1–21, ISSN Online: 2347-5099, Print: 2348-0009, DOA: 03012016.

Nace, D., & Pióro, M. (2008). Max–Min fairness and its applications to routing and load-balancing in communication networks: A tutorial. *IEEE Communications Surveys & Tutorials*, 10(4), 5–17.

Pham, N. M. N., & Le, V. S. (2017). Applying Ant Colony System algorithm in multi-objective resource allocation for virtual services. *Journal of Information and Telecommunication*, 1(4), 319–333.

Ritchie, G., & Levine, J. (2003). A fast, effective local search for scheduling independent jobs in heterogeneous computing environments. In *Proceedings of the 22nd Workshop of the UK Planning and Scheduling Special Interest Group*.

Şerifoğlu, F. S., & Ulusoy, G. (2004). Multiprocessor task scheduling in multistage hybrid flow-shops: a genetic algorithm approach. *Journal of the Operational Research Society*, 55(5), 504–512.

Shivasankaran, N., Kumar, P. S., Nallakumarasamy, G., & Raja, K. V. (2013). Repair shop job scheduling with parallel operators and multiple constraints using simulated annealing. *International Journal of Computational Intelligence Systems*, 6(2), 223–233.

Sinha, A. (2016). Cloud computing in libraries: Opportunities and challenges. *Pearl: A Journal of Library and Information Science*, 10(2), 113–118. Cybenko, George. (1989). Dynamic load balancing for distributed memory multiprocessors. *Journal of Parallel and Distributed Computing*, 7(2), 279–301.

Wagemann, J., Clements, O., Marco Figuera, R., Rossi, A. P., & Mantovani, S. (2018). Geospatial web services pave new ways for server-based on-demand access and processing of Big Earth Data. *International Journal of Digital Earth*, 11(1), 7–25.

Wang, S. C., Yan, K. Q., Wang, S. S., & Chen, C. W. (2011, April). A three-phases scheduling in a hierarchical cloud computing network. In *2011 Third International Conference on Communications and Mobile Computing* (pp. 114–117). IEEE.

10

Service Availability of Virtual Machines in Cloud Computing

Opeyemi Osanaiye and Steve Adeshina

Nile University of Nigeria, Abuja, Nigeria

CONTENTS

10.1 Introduction

Cloud computing, in recent times, has been driving massive computer deployment and processes. This is attributed to its architecture and features like resource sharing, multi-tenancy, and scalability. Its implementation is driven by key technologies like virtualization, which enables it to house different Virtual Machines (VMs) that host services offered by cloud providers to cloud users. The VMs share the available resources of the physical machine by pulling it when needed and releasing it back to the pool during idle time. Services offered by cloud providers to cloud users are guided by a well-drafted service level agreement (SLA) which ensures that a high level of availability is guaranteed when migrating to the cloud. A common way to describe availability is the number of nines the system can guarantee. Five nines (99.999%) and 24/7 concept are fast becoming a major feature of high-performance system requirement and SLAs (Wazzan & Fayoumi, 2012). Major players in the cloud computing business include Amazon with Elastic Compute Cloud (EC2), Google with Google App Engine, and Microsoft with Azure platform (Endo et al., 2010).

Virtualization entails a hypervisor or virtual machine monitor (VVM) that sits on a physical hardware to enable the deployment and coexisting of VMs. Jiang et al. (2019) described hypervisor as a software that logically replicates a physical machine's components and resources. It allows many OSs to run concurrently and share the physical machine's resources. The primary responsibility of the VMM is to dynamically schedule access to requested physical machine's hardware resources. It also handles and trap privilege or protected instructions (Mishra & Kulkarni, 2018). Virtualization is also made up of virtual interfaces and switches that enable VMs connectivity (Zhu et al., 2018), and its deployment can be either full virtualization or para virtualization (Jain, 2020).

This chapter highlights and discusses the virtualization technology, the different types of virtualization, and its applications. Furthermore, to achieve availability of services and resources, we enumerate the migration of VMs in cloud environment, with emphasis on pre-copy and post-copy migration techniques. Lastly, we propose an enhancement to the pre-copy live migration by adding intelligence to each iteration cycle of the iterative pre-copy stage. Our proposed approach, after each iteration, will predict the amount of downtime to know when to move to the stop-and-copy stage. The predicted downtime will majorly depend on the dirty rate of the memory pages and the bandwidth.

10.2 Virtualization

Virtualization is an advancement of the datacenter technology which introduces tools and techniques to dynamically provide and manage datacenter resources and infrastructure. Virtualization is the main enabling technology that drives cloud computing and is composed of four essential computing resources abstraction, namely, storage, memory, processing power, and network (Buyya et al., 2010). Virtualization ensures that virtual servers are completely unaware and independent of other virtual machines domiciled in the same physical server, therefore enabling each VM to run its own OS. For example, one VM can run Windows OS while the other run Linux OS. Virtualization ensures agile and reliable deployment that manages services to provide an on-demand cloning and live migration, thus improving reliability (Buyya et al., 2010). Other notable benefits of virtualization include the illusion of infinite resources, elastic capacity, multitenancy, and promotion of green IT through the reduction in energy wastage. Notwithstanding these, virtualization is centralized and when the hypervisor is down, it is subjected to a single point of failure.

10.2.1 Virtualization Approaches

As described in the earlier section, virtualization technology provides a virtualized CPU, storage, memory, and network component. The physical machine resources are dynamically shared and allocated to VMs. In the literature, there exist three prominent virtualization approaches, namely, full virtualization, paravirtualization, and hardware-assisted virtualization (Masdari et al., 2016).

10.2.1.1 Full Virtualization

In this approach, the guest OS is completely abstracted from the underling hardware and does not require modification. Additionally, it is not aware of it being virtualized. At the center of full virtualization is the hypervisor that functions by directly interacting with the hardware resources of the physical server. It also acts as a platform for the VM OS and ensures that all the VMs are totally independent of one another and unaware of the presence of each other running on the same physical machine. In full virtualization, the guest OS and the physical machine it exists in cannot communicate directly, except through the hypervisor. Some of the key advantages of full virtualization include its isolation feature between VMs and the hypervisor, its ability to concurrently execute multiple OSs and the fact that the guest OS does not require any modification (Chandrasekaran, 2014). Its binary translation feature ensures privilege instructions are converted to user-level during runtime by translating kernel code; however, this process affects the overall system performance. An example of full virtualization products includes VMware, VirtualBox, and Hyper-V.

10.2.1.2 Paravirtualization

The introduction of paravirtualization was proposed to improve the performance of full virtualization by eliminating privileged instruction and replacing it with specific function calls to the hypervisor (Shirinbab et al., 2014). The hypervisor, in paravirtualization, runs directly on the hardware and assigns recourses dynamically to the VM when needed. All active VMs are managed by a privileged OS running over the hypervisor.

In paravirtualization, the host and guest OSs are modified to replace the privileged operation hypercalls and cannot support unmodified OS (i.e., its portability and compatibility are limited). Paravirtualization differs from full virtualization as the guest OSs understand that they are running on a virtualized environment, where the guest OS and hypervisor communicate directly using hypercalls. Examples of paravirtualization systems are Xen Server and KVM.

10.2.1.3 Hardware-Assisted Virtualization

In hardware-assisted virtualization, its architecture ensures that the building of a VM monitor is facilitated by the hardware. It also ensures that the guest OS runs in isolation. Vendors of computer hardware such as AMD and Intel have developed additional hardware resources to support virtualization. VT-x, for example, is the virtualization technology of the processor released by Intel, while AMD also has a virtualized processor called AMD-v that supports virtualization (Chandrasekaran, 2014). When overhead is the yardstick, hardware-assisted virtualization is the most preferred as it reduces the overhead attributed to binary translation and paravirtualization; however, it does not support all vendors.

10.2.2 Virtualization Deployment

Virtualization can be further classified according to the type of resource that is being virtualized. Common among these resources are operating system, memory, storage, server, and network virtualization.

OS virtualization, which is also referred to as container-based or shared kernel virtualization, can be described as a concept where many isolated user-space instances are allowed by the kernel of an OS to exist in parallel, instead of one. This implies that the OS and not the hardware is being virtualized and the guest OS environment shares the same OS as the host physical machine (Shaoo et al., 2010). In memory virtualization, the memory of the physical machine that is virtualized is allocated to the VMs according to their demand. The hypervisor maps the physical memory to the virtual memory. The hypervisor can also be used to consolidate the main memory in a virtualized cloud datacenter to aggregate free memory of different servers into segments to create a pool of virtual memory which can be allocated to VMs when requested (Chandrasekaran, 2014). Hypervisors can be categorized into two, namely, type 1 hypervisor and type 2 hypervisor. The type 1 hypervisor, which is also known as bare metal, runs directly on the hardware of the physical host. It manages the guest OSs and the hardware resources of the physical host. Type 2 hypervisor is a distinct second layer that runs within a formal OS environment with the guest OS above the hardware running as the third layer. It is also known as hosted hypervisor.

Storage is another resource of the physical computers that is aggregated to a single virtualized storage to form a cloud storage. Storage virtualization has been deployed in advanced storage techniques, such as storage area network (SAN) and network-attached storage (NAS). Storage virtualization has ensured an enhanced process towards live migrating VM, where storage is being shared by the initiating and destination physical machines. In this instance, the disk storage will not be migrated with the server virtualization, therefore allowing the physical servers to be moved into a virtual environment. Recent physical servers can host more than one virtual server at a time, therefore the number of physical servers deployed is reduced. This in turn reduces the IT and maintenance expenditure. Finally, network virtualization creates a logical virtual network from the underling physical network consisting of switches, routers, and network interface card. Multiple virtual network components can be created from the physical network component and can be used for various purposes.

10.3 Resource Availability in Cloud Computing

When considering service and resource availability in cloud computing, it is essential to consider factors such as infrastructural failure, application failure, and security. While security concerns are related to attacks targeted at both the hardware and software components of the cloud, application failure is primarily a software-related issue while infrastructural failure is the breakdown or malfunction of the hardware component. Attacks that are directed toward cloud services and infrastructure can be either an internal or external attack; with the motive of consuming the cloud resources and disrupting its availability to intended legitimate users (Osanaiye & Dlodlo, 2015). Failure of cloud application and infrastructural component can be operational, physical, or human. Additionally, it can also be attributed to design error, software bug, power cut, network, and system failure.

In this chapter, our major focus is to ensure cloud services and resources are available, even during security attack or infrastructural failure.

10.3.1 Cloud Computing Security

Notwithstanding the many benefits cloud computing offer, some of its unique attributes expose it to some reliability and security risk. One of the most significant challenges is the

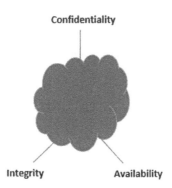

FIGURE 10.1
Security triad in cloud computing.

cloud provider guaranteeing the cloud user high availability, which has marred its general adoption (Machida et al., 2013). Cloud computing has inherited the issues attributed to its different enabling technologies, just as it has enjoyed their benefits. Top on this list is the issue of security in terms of confidentiality, integrity, and availability (see Figure 10.1). Guaranteeing confidentiality in cloud computing will mean ensuring that access to privilege information is only granted to authorized users, however, due to the cloud's multitenancy and resource sharing feature, the cloud computing environment can be subjected to information confidentiality threat. Secondly, cloud integrity can be referred to as the protection of data stored in the cloud from possible tampering, falsification, and deletion. Finally, cloud availability involves ensuring that services and resources subscribed to by legitimate cloud users must be accessible on-demand as requested. The implication of non-availability of cloud resources and services can be devastating and can possibly lead to partial or total disruption of service delivery. The security triad in cloud computing is shown in Figure 10.1.

One of the prominent security threats in accessing the available cloud resources by cloud users has been identified in the literature to be the Denial of Service (DoS) or its distributed form, Distributed Denial of Service (DDoS) attack (Osanaiye et al., 2016). This attack denies genuine users access to the pool of computing resources offered by the cloud provider.

10.4 Availability Measurement in Cloud Computing

Availability of cloud services and resources can be determined by using two key metrics, namely, mean time to failure (MTTF) and mean time to repair (MTTR). Cloud resources and services become unavailable to the users when component fails, unless restored. MTTF can be defined as the mean estimated time projected by the manufacturer of the hardware before the failure of the hardware module. In the case of software, MTTF is obtained by dividing the total amount of hours of operation by the number of resources under study. For the mean time to repair (MTTR), it can be obtained by measuring the amount of time it takes a failed module to be repaired (Longo et al., 2011). In the case of hardware module, MTTR can be defined as the average time it takes a failed hardware to be replaced and in the case of software, MTTR can be obtained by determining the time it takes it to restart, having detected a software fault.

Availability in cloud can therefore be obtained by dividing the available service time by the total time:

$$Availability = MTTF / (MTTF + MTTR).$$

10.5 Virtual Machine Migration in Cloud Computing

VM migration is a strategy used in transferring a VM between two physical hosts, to improve its reliability and performance (Medina & García, 2014). Different migration approaches have been described in the literature. Forsman et al. (2015) in their work identified cold migration, hot migration, and live migration as the three migration methods that can be used to move VMs from one physical host to the other. In cold migration, the VM is powered off or suspended for the entire duration of migrating from the source physical host to the predestined target physical host and restarted. For hot migration, rather than being shut down, as in the case of cold migration, the running guest OS is only suspended, conveyed, and restarted at the predestined target physical host. When compared, the latter is preferred to the former because the VM and all the applications running on it are not restarted completely. For live migration, it ensures an uninterrupted service delivery of the applications hosted on the VM and its running OS being migrated between two physical servers (Ahmad et al., 2015). The live migration process involves the seamless transfer of the VM and its environment between the two physical servers (Wu & Zhao, 2011).

From the migration strategies mentioned, VM live migration is the most preferred when availability is of high importance. However, it is often resource intensive, due to the large amount of network bandwidth and CPU cycles consumed. This has attracted interest from researchers on how to reduce the resources consumed during migration. Recent deployments have proposed a shared pool of storage (i.e., network-attached storage (NAS) and storage area network (SAN)) between the source and the predestined physical hosts (Das et al., 2011). With the introduction of a shared storage, it is not necessary to migrate the disk storage except content of the memory pages not present in the shared storage (see Figure 10.2). This will greatly decrease the content being transferred, hence reducing the downtime and the transmission time of applications and services in the moving VM. The performance metrics during VM live migration are the migration time, downtime, and the number of dirty pages (data) (Ruan et al., 2014). Outside the provision of high availability in virtualized environment, these metrics have also been optimized in the literature in areas such as load balancing and network resilience.

10.5.1 VM Live Migration Techniques

In VM live migration, the migrating VM continues to run its processes while a greater part of the memory and the running applications are transferred from the source host to the predestined physical host. To optimize memory-constrained disk-based paging system, the pre-paging method can be deployed. Pre-paging is a proactive approach to prefetching

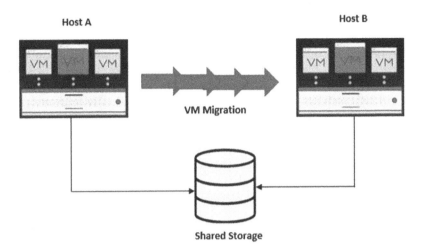

FIGURE 10.2
VM live migration between two physical servers with a shared storage.

from the disk, with the memory unit attempting to conceal the delay of local page faults by reasonably sequencing the pre-fetched pages (Hines & Gopalan, 2009). Recently deployed virtual memory has discontinued the use of pre-paging method because of its increasing DRAM capacities.

Akoush et al. (2010) in their work identified two proposed designs for live migration, namely, the pure stop-and-copy and the pure on-demand. For the stop-and-copy technique, during the VM migration process, it suspends the VM and copy the whole memory pages to the predetermined target host to reduce the migration time. This, even though effective, increases the downtime of the system. For the pure on-demand technique, it works by stopping the VM to enable it to copy the essential data from the kernel to the predestined physical host. Whatever is left in the VM address space is transferred when needed at the target host. These two methods discussed above are often characterized by poor performance, therefore prompting the proposed pre-copy live migration technique that attempts to provide an improvement and a balance between the migration time and downtime (Ruan et al., 2014). The pre-copy live migration function by iteratively moving data in the kernel between two physical hosts. In the initial iteration, all memory pages are moved while subsequently, only modified pages after the first iteration was transferred will be copied. During the iterative process, the pages dirtied while the previous iteration took place is tracked to minimize both the migration time and downtime.

In post-copy live migration technique, a VM that is suspended at the first round of the transfer process to move the device and the vCPU to a predestined physical host has been proposed (Hines & Gopalan, 2009). The transferred VM is restarted immediately at the target host and the residual memory pages are obtained from the source host on demand. Hines and Gopalan (2009) in their work proposed an adaptive pre-paging technique that eliminates the transmission of duplicate pages and dynamic self-ballooning to ensure free memory pages are not transferred.

The Pre-copy algorithm is a common VM live migration technique as seen in Xen, VMware and KVM hypervisors (Forsman et al., 2015). As stated earlier, the running VM's memory pages are iteratively copied over many circles until the dirtied pages are small enough to forcefully stop the VM temporarily at the source host and restarted at the predestined physical host. During the first round of iteration, the entire pages are copied and only the dirty or modified pages are moved in subsequent rounds. The hypervisor maintains a dirty bitmap which is used to track the modified pages.

Researchers have proposed several methods to reduce the amount of data transferred between the two physical hosts in the iterative pre-copy stage, which will subsequently limit the total migration time and downtime. The authors in Michael and Shen (2014) have proposed an efficient technique that is self-adapting and gradually migrates the database connection from the source host to the predestined target host. This technique minimizes the performance overhead of the migrating tenant by transferring only regularly accessed cache content from the source to the target host. Piao et al. (2014)have proposed a technique that use disk cache and snapshot memory compaction. This technique deployed a downtime-controlled adaptive scheme that uses history of VM memory update information in KVM hypervisor.

Callegati et al. (2014) in their work proposed a live migration technique in a cloud-based edge network, an emerging paradigm, that collectively migrates groups of similar VMs as a single unit. Clark et al. (2005) have proposed a pre-copy migration technique, consisting of six stages (*see below*), during the migration of VMs between two physical hosts:

a) Pre-migration – The source host running the VM pre-selects a destination target host that can guarantee the required resources when migration occurs.

b) Reservation – In anticipation for any VM migration, the target host reserves adequate resources to accommodate the migrated VM.

c) Iterative pre-copy – In this stage, the whole RAM is transferred from the source to the destination physical host during the first iteration while additional modified dirty pages are transmitted in subsequent iterations.

d) Stop-and-copy – Here, the VM is suspended so that the CPU state and the residual inconsistent pages are transferred to the predestined target host. At the completion of this stage, the source and the target host will be a duplicate (i.e., they will have entirely similar copies of the VM).

e) Commitment – In this stage, the destination host will notify the source that it has an entirely duplicate copy of the VM. The source host will acknowledge this before disposing the original VM. After this process, the target host will become the primary host.

f) Activation – In this stage, the post-migration codes will be run and the migrated VM activated to enable the drivers of the device to be re-attached to the new machine.

In the six stages mentioned above, what triggers when to proceed to the stop-and-copy stage after the iterative pre-copy stage, to achieve a reduced migration time and downtime, has been the focus of recent works (Ibrahim et al., 2011). This can influence the functioning of the applications running on the VM. For Xen (Akoush et al., 2010), the stop conditions used during the VM live migration for pre-copy algorithm are as follows:

a) If the amount of dirtied pages in the immediate past iteration is less than 50 pages.

b) If 29 pre-copy iterations have been performed during the migration process.

c) If more than three times the allocated RAM of the VM have already been transferred from the source to the target host during the iterative pre-copy stage.

The first stop condition described above minimizes the downtime during migration, as only limited pages are sent. However, for the second and third conditions, the stop condition forces the migration process into the stop-and-copy stage, notwithstanding the number of dirtied pages remaining at the source host. This often has a huge effect on the total downtime of the applications hosted by the VM.

10.6 VM Live Migration Evaluation

When evaluating VM live migration performance, both the downtime and the total migration time is often used. Downtime can be defined as the entire time the VM is halted during migration which affects the availability of the VM (Ruan et al., 2014), while the total migration time is the entire time it takes to transfer a VM from the source host to the predestined physical host. The performance of VM live migration is very crucial to the reliability and performance of the hosted applications. Wu and Zhao (2011) proposed an algorithm that predicts the total migration time in Xen environment using the available resources for migration and the performance of the hosted applications in the VM. Nathan et al. (2015) studied and analyzed the current prediction techniques in Xen and KVM migration. Results obtained from their analysis show that the error rate was high because the size of the writable working set, page transfer, dirty rate, and pages to be skipped were not considered. To solve this issue, a model that predicts and estimates the performance of Xen and KVM has been suggested. Voorsluys et al. (2009) have reviewed past works to study the impact of VM live migration on hosted applications in Xen. Current findings have shown that overhead during migration is inevitable, however, it requires proper attention, particularly in situations where high availability condition is of high importance.

10.7 Linear Regression-Based Smart Pre-copy Live Migration

From the review of past works, most of the proposed pre-copy live migration algorithms in cloud computing focused on reducing the migration time and the downtime and did not consider the benchmark workload of the different VMs. In this work, we are convinced that fixing a stop and copy criteria without considering the benchmark workload of different VMs will lead to a suboptimal migration time and downtime. Therefore, we present an algorithm that use regression analysis to predict the downtime by dynamically analyzing the amount of dirty pages from the previous iterations. A comparison will thereafter be done between the predicted downtime and the set downtime threshold value to know if the condition has been met to transit to the stop and copy stage.

In this section, our proposed conceptual framework, linear regression-based smart pre-copy live migration, is presented (see Figure 10.3).

10.7.1 Linear Regression Approach

Regression is a statistical method which has been used over the years for prediction. It can be used to estimate the relationship between one or more inputs (i.e., an independent variable) to estimate a dependent output. It is called simple regression if a straight line is used to establish a relationship between two variables while cases of two or more independent

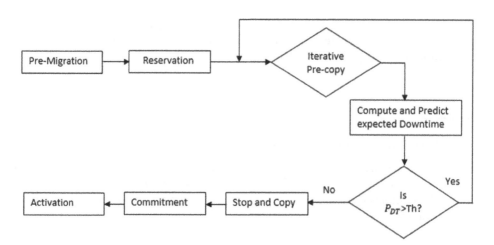

FIGURE 10.3
A conceptual live migration framework.

variables having a linear relationship with the dependent variable is referred to as multiple regression. The regression relationship in all cases can be either linear or nonlinear (Farahnakian et al., 2013). The regression is said to be linear if the relationship between the input variable x and output variable y can be represented with an s straight-line equation.

In our proposed framework (see Figure 10.3), we have adapted the pre-copy algorithm in Xen and propose a smart pre-copy live migration that adds intelligence to the system, just as in the work of (Periola et al., 2021) that discussed the use of artificial intelligence in cloud platform.

10.7.2 Smart Pre-copy Live Migration

Smart pre-copy live migration for VMs in virtualized environment, such as cloud computing, is dynamic and guarantees high availability. It enhances the iterative pre-copy stage by dynamically predicting the downtime at the end of each iteration. This is achieved using linear regression to determine when to move to the stop and copy stage. This will be determined by the available bandwidth between the physical hosts, the benchmark workload, and the dirty page rate. The block that computes and predict the expected downtime in Figure 10.3 compares the predicted downtime P_{DT} with the predefined downtime threshold, Th, at the end of each round of the iterative pre-copy stage. This will determine whether to continue with the iteration process or advance to the stop and copy stage. This process of comparing P_{DT} and Th will continue until the set condition is met to guarantee a minimum downtime.

Supposing the bandwidth between the source host and the target host is constant, linear regression can be used to determine the relationship between dirty pages which is the independent variable to predict the downtime, which is the dependent variable.

$$y = mx + b \tag{10.1}$$

where y in Equation (10.1) is the dependent variable and x is the independent variable; the regression coefficients are m and b respectively.

The degree of error can be determined to ascertain how precise the output y have been predicted

$$\varepsilon_i = y_i - \hat{y} \qquad (10.2)$$

where ε_i in Equation (10.2) is the difference between the actual output y_i and the predicted output $\hat{y}_i$ in data point i.

Equation (10.3) is used to calculate the least square criterion.

$$\min \sum \left(y_i - \hat{y}_i \right)^2 \qquad (10.3)$$

where y_i in Equation (10.3) is the actual measured downtime (dependent variable) and $\hat{y}_i$ is the estimated value of the dependent variable.

From Equation (10.1), the slope m and the intercept b can be determined using Equation (10.4) below.

$$m = \frac{\sum \left(x_i - \bar{x} \right) \left(y_i - \bar{y}_i \right)}{\sum \left(x_i - \bar{x} \right)^2} \qquad (10.4)$$

and

$$b = \bar{y} - m\bar{x} \qquad (10.5)$$

where $\bar{x}$ and $\bar{y}$ are the average value of the independent and dependent variable, while x_i and y_i are the values of the independent and dependent variable.

The linear regression approach uses historical data from previous iterations to estimate the amount of dirty pages in subsequent iterations. Equation (10.1) can be used to obtain the expression that shows the relationship between the dependent and the independent variable (i.e., downtime and workload).

10.8 Conclusion

This chapter has studied the availability of VM in cloud computing. This was achieved by first analyzing the different types of virtualization techniques and its application before studying the migration approach that transfers a VM from one physical machine to another. These migration approaches can be grouped into cold migration, hot migration, and live migration. Live migration approach has been further classified into pre-copy migration and post-copy migration. Cloud computing is highly virtualized and provides resources such as computation, storage, and networking. The requirement of high availability by end users has necessitated our proposed improvement to the pre-copy live migration by introducing intelligence to each iteration round of the iterative pre-copy stage. We predict the amount of downtime at each iteration to determine if to move to the stop-and-copy stage. The predicted downtime will majorly depend on the bandwidth and the dirty rate of the memory pages. Future work will include deploying and evaluating the framework in a real-world environment with the aim of refining and validating the framework.

References

Ahmad, R. W., Gani, A., Hamid, S. H. A., Shiraz, M., Yousafzai, A., & Xia, F. (2015). A survey on virtual machine migration and server consolidation frameworks for cloud data centers. *Journal of Network and Computer Applications*, 52, 11–25.

Akoush, S., Sohan, R., Rice, A., Moore, A. W., & Hopper, A. (2010). Predicting the performance of virtual machine migration. In *IEEE International Symposium on Modeling, Analysis and Simulation of Computer and Telecommunication Systems*, pp. 37–46.

Buyya, R., Broberg, J., & Goscinski, A. M. (Eds.). (2010). *Cloud computing: Principles and paradigms*, Vol. 87, John Wiley & Sons, Hoboken, NJ.

Callegati, F., Cerroni, W., Contoli, C., & Santandrea, G. (2014) Performance of network virtualization in cloud computing infrastructures: The OpenStack case. In *2014 IEEE 3rd International Conference on Cloud Networking (CloudNet)*, Luxembourg, 8–10 October, 2016132-137. https://doi.org/10.1109/CloudNet.2014.6968981

Chandrasekaran, K. (2014). *Essentials of cloud computing*, CRC Press, Boca Raton, FL.

Clark, C., Fraser, K., Hand, S., Hansen, J.G., Jul, E., Limpach, C., Pratt, I., & Warfield, A. (2005). Live migration of virtual machines. In *Proceedings of the 2ndConference on Symposium on Networked Systems Design & Implementation* (Vol. 2, pp. 273–286).

Das, S., Nishimura, S., Agrawal, D., & El Abbadi, A. (2011). Albatross: Lightweight elasticity in shared storage databases for the cloud using live data migration. *Proceedings of the VLDB Endowment*, 4(8), 494–505.

Endo, P. T., Gonçalves, G. E., Kelner, J., & Sadok, D. (2010). A survey on open-source cloud computing solutions. In *Brazilian Symposium on Computer Networks and Distributed Systems*, Vol. 71, pp. 3–16.

Farahnakian, F., Liljeberg, P., & Plosila, J. (2013). LiRCUP: Linear regression based CPU usage prediction algorithm for live migration of virtual machines in data centers. In *39th Euromicro Conference on Software Engineering and Advanced Applications*, pp. 357–364.

Forsman, M., Glad, A., Lundberg, L., & Ilie, D. (2015). Algorithms for automated live migration of virtual machines. *Journal of Systems and Software*, 101, 110–126.

Hines, M. R., & Gopalan, K. (2009). Post-copy based live virtual machine migration using adaptive pre-paging and dynamic self-ballooning. In *Proceedings of the 2009 ACM SIGPLAN/SIGOPS International Conference on Virtual Execution Environments*, pp. 51–60.

Ibrahim, K. Z., Hofmeyr, S., Iancu, C., & Roman, E. (2011). Optimized pre-copy live migration for memory intensive applications. In *Proceedings of 2011 International Conference for High Performance Computing, Networking, Storage and Analysis*, pp. 1–11.

Jain, S. M. (2020). Virtualization basics. In *Linux containers and virtualization*, Apress, Berkeley, CA, pp. 1–14.

Jiang, C., Wang, Y., Ou, D., Li, Y., Zhang, J., Wan, J., Luo, B., & Shi, W. (2019). Energy efficiency comparison of hypervisors. *Sustainable Computing: Informatics and Systems*, 22, 311–321.

Longo, F., Ghosh, R., Naik, V. K., & Trivedi, K. S. (2011). A scalable availability model for infrastructure-as-a-service cloud. In *IEEE/IFIP 41st International Conference on Dependable Systems & Networks (DSN)*, pp. 335–346.

Machida, F., Kim, D. S., & Trivedi, K. S. (2013). Modeling and analysis of software rejuvenation in a server virtualized system with live VM migration. *Performance Evaluation*, 70(3), 212–230.

Masdari, M., Nabavi, S. S., & Ahmadi, V. (2016). An overview of virtual machine placement schemes in cloud computing. *Journal of Network and Computer Applications*, 66, 106–127.

Medina, V., & García, J. M. (2014). A survey of migration mechanisms of virtual machines. *ACM Computing Surveys (CSUR)*, 46(3), 1–33.

Michael, N., & Shen, Y. (2014). Downtime-free live migration in a multitenant database. In *Technology Conference on Performance Evaluation and Benchmarking*, Springer, Cham, pp. 130–155.

Mishra, D., & Kulkarni, P. (2018). A survey of memory management techniques in virtualized systems. *Computer Science Review*, 29, 56–73.

Nathan, S., Bellur, U., & Kulkarni, P. (2015). Towards a comprehensive performance model of virtual machine live migration. In *Proceedings of the Sixth ACM Symposium on Cloud Computing*, pp. 288–301.

Osanaiye, O., Choo, K. K. R., & Dlodlo, M. (2016). Distributed denial of service (DDoS) resilience in cloud: Review and conceptual cloud DDoS mitigation framework. *Journal of Network and Computer Applications*, 67, 147–165.

Osanaiye, O., & Dlodlo, M. (2015). TCP/IP header classification for detecting spoofed DDoS attack in Cloud environment. In *Proceedings of 16th IEEE International Conference on Computer as a Tool (EUROCON 2015)*, Salamanca, Spain, pp. 1–6.

Periola, A. A., Osanaiye, O. A., & Olusesi, A. T. (2021). Future cloud: Spherical processors for realizing low-cost upgrade in underwater data centers. *The Journal of Supercomputing*, 77, 7046–7072.

Piao, G., Oh, Y., Sung, B., & Park, C. (2014). Efficient pre-copy live migration with memory compaction and adaptive VM downtime control. In *Proceedings of 4th IEEE International Conference on Big Data and Cloud Computing (BdCloud)*, Sydney, Australia, pp. 85–90.

Ruan, Y., Cao, Z., & Cui, Z. (2014). Pre-filter-copy: Efficient and self-adaptive live migration of virtual machines. *IEEE System Journal*, 10, 1459–1469.

Sahoo, J., Mohapatra, S., & Lath, R. (2010). Virtualization: A survey on concepts, taxonomy and associated security issues. In *Second International Conference on Computer and Network Technology*, pp. 222–226.

Shirinbab, S., Lundberg, L., & Ilie, D. (2014). Performance comparison of KVM, VMware and XenServer using a large telecommunication application. In *Cloud Computing*. IARIA XPS Press.

Voorsluys, W., Broberg, J., Venugopal, S., & Buyya, R. (2009). Cost of virtual machine live migration in clouds: A performance evaluation. In *Proceedings of the 1st International Conference on Cloud Computing*, Beijing, China, pp. 254–265.

Wazzan, M., & Fayoumi, A. (2012). Service availability evaluation for a protection model in hybrid cloud computing architecture. In *International Symposium on Telecommunication Technologies*, pp. 307–312.

Wu, Y., & Zhao, M. (2011). Performance modeling of virtual machine live migration. In *Proceedings of theIEEE International Conference onCloud Computing (CLOUD)*, Washington, DC, USA, pp. 492–499.

Zhu, K., Yao, Z., He, N., Li, D., & Zhang, L. (2018). Toward full virtualization of the network topology. *IEEE Systems Journal*, 13(2), 1640–1649.

11

Analysis of Security Challenges and Threats in Social Network and Cloud Computing

K.P. Bindu Madavi
Dayananda Sagar University, Bengaluru, India

P. Vijayakarthik
Sir M. Visvesvaraya Institute of Technology, Bengaluru, India

CONTENTS

11.1 Introduction

Social networking is an online platform where people can interact and communicate. In societies, the usage of social networks has rapidly increased. Social media networks have transformed how individuals stay in contact with family, friends, and also, how data are dispersed across the globe. People will share documents, pictures, and videos in the cloud via the Internet. The most popular content in social networks is photos and videos which require maximum space to store. Social networks use cloud technologies as on-demand self-service where no human intervention needs to get resources. Users can access a massive amount of structured and unstructured data from anywhere. The cloud is also useful in data recovery and backup. The user's private and sensitive data are maintained by social networking sites which might be attractive targets for the different attacks. This brings new threats to the user's privacy. The most commonly used social networks are Instagram, Facebook, and Twitter.

DOI: 10.1201/9781003213888-11

Multiple numbers of online users have been enrolled in the social network. Users have access to their information and can post it on social media. Therefore, computation has increased the independence of interaction. Many privacy issues exist in using cloud data centers. Cloud providers must trust social network providers with their data. It may be a smart idea to combine private and public cloud data centers. The Amazon, Azure, and Google Cloud are only a few of the cloud service providers with various data centers that help with storing and handling private data. This research examines the security and privacy issues that arise from the use of cloud technologies in social networks. Since social networking sites have millions of users in various places, this is the reason they are generally appropriate for cloud adaptation. Since they store rich multimedia content inside cloud networks, social networks have also aided in improving web usability. For example, audio and video files take up a lot of memory and can slow down any website. Amazon and Salesforce are two examples of vendors that provide this service. Backup and data recovery costs have been drastically reduced by cloud computing. Cloud computing technology was used daily, whether to send messages, upload videos, or store photographs. The main goal of social networking is to reach out to a specific audience, which is exactly what you would expect to do if you store your data in the cloud. This is because while data is processed in the cloud, anybody with Internet access can access it.

11.2 Literature Survey

Every year, the number of people who use social networking sites has risen dramatically in recent years. Statista report provides several social networking sites used globally from 2010 to 2020 with the predictions until 2022 which is shown in Figure 11.1. In 2020, worldwide 8.2 billion users are using social media. The tremendous increase in sign-ups of social networks has resulted in security and privacy issues for users. This affects confidentiality, privacy, and authentication of users. This section aims to compile a list of the most recent survey articles on social networks and cloud data protection.

Praveena and Smys (2018)suggested a method for securing data in cloud-based social networks. It focuses on encryption strategies based on Revocable-Hierarchical-Identity (RHIBE). Before the data are stored in the cloud, they will be encrypted. To decrypt the data, the user uses a private key. Collusion is avoided because the proposed system does not share the user's private key.

Huang et al. (2018) introduced a Secure Identity-based Data Sharing and Profile Matching scheme for cloud-based mobile health social networks (MHSN). In mobile health social networks, the proposed scheme guarantees data security and availability. Identity-based broadcast encryption (IBBE) techniques are used to secure the patient data and share those dose data with doctors. The attribute-based CPRE technique is used to not leak any sensitive information. The analysis of the paper shows the reduction in computation cost to patients.

A privacy-preserving similarity computation scheme is proposed by Zhang et al. (2020) for cloud-based mobile social networks. The author is focused on partially homomorphic encryption to improve efficiency.

A survey was conducted on the challenges and opportunities of cloud computing in social networks by Alazie Dagnaw and Ebabye Tsige (2019). The author proposes the

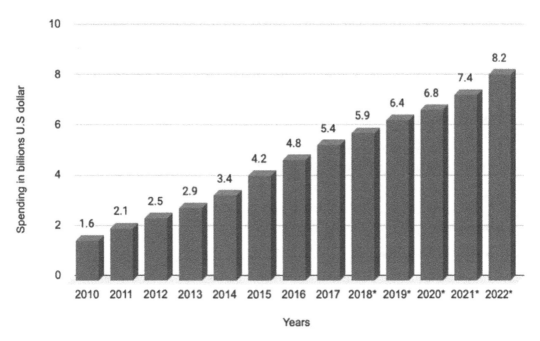

FIGURE 11.1
Usage social network world wide (Steven, 2021).

development of a dynamic 'Social Cloud' that allows sharing resources with friends in the framework of a social network by leveraging pre-existing trust established through friendship. They believe that a much more sustainable resource-sharing system could be created by integrating trust relationships with appropriate reward structures.

Vora and Nayak (2017) address the major privacy concerns and strategies for maintaining privacy in the Social-Networking, Mobile, Analytics, and Cloud Environments, as well as the methods used in each context, as well as their benefits and drawbacks. Although there are several methods for protecting sensitive data, the author discovered that not all of them are foolproof in practice.

Stergiou et al. (2018) focused on the security concerns surrounding social networks, Big data, and Cloud computing technologies. They want to combine the benefits of both technologies, especially big data and social networking. The new framework has been proposed in the cloud through which the different social network users can transfer information and data. The proposed framework improves social network user connectivity while also providing security and accuracy in a Cloud.

Zheleva and Getoor (2011) review the literature on social network privacy. They concentrate on both online social and online affiliation networks and identify potential privacy violations and explain the attacks that have been investigated. Privacy concepts in the sense of anonymization and current anonymization techniques are discussed in the paper.

Khalid et al. (2018) provided an overview of different types of attacks on social networks as well as security strategies for users. The numerous threats that can compromise user protection and privacy have been addressed and divided into categories. In addition to these attacks, strategies to defend against them are also given.

Rathore et al. (2017) examined the various privacy and security threats that affect any user of social networking. They concentrate on different risks that occur as a result of the distribution of multimedia material on a social networking platform separately. The most up-to-date security options for protecting social network users from these attacks were explained in the article.

Fire et al. (2014) have done a comprehensive analysis of the various privacy and security threats that endanger the well-being of OSN users. They provide an overview of existing solutions that can improve OSN users' safety, security, and privacy.

Chakrabarti et al. (2018) discussed the most important security flaws and security specifications of a current Cloud framework. They provide a broad overview of these issues to emphasize the importance of understanding the security vulnerabilities in the Cloud computing environment and developing appropriate countermeasures.

11.3 Social Networks

Social networking has transformed the Internet in the last few years. In reality, it has altered the entire marketing landscape. So, it is essential for your business system to implement these new communication methods as soon as possible. The most significant is to promote your brand on social media. This is an additional marketing tool for raising brand awareness. It has the maximum exposure due to worldwide access sharing capabilities. It provides the most recent information about what is going on in our country and around the world. We recognize the importance of social media for connectivity and contact in this corona era since we are unable to leave our homes to meet our friends, family, relatives, and others with whom we are connected. Figure 11.2 shows the reasons to use Social Networks.

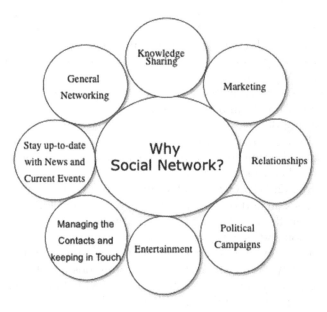

FIGURE 11.2
Reasons to use social networks.

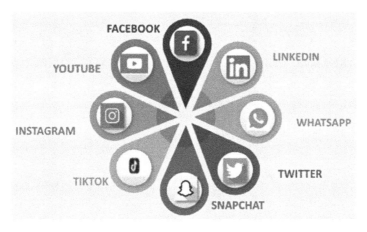

FIGURE 11.3
Top popular social media platforms in 2021.

11.3.1 Popular Social Media Platforms in 2021

Figure 11.3 shows the top popular social media platforms in 2021. LinkedIn can be categorized as a social network for professionals. In LinkedIn, the user can post their learning and also learn through networking. It can also be used for marketing and job postings. The user in LinkedIn will post all the data including educational information and personal information. On Facebook, users can upload pics and videos to reflect their emotions. This is also the tool that can be used to network with friends and families across the globe. YouTube is a video platform and it can be used for media-based communication. Users can also learn and share their experiences. It also works as a medium by various media networks to keep the users updated with the latest information happening across the globe. TikTok had one of the highest growth rates in 2020. TikTok is a short media-sharing social network platform. It is used to entertain friends and family. It is also used as a popular source of entertainment. Twitter apps exist to make your life simpler as well as to give you an insight into the platform's potential through the lens of a particular artistic vision. WhatsApp is a messaging platform. Currently, WhatsApp is used for business by selling regular updates to the interested customer directly. It uses the personal phone number to create the account. In Snapchat, users will send videos, pictures, and messages to their contacts, and those pictures will disappear after a few seconds once it is viewed.

11.4 Cloud in Social Networks

Social media has its cloud application. So, the user can update information and photos from anywhere across the globe via an Internet connection. The social media apps themselves have their own data centers. Instagram has 1 billion monthly active users. Just put that in perspective Facebook has 2 billion monthly active users, and we are seven billion people on this planet so that is one-seventh of the population using Instagram and on average a user spends about roughly an hour on Instagram daily. Instagram is a photo-sharing app that uploads photos and other users react to it mainly through likes and comments.

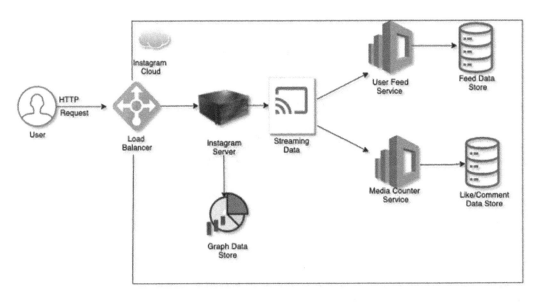

FIGURE 11.4
Architecture of photo sharing in Instagram (Takshila, 2020).

The user is interacting with the Instagram Platform in the form of action and it can be posting a picture, loading the user feed, or posting a comment on someone else's photo.

The process of Sharing a picture in Instagram is depicted in Figure 11.4. The request from the user will land into a front-end Load Balancer, which will then be forwarded a feed of highly scalable Instagram web servers that are running applications to handle this operation. Streaming services provide the flexibility to scale out the system by adding additional microservices. Stream data is consumed by feeds of microservices. For instance, like likes event data is consumed by the media counter services to upload the likes count or the post. The user feed Service puts the event to generate the user feed for all the followers of the ads. Graph databases are very effective in storing Complex relationships and are super extensible. Cassandra is an aggregate-oriented database used to store data like likes and follower comments and any post.

11.5 Social Network Attacks

Accessing social networking sites is increasing day by day, which is providing new opportunities for attackers to have access to other accounts. Security and privacy-related issues are raised when more information is posted on social media.

Figure 11.5 shows the different types of Social Network Attacks. Unauthorized data transmission from within an organization to an external destination is known as information leakage. It's also known as slow and low data theft, and it's a big problem for data security, with catastrophic implications for any business, regardless of size or industry. Vishing is a type of attack that tries to fool victims into handing over confidential personal details over the phone. Ransomware is a type of malicious software that encrypts your information or blocks access to your computer or mobile device until you pay a ransom to

FIGURE 11.5
Different types of social network attacks.

regain access to your device or data. A zero-day vulnerability is a previously unknown and unpatched software flaw that can be used by a threat actor to gain access to a target network. It exploits a weakness that a vendor or developer was unaware of. Smishing is a cyber-attack that uses Misleading text messages to trick users into sharing secret data and downloading Malware. Web-based threats, also known as online threats, are malicious programs that can attack you when you're online. A variety of malicious software programs designed to infect victims' computers are included in these browser-based threats. Man-in-the-middle attack cyber terrorists carry on this type of Cyber Attack indifferent ways, including hijacking, active eavesdropping, IP spoofing, and replay. The common solution of the Man-in-the-middle attack Encryption, Tamper Detection, authentication of identification of digital certificates. The Phishing attack is where the cyber-terrorism attack sends you fraudulent emails with Clickable links. These attackers aim to steal your personal information. Cyber-terrorist also use this type of Cyberattacks to install on your computer. Cyber terrorists frequently use driver attacks to spread Malware that targets insecure websites. Once they find a potential victim, they inject malicious scripts into the HTTP or PHP code of the website page. This script directly compromises the computer network of the site visitor. Cyber terrorists use social engineering to access the personal data of victims; they also use this type of attack for hijacking the accounts, characters, or identity impersonation or to perform authenticated payments, and more. SQL Injection attack happens when a Cyber terrorist injects malicious code into an SQL server. This injection attacks the server to divulge information it doesn't usually disclose. Malware attacks are different types of Cyberattacks using malicious software in computer security. Use good antivirus software, be careful when opening emails from unknown sources, avoid clicking on malicious pop-ups and keep your Firewall up to date. These are the steps to prevent malware. In a cross-site scripting attack, a third-party website is used to inject malicious JavaScript code into the victims' web browsers. It can also be used to take screenshots, learn about and collect network information, and gain remote access to and control over the victim's computer network. Password attacks leverage on the password authentication mechanisms to gain access to a user's information. It can take several forms; brute force commonly does this with advanced programs which help decipher passwords based on certain factors. Distributed Denial of service attacks occurs when many compromised network devices. All over the world, the bandwidth of the target system's and DDOS attacks can occur through session hijacking and Botnets. Inside attacks and data breaches commonly occur through the activities of disgruntled employees or ex-employees. Always monitor your privileged access network for current employees. An eavesdropping attack occurs when the attackers intercept a user's network traffic. This type of Cyberattacks enables the cyber-terrorist to perform cyber-terrorism acts like accessing the user password and other personal and financial information.

11.6 Cloud Security

Consider the following three well-known companies: LinkedIn, Sony, and iCloud. LinkedIn was the target of a cyber-attack in 2012, during which hackers exposed 6.5 million usernames and passwords. Following that, Sony was the target of the world's most severe Cyberattacks. Hackers made their highly confidential files public, including their financials and potential film projects, causing major damage to their company. iCloud was the victim of a cyber-attack in which hackers exposed the private images of users. All three businesses have a security breach that needs to be resolved. New threats emerge every day, the security mechanisms used to protect the application should be modified as frequently as possible. We must be able to address these issues, so everyone should upgrade their security as frequently as possible.

11.6.1 Cloud Security Challenges in 2021

Figures 11.6 show the top cloud security challenges in the year 2021. The different cloud security challenges and also solutions are listed.

Data Privacy and Security: The safety of data is one of the key concerns about the cloud. If security and privacy are neglected, each user's private information is at risk.

Insider Threats: Any type of malicious activity is an insider threat, against an organization coming from users with legitimate access to network applications or databases of the organization.

Lack of IT Experts: As cloud technologies evolve at a rapid pace, companies gradually put more workloads on the cloud. Because of these factors, organizations cannot

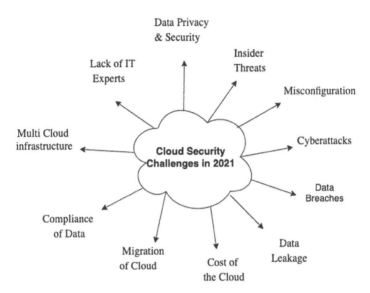

FIGURE 11.6
Cloud security challenges.

keep up with tools. The demand for skills is also steadily increasing. Additional preparation for IT and development will help alleviate these problems.

Multi-Cloud Infrastructure: The condition of multi-cloud has changed exponentially in recent years. Enterprise's merge or migrate to private and public clouds. 81% of enterprises have a multi-cloud strategy, according to the report. Hybrid cloud organizations decreased from 58% in 2017 to 51% in 2018, while companies that use multiple public clouds.

Misconfiguration: Data breaches in the cloud are often caused by incorrectly configured cloud security settings. Many companies' cloud protection health management policies are insufficient to protect their cloud base.

Data Leakage: The unauthorized transfer of data from an internal to an external destination is called a data breach. The risks of data loss are most common through the Internet and email.

Migration of Cloud: In recent years, the cloud industry has migrated into one of the most challenging problems. This is the way an application is transferred to the cloud.

The Cost of the Cloud: Many mistakes are made by companies that can lead to higher costs. IT professionals, such as developers, often forget to deactivate a cloud instance that is supposed to be used for a certain period. And some companies get confused with secret cloud plans that offer multiple discounts that they may not be able to take advantage of.

Compliance of Data: Compliance is one of today's threats faced by cloud computing. For someone using cloud storage or support services, this is a problem. Whenever a company transfers data from internal storage to the cloud, it must comply with the rules of the industry.

Cyber-attacks: Based upon how profitable their attacks are supposed to be, cybercriminals choose their objectives. Cloud technology is directly accessible through

TABLE 11.1
Provides the Necessary Solution and Prevention to Secure and Protect the Data in the Cloud

Cloud Security Challenges	Solution
Data privacy and security	1. Use multi-factor authentication.
	2. Implement a risk-based approach to security.
	3. Monitor access to sensitive data.
	4. Create Achievable Policies and SLAs with Third Parties
	5. Identify sensitive data and classify it.
	6. Use endpoint security systems to protect your data.
Insider Threats	1. Implement physical protections in the workplace
	2. Implement security software, Appliances, Secure Backup, Archiving & Recovery Processes.
	3. Enable surveillance.
Lack of IT experts	1. Diversify & broaden the technical expertise of your workforce
	2. Develop a strong business sense
	3. Focus on problem solving and out-of-the box attitude.
Multi-Cloud Infrastructure	1. Map workloads to cloud services
	2. Incorporate hybrid cloud concepts
	3. Create a robust integration framework
	4. Benchmark service levels
Misconfiguration	1. Verify the permission controls
	2. Audit for misconfiguration and compliance continuously
	3. Use security encryption techniques.
	4. Before provisioning, check for policy compliance select the appropriate security solution
Data Leakage	1. Identifies the sensitive data sent violating the policy.
	2. Endpoint checkpoints can block the attempts of communication concerning sensitive data.
	3. Encryption, data retention, and access control policies are implemented.
	4. DLP systems will monitor the unauthorized activities of users either intentionally or not.
	5. Identifies which data needs to be blocked by ML or metadata.
Migration of Cloud	1. Conduct research on different migration cycle and related requirements.
	2. Determining a project plan and budget with consideration of migration.
	3. Hiring cloud service providers with a comprehensive portfolio in migration programs.
Cost	1. Develop an optimization strategy
	2. Pay attention to software licenses
	3. Create a discount strategy that includes the correct form and amount of discounts.
	4. Make cloud spending optimization a continuous operation.
	5. Using a variety of technical tools to help with cloud cost control.
Compliance of data	1. Creating security architecture compliance protocols
	2. Concentrating on data circulation & related data security
	3. Deploying a cloud management solution that complies with regulatory requirements to ensure optimal data protection.
Cyber-attacks	1. Multi-Factor Authentication
	2. Malware scanners
	3. Full-disk encryption
	4. Lockdown your IP address
	5. Adopt proactive measures to detect and respond to advanced cyber threats
	6. Conduct Phishing Simulations
	7. Detecting Insider Threat.

the public Internet and is often insecure and contains a lot of information that is confidential and useful. Moreover, since the cloud is utilized by several organizations, it will most likely replicate a successful attack (Table 11.1).

11.7 Recommendation for Security and Privacy in Social Networks

- Two-factor authentication: It is an additional layer of protection that guarantees people who are signing in are who they say they are by adding an extra layer of security to ensure anyone attempting to access an online account is who they say they are. The user must first enter the username and password. Before being accepted, they will have to provide yet another piece of information. This quote is connected to your account and generated by a token smartphone or sent to you via text message. With 95 percent of account takeover breaches involving two-factor authentication, it is the most efficient tool for protection. The more modern and reliable form of two-way authentication uses a mobile app to send an approval message to a smartwatch with the least amount of hassle possible. It's time for everyone in the industry, government, and you to take the simple and efficient step of allowing two-factor authentication on all accounts. If the account uses a password, two-factor authentication is needed.

- Keep an eye on third-party apps: Malware attacks on Android devices are increasingly coming from third-party apps. So, before you download any applications, make sure your data is safe and secure.

- Upload just a small amount of private information on social networks: It is recommended that you do not post private data such as your birth date, Location, or cellphone number on social networking sites. Strangers may use this knowledge to engage in risky behaviors.

- Option to sign in and check out of the venue: Some sites can check an individual's geographic location. Most of us will be unconcerned about this choice, but it will reveal our position to others. You're just letting them know where you are when you're not at home.

- Limit who you share information with: Don't give out personal information to strangers. Customize your social media settings so that your messages and photos are only shared with your friends and not strangers.

- Keeping up with privacy policy changes: Privacy policies change periodically from site to site, so keep an eye out for updates and check your privacy settings regularly.

- Unique and strong passwords: For each social networking website, it is always recommended to use unique and strong passwords. Hackers would have an easier time gaining access to all of your accounts if you use a single password.

- Not Linking to Other Social Media Accounts: Several social media sites let you fill out a profile field that links to your other social media accounts. Maintaining a distinction between accounts, particularly if they include separate personal and professional identities, is a good idea.

11.8 Best Practices to Protect the Data

- Strong access controls and authentication managed and unmanaged software federated.
- Adaptive access controls selectively grant access to specific activities based on the user, app, instance, computer, place, date, and destination.
- A Network of Zero Confidence Access to private applications in data centers, and public cloud facilities to minimize network lateral movement and reduce app visibility.
- Continuous security assessments of public cloud systems to identify misconfigurations and publicly exposed data, as well as data-at-rest storage scans for data and threat protection.
- Data movement to and from applications, cases, users, websites, computers, and locations is protected by seven granular policy controls.
- Cloud data protection for sensitive data from internal and external threats.
- Isolate cloud data backups to prevent ransomware threats.

11.9 Conclusion

Social networks provide a virtual spot in which individuals can share their data and interact with others with cloud computing technologies. With the growing number of users in social media, users need to adopt cloud computing technologies to achieve scalability, flexibility, and architectural cost. Major issues and problems relating to security and privacy in social networks and cloud computing were addressed. The most common attacks on social networking sites, including Viruses, Phishing Attacks, Malware attacks, etc. are reviewed. The clients have a critical role in ensuring their data by sticking to a bunch of security guidelines. Users are responsible for posting sensitive and personal information on online social network platforms. The user needs to adopt necessary recommendations and best practices to secure personal and sensitive information from strangers. With the introduction of 5G connectivity, the globe will grow smarter. It's vulnerable to cyber-attacks. The future direction includes the need for users to explore and protect the reasons for these attacks. Training the user and making them aware of attacks is the best defense.

References

Alazie Dagnaw, G., & Ebabye Tsige, S. (2019). Challenges and Opportunities of Cloud Computing in Social Network; Survey. *Internet of Things and Cloud Computing*, 7(3), 73. https://doi.org/10.11648/j.iotcc.20190703.13

Praveena, A., & Smys, S. (2018). 2018 Second International Conference on Electronics, Communication and AerospaceTechnology (ICECA 2018). *Proceedings of the 2nd International Conference on*

Electronics, Communication and Aerospace Technology, ICECA 2018, Coimbatore, India, 29–31 March 2018, 981–1982, IEEE Catalog Number: CFP18J88-POD, ISBN:978-1-5386-0966-8.

Chakrabarti, S., Saha, H. N., University of Nevada, Institute of Engineering & Management, IEEE-USA, Institute of Electrical and Electronics Engineers Region 6, & Institute of Electrical and Electronics Engineers. (2018). *2018 IEEE 8th Annual Computing and Communication Workshop and Conference (CCWC),* 8th–10th January 2018, University of Nevada, Las Vegas, NV, USA.

Fire, M., Goldschmidt, R., & Elovici, Y. (2014). Online Social Networks: Threats and Solutions. *IEEE Communications Surveys and Tutorials,* 16(4), 2019–2036. https://doi.org/10.1109/COMST.2014.2321628

Huang, Q., Yue, W., He, Y., & Yang, Y. (2018). Secure Identity-Based Data Sharing and Profile Matching for Mobile Healthcare Social Networks in Cloud Computing. *IEEE Access,* 6, 36584–36594. https://doi.org/10.1109/ACCESS.2018.2852784

Khalid, Z., Sheraz, M., Malik, A., Usman, M., Abid, M., & Shoukat, I. A. (2018). Comparative Study of Various Social Network Attacks: Comprehensive Survey. *International Journal of Computer Science and Network Security,* 18(12), 170–180.

Rathore, S., Sharma, P. K., Loia, V., Jeong, Y. S., & Park, J. H. (2017). Social Network Security: Issues, Challenges, Threats, and Solutions. *Information Sciences,* 421, 43–69. https://doi.org/10.1016/j.ins.2017.08.063

Stergiou,C., Psannis, K. E., Xifilidis, T., Plageras, A. P., & Gupta, B. B. (2018). *IEEE INFOCOM 2018 – IEEE Conference on Computer Communications Workshops (INFOCOM WKSHPS).*

Steven, K. (2021, January 21). Is Affiliate Marketing Dead 2021? See What's New! Retrieved June 24, 2021, from https://khrisdigital.com/is-affiliate-marketing-dead/

Takshila, T. (2020, September 9). Design Photo Sharing Platform – Instagram Tech Takshila. Retrieved June 24, 2021, from https://techtakshila.com/system-design-interview/chapter-4/

Vora, D., & Nayak, D. (2017). Privacy Preservation in SMAC-Social Networking, Mobile Network, Analytics, and Cloud Computing. In *Proceedings of the International Conference on IoT in Social, Mobile, Analytics, and Cloud, I-SMAC 2017,* 801–806. https://doi.org/10.1109/I-SMAC.2017.8058289

Zhang, J., Hu, S., & Jiang, Z. L. (2020). Privacy-Preserving Similarity Computation in Cloud-Based Mobile Social Networks. *IEEE Access,* 8, 111889–111898.

Zheleva, E., & Getoor, L. (2011). *Social Network Data Analytics.* https://doi.org/10.1007/978-1-4419-8462-3

12

Secured Trusted Authentication with Trust-Based Congestion Scheme for V2V Communication

H.N. Jithendra and D. Rekha

Vellore Institute of Technology, Chennai, India

CONTENTS

12.1 Introduction

Vehicular Ad-hoc Network (VANET) is widely used to provide on-demand wireless communication infrastructure between the vehicles by using the wireless communication links (Bali et al., 2017). The vehicles of the VANET are behaved as router and transmit the data packets by using the wireless communication devices namely On-Board Units (OBU) as well as each vehicle switches the data packets between other vehicles. The OBU transmits a different kind of data such as traffic volume remarks, vehicle location, current time,

DOI: 10.1201/9781003213888-12

speed, direction, acceleration and deceleration. The messages from the OBU are transmitted to other vehicles or roadside units for accomplishing the Vehicle-to-Vehicular (V2V) or Vehicular-to-Infrastructure (V2I) communication respectively (Sugumar, Rengarajan & Jayakumar, 2018). VANET is considered as an intelligent transportation system due to its movement predictability, strong computing, adequate node energy, and storage capability. VANET provides real-time traffic information to the traffic participants by collecting, analyzing, processing, and disseminating traffic information obtained from the vehicles. This data traffic transmission is used for improving the road safety and driving conditions.

The delay and reachability issues are created in the VANET due to the restricted wireless channel bandwidth, non-uniform vehicle densities, and high mobility. The vehicles in the VANET have high mobility with restricted transmission range and this higher vehicle mobility causes frequency changes in the network topology during communication. Hence, the reliable data transmission over the VANET is difficult due to the higher vehicle mobility, unpredictable network topology, and unstable links (Rana, Tripathi & Raw, 2020). Therefore clustering is used in the VANET for dividing the network into numerous clusters which leads to obtain high connectivity rate between the vehicles. But the selection of cluster head from an each cluster is a difficult task due to the high velocity of vehicles. Besides, the cluster head is used to maintain intra- and inter-cluster communications. Moreover, the security is considered as a main threat due to the openness, dynamic, and distributed nature of the VANET. For example, malicious vehicle utilizes the authenticated vehicles to determine the travel route and analyze the habits of drivers. Additionally, theft or other crime may occur by overhearing the VANET communication.

The major contribution of this research work is given as follows.

- The trust degree-based secure data transmission is accomplished for the cluster-based VANET. The nodes in the VANET are clustered by using the K-means clustering algorithm and the cluster heads are selected by using the trust degree.

- The sender node signs a digital signature to the messages and the key from the trusted authority is used to encrypt the message transmitted by the sender node.

- The performance of this research work is improved by placing the Trust based congestion control (TCC) and Trusted authentication (TA) using AODV protocol.

This research work is structured as follows: Section 2 surveys several existing research papers based on routing protocol and security over VANETs. In Section 3, a brief explanation of a TCC-TA method is presented to improve the performance of VANETs. In Section 4, comparisons of the experimental results of existing methods are presented. The conclusion is made in Section 5.

12.2 Literature Review

There are numerous existing researches are developed for improving the VANET security to enhance the vehicle, passenger safety, and so on. This section shows the description about the existing researches about secure communication in VANET along with its limitations. Generally, the data is created by the vehicles namely instant messaging between the vehicles. This message contains the information about the accident on the roads, congestion, traffic light and parking information. The communication among the vehicle and infrastructure components is referred as Vehicle-to-Infrastructure (V2I) communication. Moreover, the VANET utilizes the dedicated short-range communication to transmit the data through the network. The VANET uses the navigation mechanism for collecting the online road information about vehicles. The collected information is used to reach the desired destination in real time (Chim, Yiu, Hui & Li, 2014).

Baskar and Dhulipala (2018) presented the trusted nodes association and QoS-based energy multipath routing protocol namely TCAQEMR for improving the VANET data transmission. The neighbor nodes were analyzed by using the trusted nodes and multipath routing protocol is used to transmit the data to the destination node. The message contains private information in VANET for better security and privacy.

Jain, Kushwah and Tomar (2019) developed the Named Data Networking (NDN) to transmit the data packets through the network. The NDN transmits the data by determining the trust value of each node. Moreover, the trust value was calculated based on the interaction between the nodes.

Minimum multipoint relays (MMPR) protocol is used to increase the channel utilization and reduce the flooding effects. The optimal security level was obtained based on the effective usage of mission with channel utilization. The effective method can be used to maintain the network by varying simulation time and network size.

Elliptical Curve Digital Signature Algorithm (ECDGA) approach to obtain the private data transmission between the vehicles. The signature verification time was minimized by using the signature verification method. The time of signature verification was reduced while improving the design scalability. The updation of routing tables should be done in an effective manner.

Tripathi and Sharma (2020) presented the trust-based model namely Trust-AODV for identifying the malicious/rogue nodes in the VANET. The rogue node's identifies were used for calculating the trust value of the nodes. The trustworthy nodes through the VANET were selected to switch the data during the routing process using the AODV protocol. The lesser computations of trust-based model were created this trust model as lightweight for detecting the faulty nodes in the network. The throughput and control overhead was varied with respect to the varying malicious nodes.

Santhi and Sheela (2020) developed Index-Based Voting Algorithm (IBVA), used to improve the reliability of short-range communications in hostile situations. This IBVA method was developed to remove the hybrid jamming attack in VANET. Since, the hybrid jamming attack was the combination of characteristics of the deceptive, random, and constant jamming attacks. Moreover, the recursive candidate elimination algorithm was used to identify the authenticity of the vehicular nodes. Here, the verification for local base station transmission was not considered during the data transmission.

12.3 Problem Definition and Solutions

Current problems of the VANETs are analyzed in this section and also it gives how TCCTA-AODV method overcomes the stated problem. The highway and roads are susceptible to the congestion and security due to the everyday increment of vehicles on the roads. The malicious attacks and congestion cause the packet drop and higher delay during communication. This affects the people's safety, security and degrades the performance of the VANET. The TCC and Trusted Authentication (TA) based secure routing is proposed to overcome the issues related to the security and congestion. In the TA method, the vehicles in the network are monitored by using the verifiers. Moreover, the data is digitally signed by the sender and the public/private key from the trusted authority is used to encrypt the data. Subsequently, the data is decrypted at the destination.

12.4 Method for Secured Vehicular Ad-hoc Network1 Soil Analysis

In the VANET system, the data transmission between the vehicles and vehicles to the RSU is obtained by using the standard wireless medium WAVE. This helps to obtain the huge range of communication to the travelers and drivers. The safety application is accomplished for providing comfortable driving and improving the safety on roads. Figure 12.1 shows the VANET system architecture that includes the Vehicle-to-Vehicle (V2V) or Vehicle-to-Infrastructure (V2I) communications. The main components in the VANET are RSU, On Board Unit (OBU), and Application Unit (AU). The major processes of the OBU are IP mobility, network congestion control, data security, ad-hoc and geographical routing, wireless radio access, and reliable message transfer.

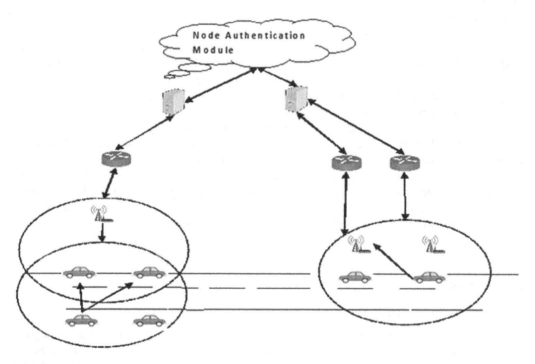

FIGURE 12.1
System architecture of V2V and V2I network.

12.4.1 Real-Time Traffic Generation

In VANET, the simulation and modeling plays main roles in generating the real-time traffic to the network. The generation of network scenarios with hardware deployment is expensive in developing countries (e.g., India). Therefore, the Open Street Map (OSM) is used for generating the real-time traffic in VANET. This OSM contains the position or longitude of vehicle, latitude, and so on. The OSM file is downloaded from the open street map for developing the VANET in the urban environment. Consequently, the scenario of real-time road traffic is created by using the Simulation of Urban Mobility *(SUMO-0.12.3)* simulator. The generated mobility of traffic data from SUMO software is transferred to the NS2 simulator to analyze the performances of VANET. The SUMO commends such as net convert and poly convert are used to configure the OSM data into the Configuration (cfg) file and these configuration files are utilized to save the settings and information. Moreover, the trace files are generated by using the cfg file that is considered as a significant step for generating the network scenario in the network simulator. SUMO simulator contains an inbuilt utility namely sumo trace exporter for creating the trace files. The VANET mainly requires two simulation types for smooth functioning such as network simulation and traffic simulation.

12.4.2 Trust-Based Congestion Control and Secure Routing Using Trusted Authentication Scheme

In this TCCTA-AODV method, For VANETs that are built on clusters, a trust-based authentication system is being developed. Initially, the vehicles are grouped and the trust degree of every node is determined for obtaining the secure data transmission. The trust degree determined for every node is the integration of the direct trust degree and indirect trust degree. The past interactions are used for calculating the direct trust degree from the neighbor nodes. Next, the indirect trust degree is the recommendation trust degree from the most adjacent neighbor nodes of the network. The selection of Cluster Head (CH) mainly depends on the calculated trust degree and a verifier is used for monitoring the behavior of each vehicle in the VANET. Additionally, the digital signature is incorporated into the message which is signed by the sender node. Next, the public/private key from the trusted authority is used to encrypt the message.

12.4.2.1 Clustering of Vehicle

The VANET has numerous Certificate Authorities (CAs) which used to authenticate the vehicles positioned inside the transmission range. The CA is a trusted third party which maintains the node identifies, authorizations of vehicles, and cryptography keys. At first, the vehicles in the highway environment are separated into various clusters with two bands and each band of the vehicle has three different lanes. Here, each cluster has one CH and cluster members. The vehicle that exists in the one cluster communicates directly and the vehicle between different clusters are communicated by using the CH. Each vehicle of the VANET plays the CH role or member or gateway. The vehicle node is referred as a gateway, when it is located in two or more clusters. Moreover, each vehicle of the VANET maintains information about the gateways and cluster members. The clustering algorithm controls the communication in is communication range and transmits the data packets to the gateway nodes. The CH is used to control the adjacent communication among the cluster members.

The process of K-means clustering algorithm is given as follows.

Initially, the k amount of clusters is created from the amount of nodes and the fitness function is optimized by using the clustering algorithm. The squared error function is used as a fitness function for K-means clustering which is shown in Equation (12.1).

$$F = \sum_{j=1}^{k} \sum_{i=1}^{n} \left\| x_i - c_j \right\|^2 \qquad (12.1)$$

where c_j represents the jth cluster center, x_i represents the ith sample's data point and the $\|x_i - c_j\|^2$ represents the distance from the node to the cluster center.

The main processes of K-means clustering algorithm are given as follows:

1. At first, amount of centroids is randomly identified to cluster the nodes into clusters.

2. The k initial clusters are generated by calculating the Euclidean distance from the centroid to nodes. The formula for Euclidean distance is shown in Equation (12.2).

$$\text{Eucildean distance} = \sqrt{(x_1 - x_2)^2 + (y_1 - y_2)^2} \qquad (12.2)$$

where x_1, x_2 and y_1, y_2 are the coordinates of x and y axis respectively.

3. Each node's position is verified from the previous position and the position of the cluster is calculated again in the VANET.

Step 2 is processed again to obtain an effective cluster when the centroid's location is changed through the network. Then the centroid from the K-means clustering is considered as an optimal CH for cluster groups and PSO is used for optimizing the different CH in the ad-hoc network.

12.4.2.2 Estimation of Trust Degree

The calculation of trust degree is accomplished by selecting the CHs from the nodes. The trust relationship obtained from the direct interactions is referred to as direct trust. Then the indirect trust node is the trust relationship created from the trusted node or the chain of trusted nodes. Equation (12.3) shows the direct trust degree from the pth vehicle to qth vehicle.

$$T_{new}^d(p,q) = \left\{ T_{new}^d(p,q) + RF, (ST > O) \right\} / \left\{ T_{old}^d(p,q) - PF, (FT > O) \right\} \qquad (12.3)$$

where the previous trust degree is represented as T_{old}; RF is the Reward factor; PF is the penalty factor; the amount of successful and failed transmissions among the T_{old} and T_{new} at time interval (Δt) are presented as ST and FT respectively. The value of T_{old} is computed while selecting the CH from the network. Equation (12.4) shows the indirect trust degree from the pth vehicle to *the* vehicle.

$$T_{p,q}^r = \sum_{k \in m} T^d(k,q) * s(p,k) \Big/ \sum_{k \in m} s(p,k) \qquad (12.4)$$

where common neighbor vehicle is represented as k; the vehicle's similarity between the pth vehicle and kth vehicle is represented as $s(p,k)$ and amount of adjacent nodes of p and q is m.

The trust degree evaluation is the addition of direct and indirect trust degrees which is shown in Equation (12.5).

$$T(p,q) = \propto *T^d(p,q) + \beta * T^r(p,q) \tag{12.5}$$

where the weighing factors of direct and indirect trust degree are specified as $\propto$ and β, respectively.

12.4.2.3 Vehicle Monitoring

The behavioral information of vehicles in the cluster is collected by using the set of verifier nodes in the monitoring phase. If T(VH_i)>T(VH_j), the vehicle VH_i is considered as verifier for vehicle VH_j. Here the total trust degree from the neighbor table of each node is specified as T. In vehicle monitoring, the T_min is considered as minimum threshold of trust degree.

12.4.2.4 Node-Node Authentication and Trust-Based Authentication

Consider the pairs of keys and certificates are disseminated to the authorized nodes which are required to transmit the information through VANET. The Digital Signature (DS) is used for protecting the data packets transmitted by the vehicle. The DS is inserted in control message end by using the sender. The DS has the value which is only recognized by the signer and the information of data packet signed while transmitting the data packets. In the DS scheme, the sender node signs the data by private key and the receiver node verifies the data with the public key. The node tried to validate the identity and verify the authorized node during the authentication process. The public key of CA is used to verify the authorized node in the VANET. The secret keys are exchanged between the nodes at the end of the handshake signal during the communication. The vehicle monitoring is shown in Figure 12.2

The overall process of the trust-based authentication is given as follows:

1. At first, the vehicles are clustered using the K-means clustering technique.
2. The direct and indirect trust degrees are used for calculating the node's trust degree.
3. A weighted sum approach is used for selecting the CH from each cluster.

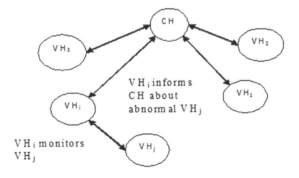

FIGURE 12.2
Vehicle monitoring.

4. The set of verifiers is initialized in each cluster for monitoring the vehicle's behavior.

5. The CH is used for monitoring the vehicle's trust degree with abnormal behavior.

6. The CA is used for isolating the abnormal node with less trust degree.

7. A DS is inserted in the data packets signed by the sender node and the public/private key from the trusted authority is used to accomplish the secure data transmission at node-to-node authentication.

8. The sender node signs the message by using the private key and the public key is used for validating the message at receiver node.

9. The faster re-association is obtained by exchanging the secret keys at the end of handshake signal.

12.5 Results and Discussion

The TCCTA-AODV method is used for avoiding congestion and maintaining a stable path in presence of node failure as well as this TCCTA-AODV method is simulated by using the NS-2. The TCCTA-AODV method is analyzed in terms of throughput, Packet Delivery Fraction (PDF), and control overhead. The performances are analyzed by varying malicious nodes. The Setting and parameters used in this simulation are displayed in Table 12.1.

12.5.1 Parameters Used for Traffic Model

The total time taken for the Nam simulation is 500 seconds. Type of traffic and data set in TCL code is Constant Bit Rate/User Datagram Protocol (CBR/UDP). The packet size and rate is set as 500 bytes and 500kb, respectively, with 500 m × 500 m area size.

TABLE 12.1

Simulation Parameters

Parameters	Value
Simulation time	600 seconds
Transport protocol and application type	UDP and CBR
Packets size and rate	500 and 500
Area size	500m × 500 m
Mobile speed	10–40 m/s
Map model	Open street map (real-time map)
Propagation model	Two-ray ground
Network interface type	Wireless (vehicular ad-hoc)
Number of vehicles	100
Number of malicious nodes	0, 5, 10, 15, 20, and 25
Mobility model	Random waypoint
Network simulator	NS2.35
Traffic simulator	SUMO – 0.12.3

12.5.2 Parameters Used for Physical and Link Layers

The MAC protocols used is IEEE 802.11 with a two-ray ground propagation model, antenna as Omni-antenna, and network interface type is wireless.

12.5.3 Parameters Used for Mobility Model

Number of Wireless Nodes is based on random deployment of nodes. The mobility model used is a random waypoint. The Sensor nodes (i.e., vehicles) are randomly distributed in the area. In this experiment, the data packet is transmitted from the random source node and the vehicles are initialized with random speed. The mobility and traffic generation, the type of antenna are defined. The two-ray ground radio-propagation model is used. The pairs of sender-receiver nodes are randomly initialized through the network and UDP/CBR traffic sources are utilized in VANET.

12.5.4 Performance Analysis

The TCCTA-AODV method is implemented to achieve better performance in terms of throughput, PDF, and control overhead by varying malicious nodes. Hence, the performance of the TCCTA-AODV method is compared with the two existing algorithms such as Trust-AODV (Tripathi & Sharma, 2020) and IBVA (Santhi & Sheela, 2020).

12.5.4.1 Throughput

Throughput is defined as the amount of packets received by the destination node at total network time and it is expressed in Equation (12.6). Generally, throughput is measured in bits per second (bps).

$$\text{Throughput} = \frac{\text{Total number of packets delivered successfully}}{\text{Total time internal}} \qquad (12.6)$$

Figure 12.3 shows the throughput comparison for the TCCTA-AODV with the Trust-AODV (Tripathi & Sharma, 2020) and IBVA (Santhi & Sheela, 2020). From Figure 12.3, it is known that the throughput of the TCCTA-AODV method is high when compared to the Trust-AODV (Tripathi & Sharma, 2020) and IBVA (Santhi & Sheela, 2020). The number of packets transmitted to the TCCTA-AODV method is increased by using secure communication through the VANET. But, the throughput of the Trust-AODV (Tripathi & Sharma, 2020) is affected due to an increment in malicious nodes.

12.5.4.2 Packet Delivery Fraction

PDF is defined as the ratio among the amount of received packets to amount of transmitted packets through the network and this PDF is expressed in Equation (12.7).

$$\text{PDF} = \frac{\text{Total received Packets}}{\text{Total send packets}} * 100 \qquad (12.7)$$

The comparison of PDF for the TCCTA-AODV, Trust-AODV (Tripathi & Sharma, 2020), and IBVA (Santhi & Sheela, 2020) is shown in Figure 12.4. Figure 12.4 shows that the TCCTA-AODV has a higher PDF than the Trust-AODV (Tripathi & Sharma, 2020) and IBVA (Santhi & Sheela, 2020).

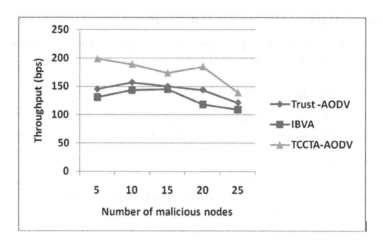

FIGURE 12.3
Comparison of throughput for varying malicious nodes.

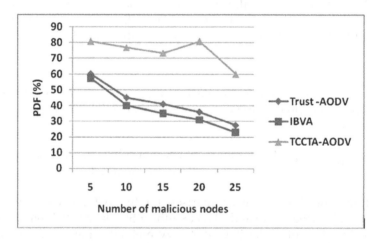

FIGURE 12.4
Comparison of PDF for varying malicious nodes.

The TCC and TA used in the TCCTA-AODV method are used to avoid congestion and malicious nodes during the data transmission. This congestion and malicious node causes the packet drop through the VANET communication.

12.5.4.3 Control Overhead

Control overhead is defined as the ratio between the transmitted control packets to the total data packets transmitted to the destination as well as control overhead is expressed in Equation (12.8).

$$\text{Control overhead} = \frac{\text{Total control packets sent}}{\text{Total received Packets}} \tag{12.8}$$

Figure 12.5 shows the control overhead comparison for the TCCTA-AODV with the Trust-AODV (Tripathi & Sharma, 2020) and IBVA (Santhi & Sheela, 2020). From Figure 12.5, it is

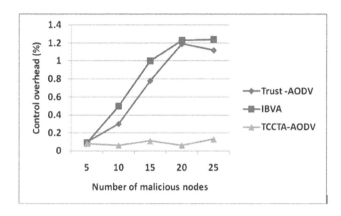

FIGURE 12.5
Comparison of control overhead for varying malicious nodes.

known that the control overhead of the TCCTA-AODV method is less when compared to the Trust-AODV (Tripathi & Sharma, 2020) and IBVA (Santhi & Sheela, 2020). The control overhead for the TCCTA-AODV method is minimized by avoiding the malicious nodes and congestion while transmitting the data packets.

12.6 Conclusion

In this paper, the trust degree-based secure authentication method is developed for the cluster-based VANET. The K-means clustering algorithm is used to divide the network into various clusters. Then the trust degree for each vehicle is determined by using the trust degree value which is an integration of direct trust degree and indirect trust degree. The identified trust degree is used for selecting the optimal CHs from the clusters as well as a set of verifiers are initialized to monitor the vehicle's behavior. Additionally, the digital signature is incorporated for the data signed by the sender and the key from the trusted authority is used to encrypt the data packets. The encrypted data packet is decrypted at the destination node. This trust-based secure communication is used to verify the sender and receiver node as authenticated nodes or not during the data transmission. From the performance analysis, it is known that the throughput, PDF, and control overhead are improved when compared to the Trust-AODV and IBVA. The throughput of the TCCTA-AODV is 139 for 25 malicious nodes, it is high when compared to the Trust-AODV and IBVA.

References

Bali, R.S., Kumar, N. and Rodrigues, J.J., 2017. An efficient energy aware predictive clustering approach for vehicular ad hoc networks. *International Journal of Communication Systems*, 30(2), p. e2924.

Baskar, S. and Dhulipala, V.S., 2018. Collaboration of trusted node and QoS based energy multi path routing protocol for vehicular ad hoc networks. *Wireless Personal Communications*, 103(4), pp. 2833–2842.

Chim, T.W., Yiu, S.M., Hui, L.C.K. and Li, V.O.K., 2014. VSPN: VANET-based secure and privacy-preserving navigation. *IEEE Transactions on Computers*, 63(2), pp. 1–14.

Jain, V., Kushwah, R.S. and Tomar, R.S., 2019. Named data network using trust function for securing vehicular ad hoc network. In *Soft Computing: Theories and Applications* (pp. 463–471). Springer, Singapore.

Rana, K.K., Tripathi, S. and Raw, R.S., 2020. Opportunistic directional location aided routing protocol for vehicular ad-hoc network. *Wireless Personal Communications*, 110(3), pp. 1217–1235.

Santhi, G.B. and Sheela, D., 2020. Reliability refinement in VANET with hybrid jamming attacks using novel index based voting algorithm. *Peer-to-Peer Networking and Applications*, 13, pp. 2145–2154.

Sugumar, R., Rengarajan, A. and Jayakumar, C., 2018. Trust based authentication technique for cluster based vehicular ad hoc networks (VANET). *Wireless Networks*, 24(2), pp. 373–382.

Tripathi, K.N. and Sharma, S.C., 2020. A trust based model (TBM) to detect rogue nodes in vehicular ad-hoc networks (VANETS). *International Journal of System Assurance Engineering and Management*, 11, pp. 426–440.

13

MQTT Protocol-Based Wide-Range Smart Motor Control for Unmanned Electric Vehicular Application: A Case Study in IoT

Arunava Chatterjee

Raghunathpur Government Polytechnic, Purulia, India

Biswarup Ganguly

Meghnad Saha Institute of Technology, Kolkata, India

CONTENTS

13.1 Introduction

Unmanned electric vehicles for autonomous driving are coming up especially for short-range drives as well as for special applications. This chapter presents a case study of an application of the internet of things (IoT) in extensive motor control for an unmanned electric vehicle (EV) for different ranges of speed. The main aim of this chapter is controlling and monitoring of DC motor-based drives for unmanned electrical vehicles with a focus on the IoT protocol, Message Queuing Telemetry Transport (MQTT). MQTT is light and follows publish and subscribe feed model. It transfers messages between devices. MQTT is also quite secure for IoT control with friendly end-user-based support and lossless and bi-directional connection provision. A cloud server may be used for the same which is the

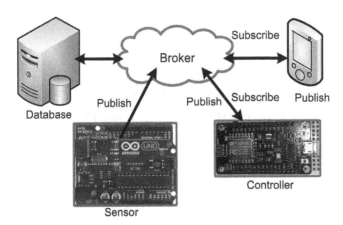

FIGURE 13.1
Typical message queuing telemetry transport (MQTT) architecture.

broker. The broker resources can be used by different clients for communication. Typical MQTT architecture is shown in Figure 13.1.

In an unmanned EV, mostly DC motor drive is used. The technique can provide below rated to twice the rated speed control with a reduction in torque ripple vibrations at higher speeds. The control is brought about by an ESP8266 Wi-Fi controller which fully supports MQTT and aids in controlling the motor driver. The controller is cost-effective as well as robust and can be used with open-source dashboard controllers effectively with encrypted security. The controller dashboard can be a smartphone or any other display device which allows Wi-Fi support with a secure working internet connection. Speed control is brought about using a speed estimator and controller which suitably reduces speed error giving a wider range of speed control. Another challenge is collision avoidance in the case of an unmanned EV and it is brought about by a suitable intelligent control scheme which is also supported by the IoT platform. Direction control for the drive is done using a servo-based drive which efficiently controls the unmanned EV direction avoiding collision. An experimental prototype is built for the purpose of the same and tested in a laboratory scale. The vehicle contains an unmanned vehicle control unit (UVCU) which will accept speed reference, direction angle with commands and the output will be obtained via closed-loop control.

The drive also incurs lower power requirement than conventional closed loop-controlled DC motor drives for EV applications. A laboratory prototype is tested with lithium-ion-based batteries; however, inverter-chopper-based source can also be used for regenerative power recovery during braking applications in future. This also substantially helps in saving power during braking application for the drive. The proposed control also achieves improved accuracy requiring lesser maintenance.

13.2 Literature Review

Electric motors and associated drives play a significant role in the functioning of electric vehicles. Conventional and brushless DC motor (BLDCM) drives, servos, permanent magnet DC (PMDC) motors, are frequently used for DC motor-based EVs. Thus, an important

TABLE 13.1

Comparison of Different Communication Techniques for IoT Application

Name	Power Consumption	Range (m)	Data Transfer Rate	Data Transfer Cost	Reliability	IEEE Standard
Wi-Fi	Medium	400	Medium	Low	High	802.11
Zigbee	Low	10–100	Low	High	Low	802.15.4
Bluetooth	Medium	10–100	High	Medium	Low	802.15.1
RFID	Medium	5	Low	Low	Medium	802.15

facet is control of these motors in modern drives. Most of the speed and position control techniques for EVs use conventional Bluetooth (Mora et al., 2015), hardware-based global positioning system (GPS) (Rangan, 2017) or radio frequency identification (RFID) (Choy et al., 2020), etc., for such control. Generally, Wi-Fi has wider applications and is quite advantageous than other connectivity methods used in IoT applications as shown in Table 13.1. Traffic signal feedback-based speed control (Malik et al., 2014) is proposed which uses signal and data processing for accurate control. A robust vehicle tracking is proposed which is resilient to attacks (Rana, 2017) and grounded on the internet of things (IoT) framework. Global positioning system (GPS) and Zigbee module are also used for sensing and tracking for such drives (Kochar & Supriya, 2016). Speed violation sensor-based method is used (Gallen et al., 2013) previously which is implementation friendly but not cost-effective and requires expensive hardware. Instead of true speed control, the proposed techniques mainly focus on overspeeding and its detection. IoT can be used for position control evading collisions along with vehicle true speed control. A vibration sensor-based controller is employed for acceleration fault detection (De Novellis et al., 2014) where the speed estimation is precise though it is dependent on the driving atmosphere whose forecasting is difficult.

In this chapter, MQTT protocol-based-wide range smart motor control allowing precise remote speed control of unmanned EV is proposed.

The principal advantages of the proposed scheme include,

- A closed-loop speed control of unmanned EV by means of MQTT broker hierarchical control.
- The closed-loop speed estimation reduces speed error and provides a wider range of speed control. The end-user control is also flexible via IoT enabled dashboard.
- Lower drive power requirement than conventional control can also be achieved using the control scheme.

13.3 Electric Vehicle (EV) Configuration

Electric vehicles (EV) use electrical motors for traction purposes. The motor is usually driven by energy sources like batteries, fuel cells, ultracapacitors, and flywheels. EVs are mainly converted versions of the older internal combustion engine vehicle (ICEV). The EV is derived from ICEV by substituting the IC engine with an electrical motor drive retaining

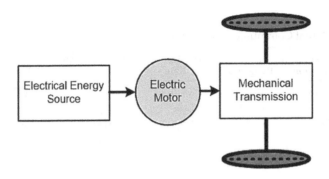

FIGURE 13.2
Basic EV configuration.

other components. Another major change is the replacement of fuel tanks with that of the energy sources or their combination as mentioned. The basic EV using this replacement is shown in Figure 13.2.

This type of EV is bulky and less flexible making it a degraded performer with the upcoming modern EVs. The modern EV has a novel drive train consisting of different subsystems. There is an electric motor propulsion system connected to energy source and sometimes there are auxiliaries. Mainly the change is in the electric motor propulsion system which has a controller unit along with power converter, electric drive motor, and the mechanical transmission system.

The energy source can be a simple unit but sometimes it consists of a combination of the energy source with an energy management system. The auxiliary system is present in higher order control EVs which require power steering, auxiliary supply, and other controls. A block diagram of modern EV drive is shown in Figure 13.3.

The accelerator controlling the speed and the brakes act like control signal inputs based on which the proper control signals are sent to the controller which sends command to the

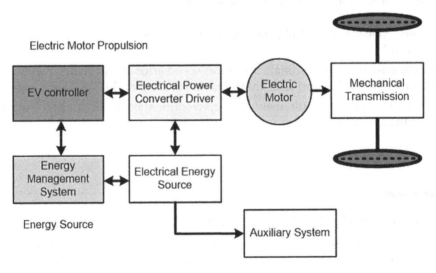

FIGURE 13.3
Block diagram of modern EV drive.

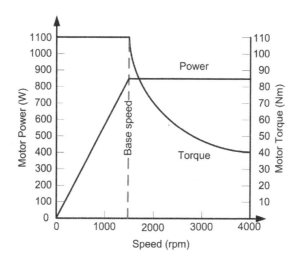

FIGURE 13.4
Characteristics of a typical drive motor.

power converter to control the motor drive. The converter can also be used during vehicle regenerative braking which will allow for backward flow of power from the drive motor to the energy source. Most of the electrical energy sources used for fueling the EV are receptive i.e., they can readily receive regenerative energy allowing efficient use of power. The entire coordination for the energy flow is done by the energy management system present in the EV along with the vehicle controller.

In a modern EV, the design of the drive train, selection of the motor, and transmission parameters are the primary factors for determining its performance. The acceleration time, speed, and gradeability are its performance parameters (Ehsani et al., 2004). The design is dependent on the mechanical characteristics of the drive motor. This is primarily the motor torque versus speed characteristics and is like that of any traction motor that are used in vehicle drives. In general, the traction motor characteristics are shown in Figure 13.4. At below base speeds, the drive motor has constant torque. The voltage supply to the motor increases with speed increase while the flux is kept at constant value. For speeds above base or rated speed, the motor drives with constant power. Here, usually the flux is weakened keeping the supply voltage at a constant value (Gao et al., 2003). This is true for most of the DC motors used in smaller ranges in EVs and in unmanned EV drives.

13.4 System Planning

For an electric vehicle (EV) it is essentially imperative to control its speed by monitoring the motor drive, be it a battery-operated electric vehicle (BEV) or a hybrid electric vehicle (HEV) drive. A vehicle may be controlled based on the requirements and conditions. Based on the conditions and requirement, vehicle start-strop, brake, electric launch, power assist, optimization of energy, etc., can be controlled. A smart Wi-Fi module can be used for remotely controlling the vehicle speed and direction precisely which is brought about by controlling the DC motor. The Wi-Fi module is IoT enabled and the control is flexible.

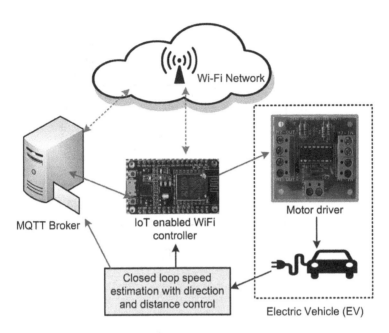

FIGURE 13.5
Block diagram of control technique.

Motor parameters can be controlled using this module remotely. It correspondingly entails a console or a dashboard through which the control is done, and it acts like an end-user interface. The dashboard can simply be a smartphone with a pre-installed application that can directly send control commands via the MQTT communication

protocol. The Wi-Fi controller has lower power consumption than other popular IoT network connections like Bluetooth and has better power transfer rate than Zigbee. Most Wi-Fi controllers also have better range of operation and are cost-effective (Zhang et al., 2020). IoT based control, other than for controlling vehicles are also popularly used for wider range of applications from healthcare (Haghi et al., 2020), energy harvesting (Islam & Chatterjee, 2019), farming (Chatterjee & Ghosh, 2020), residential load monitoring (Ghosh et al., 2021) to vehicle state estimation (Rana, 2020).

An ESP8266 board-enabled Wi-Fi module can be used for the control. The DC motor used in the vehicular drive is driven using an L293D H-bridge driver and is powered by means of a battery. The L293D controller inherently can drive the DC motor in both forward and backward directions allowing movement of the vehicle in both directions. The Wi-Fi network can be any secured internet router. The block diagram of the control technique is shown in Figure 13.5.

13.5 Unmanned EV Model

A mathematical model may be built for an EV system (Ehsani et al., 2004). This model is applicable to almost all types of EVs and can be extended to modern EV models. The same is shown in Figure 13.6 and will be used for unmanned EV. The model can later be used to derive the dynamic characteristics of EV.

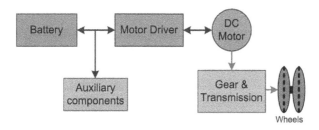

FIGURE 13.6
Model of an unmanned EV.

A rolling force is assumed at the center of the wheel to keep the vehicle moving. This force is defined as force of rolling and is shown as,

$$F_r = Pf_r = \frac{R_r}{r} \tag{13.1}$$

where R_r is rolling resistance, r is tire radius, P is load normally acting on center of the tire and f_r is rolling friction coefficient. In (13.1), gradient or slope is not considered, in other words, the road is assumed to be flat. If the vehicle is moving on a concrete road, the coefficient of rolling friction converts to a function of speed of vehicle (Ehsani et al., 2004),

$$f_r = 0.01\left(1 + \frac{V}{160}\right) \tag{13.2}$$

where V is the vehicular speed in m/s. The aerodynamic drag force or the air friction drag force between vehicle and air molecules is expressed as,

$$F_w = \frac{1}{2}\rho A C_D \left(V + V_{air}\right)^2 \tag{13.3}$$

where ρ is air density in kg/m³, A is vehicle frontal area m²C_D is coefficient of drag and V is speed of the EV. V_{air} is velocity of air in opposing direction and is measured in *m/s*. During vehicle acceleration, another force is experienced by the vehicle known as acceleration resistive force, which is expressed as,

$$F_a = \lambda M \frac{dV}{dt} \tag{13.4}$$

where λ is rotational inertia constant which includes the inertia of every component of the EV which are revolving. M is the vehicular mass in kg. The total driving force F_r is summation of (13.1), (13.3) and (13.4). Thus, drive power is,

$$P_r = F_r V \tag{13.5}$$

Finally, the dynamic equation of the EV in longitudinal direction is,

$$M \frac{dv}{dt} = F_{tf} - \left(F_r + F_w + F_a\right) \tag{13.6}$$

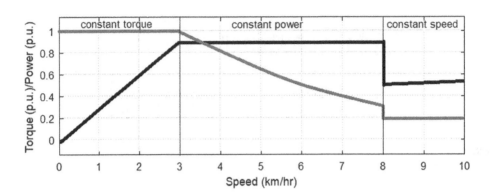

FIGURE 13.7
Different zones of operation of EV according to drive motor characteristics.

where F_{tf} is the full tractive effort in the forward direction. A model can be constructed to for dynamic response of the EV from the above equations.

Figure 13.7 shows the three different zones of operation for the EV according to drive motor characteristics. These three operation zones are constant torque zone, constant power zone, and constant speed zone. It is evident that the speed control of the EV is possible only during the constant torque zone and constant power zone.

13.6 MQTT Protocol Background

The MQTT is a hierarchical communication protocol which has three layers. An application layer is added to the existing physical and network layers for the MQTT communication. The physical layer consists of the hardware which support IoT and the network layer consists of the internet gear over which the communication is made. A closed-loop control for the unmanned EV is then used for complete speed control of the vehicle. A similar control is attempted (Ganguly & Chatterjee, 2020) but collision avoidance and direction control are not achieved which are essential for an unmanned drive.

In general, MQTT communication protocol is also used in resource allocation-based algorithms which can be applied in smart residences for reducing grid demand (Jamborsalamati et al., 2019). It also has other wide applications including smart farming, smart grid, and applications which require secure communication. MQTT is a secure communication protocol however additional security layers can also be added in the form single packet authorization processes which will make cyber-attacks tougher (Refaey et al., 2019).

13.6.1 MQTT Protocol Based Speed Control

The speed control for the motor for the unmanned EV is done using MQTT protocol which is an integral part of IoT as described. This protocol has a bi-layer hierarchical structure for communication in which an application layer can be added. The structure is based on transmission control protocol (TCP) which allows digital computers to communicate at long distances. MQTT requires a broker or a server which allows message storage and retrieval.

The broker accepts communications from publishers and sends them to clients which here is the ESP board. The clients are also known as subscribers. The data subscription in the case of motor speed control is variation in speed data which can be supervised by a suitable sensor. The IoT-based control also requires an end-user control panel as graphical user interface with remote control features. This can be achieved using various open-source software. One such application is Blynk IoT platform that can be installed in any android enabled smartphone. Blynk uses some libraries which can be freely downloaded in the programming environment. Using precise code, the same can be used as a dashboard to connect to the ESP board and control the hardware. This method of control is quite secure and will allow control over only a single dashboard user interface.

Blynk can be configured for input signal control. Push-button switch or slider controller can be added and configured for smoother wide-range speed control of the DC motor. Figure 13.8 shows the Blynk dashboard for configuration of a slider controller and push-button controller. The slider controller can be used to vary speed smoothly for the DC motor over a range whereas the push button can be used for starting/stopping the motor.

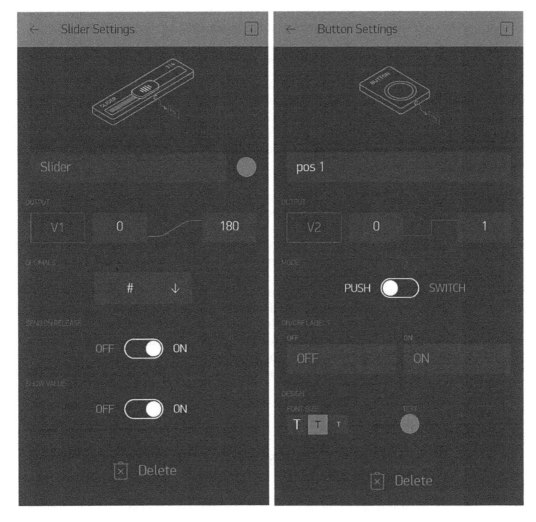

FIGURE 13.8
Blynk dashboard for configuration of a slider controller and push-button controller.

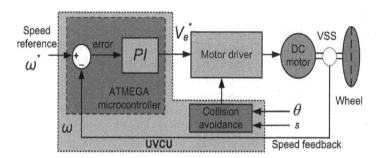

FIGURE 13.9
Closed-loop speed control.

For precise and wide-range speed control for the DC motor, a closed-loop speed control with IoT is devised. The control is based on MQTT with the use of vehicular speed sensor (VSS) tachometer and *ATMEGA* based microcontroller. This closed-loop speed control is quite like normal DC motor speed control which is discussed in detail in the next sub-section.

13.6.2 Closed Loop Speed Control of EV Using IoT

A closed-loop speed control is proposed for better, precise, and wider range speed control for the DC motor enabling better control for the unmanned EV. The control is achieved using an inner loop with a speed sensor. *ATMEGA* microcontroller is employed which access data from the sensor and compare this data with set point value. This information is sent to the driver for driving the motor. The closed-loop control for the unmanned EV is shown in Figure 13.9.

Only one wheel and motor are shown for simplicity for the proposed drive. However, similar control is applicable also for multimotor drives. The microcontroller along with the directional information is sent to the unmanned vehicle control unit (UVCU). The direction information (θ) is received and controlled via a servomotor which is appropriately placed in the unmanned EV. The speed denoted by ω is sensed via a vehicular speed sensor (VSS) tachometer which reads the speed from the rotation of the EV wheel connected to the DC motor. This sensor is based on potentiometric speed sensing unit and it is also cost-effective for use in unmanned vehicular drives. The sensed speed is then communicated to the broker via the Wi-Fi controller. The sensed speed is then compared to a preset value using the microcontroller. The error is fed back to the microcontroller configured proportional-integral (PI) controller. The error voltage reference (V_e^*) is then supplied to motor driver. The data attained from the speed sensor is pre-processed for precise estimation. Collision can also be avoided in the present scheme using an ultrasound distance sensor. This is mainly used for sensing distance 's' for close-range speed control.

13.7 Expected Output of the Control Scheme

13.7.1 Expected Outcome

With the proposed control, an unmanned EV can be easily controlled with better control accuracy. The controller requires lower power even at rated load. This also reduces the system power requirement. Some small adjustments can be made which further reduces the system power requirement. Rectifier-inverter-chopper-based sources can be used to help in regenerative power recovery during braking which can further reduce power requirement. The energy stored in such case can be later retrieved during requirement. Enhancement of the control range is also another advantage in the proposed control. Detailed discussion on a laboratory prototype is done in the next section. It is expected that the control structure will replicate its efficacy in real-life vehicular control especially when the control is done remotely or with unmanned drives.

13.7.2 Discussion on Prototype

A laboratory-scale prototype was constructed and controlled via the proposed control scheme. It is observed that the system is reliable in comparison to conventional PI-based control and open-loop IoT-based control systems. The same can be observed in Figure 13.10.

As observed from Figure 13.10, the control accuracy and range are increased substantially for the proposed closed-loop IoT-based control albeit increased system cost. It is expected than the system cost will decrease over time and usage and the same can be used to conserve much more energy over wide operational lifetime. Also, the maintenance requirement and cost are not high and thus it is also sustainable. The prototype is constructed with lithium-ion-based batteries and with storage allowing backward flow of regenerative energy, power requirement can be greatly reduced.

A comparative analysis is also done for the proposed control scheme and conventional speed control for the DC motor drive used for the unmanned EV. The conventional control is PI controller-based closed-loop DC motor speed control which is tested with an experimental laboratory prototype with similar ratings as that of the proposed control. The PI control parameters are tuned using the popular Ziegler-Nichols tuning methodology. In general, the power requirement at different speeds for the proposed control setup is shown in Figure 13.11.

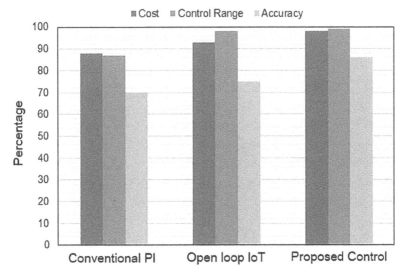

FIGURE 13.10
Comparison of three different methods of control for unmanned EV.

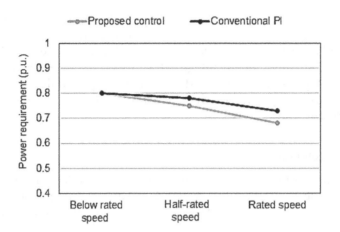

FIGURE 13.11
Power requirement at different speeds for the unmanned EV.

For open-loop control, the speed range cannot be suitably modified for wider range of control. This is because in the case of open-loop control, speed control is done via input voltage control of the DC motor. In case of closed-loop control, smoother wide range of speed control can be achieved with different values of set point speeds. For a DC motor drive operating within base speed region, the proposed control is more efficient.

Even precise wider range of speed control may be achieved using power electronic devices where both armature voltage control and field current control may be separately done. This can also be done with IoT integration. The speed range variation with the proposed control and the conventional control is shown in Figure 13.12. Here conventional control is referred to normal armature voltage control for DC motor speeds below rated speed which is generally the preferred method of speed control for EVs. Other methods of speed control for motoring applications are seldom used.

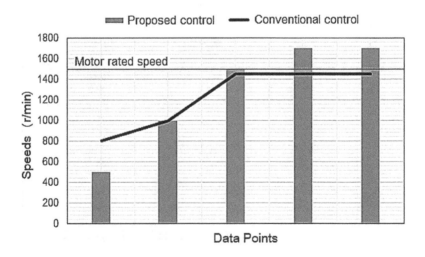

FIGURE 13.12
Speed range variation for proposed control and conventional control.

The proposed control scheme laboratory implementation thus gives promising results as regards enhancement in speed control range and reduction of drive power requirement for the unmanned EV. IoT-based control also gives better accuracy in control which is suitable for unmanned applications. The unmanned EV are most suitable for small-scale applications for precise vehicular control, in remote explosive disposal units and in military surveillance systems requiring remote control and observation support.

13.8 Conclusions and Future Scope

A case study on MQTT-based smart speed control of a DC motor suitable for unmanned EV is devised in this Chapter. The closed-loop speed control can help extend the motor control range and accuracy than conventional and open-loop control techniques. The controller incurs lower cost than other IoT-based communication systems. The control scheme is also implemented in laboratory and gives promising results as regards range of speed control enhancement and reduction of power requirement. The proposed control incurs some initial cost which can be mostly bearable keeping in mind the extended range of control and accuracy.

In future, regenerative braking can be studied for the DC motor-based drive for unmanned EV. This will further reduce the power requirement for the drive enabling further conservation of power. Studies can be extended for optimized position control with MQTT for increased position control accuracy. Modern optimization algorithms can also be used along with IoT for testing the control accuracy for such drives. Finally, renewable sources integration like usage of photovoltaics energy for the proposed unmanned EV can be studied for powering as it can further bring down the energy costs.

References

Chatterjee, A. and Ghosh, S. (2020). PV based isolated irrigation system with its smart IoT control in remote Indian area. In *Proceedings of the International Conference on Computer, Electrical & Communication Engineering (ICCECE)*, Kolkata, India, 1–5.

Choy, J., Wu, J., Long, C. and Lin, Y. (2020). Ubiquitous and low power vehicles speed monitoring for intelligent transport systems. *IEEE Sensors J.*, 20, 5656–5665.

De Novellis, L., Sorniotti, A., Gruber, P. and Pennycott, A. (2014). Comparison of feedback control techniques for torque-vectoring control of fully electric vehicles. *IEEE Trans. Veh. Technol.*, 63, 3612–3623.

Ehsani, M., Gao, Y., Gay, S. and Ehmadi, A. (2004). *Modern electric, hybrid electric, and fuel cell vehicles – fundamentals, theory and design*, 1st Ed., CRC Press, Boca Raton, FL.

Gallen, R., Hautière, N., Cord, A. and Glaser, S. (2013). Supporting drivers in keeping safe speed in adverse weather conditions by mitigating the risk level. *IEEE Trans. Intell. Transp. Syst.*, 14, 1558–1571.

Ganguly, B. and Chatterjee, A. (2020). MQTT protocol based extensive smart motor control for electric vehicular application. In *Proceedings of the IEEE 7th Uttar Pradesh Section International Conference on Electrical, Electronics and Computer Engineering (UPCON)*, 1–5, doi: 10.1109/UPCON50219.2020.9376452.

Gao, Y., et al. (2003). Investigation of proper motor drive characteristics for military vehicle propulsion. *Society of Automotive Engineers (SAE) Journal*, Paper No. 2003-01-2296, Warrendale, PA.

Ghosh, S., Manna, D., Chatterjee, A. and Chatterjee, D. (2021). Remote appliance load monitoring and identification in a modern residential system with smart meter data. *IEEE Sensors J.*, 21, 5082–5090.

Haghi, M., et al. (2020). A flexible and pervasive IoT-based healthcare platform for physiological and environmental parameters monitoring. *IEEE Internet Things J.*, 7, 5628–5647.

Islam, M. and Chatterjee, A. (2019). Analysis of a hybrid energy system for supplying a remote critical load in onshore coastal India. In *Proceedings of the 5th Jubilee Virtual International Conference on Science, Technology and Management in Energy*, Republic of Serbia, 1–5.

Jamborsalamati, P., et al. (2019). MQTT-based resource allocation of smart buildings for grid demand reduction considering unreliable communication links. *IEEE Syst. J.*, 13, 3304–3315.

Kochar, P. and Supriya, M. (2016). Vehicle speed control using Zigbee and GPS. In *Proceedings of the International Conference on Smart Trends for Information Technology and Computer Communications.* Jaipur, India, 847–854.

Malik, S., et al. (2014). Automated over speeding detection and reporting system. In *Proceedings of the 16th International Power Electronics and Motion Control Conference and Exposition*, Antalya, Turkey, 1104–1109.

Mora, A., Yagama, H., Zorro, D. and Jiménez, L. (2015). Speed digital control for scale car via Bluetooth and Android. In *Proceedings of the Chilean Conference on Electrical, Electronics Engineering, Information and Communication Technologies (CHILECON)*, Santiago, Chile, 129–134.

Rana, M. (2017). Attack resilient wireless sensor networks for smart electric vehicles. *IEEE Sensors Lett.*, 1, 1–4.

Rana, M. (2020). IoT-based electric vehicle state estimation and control algorithms under cyber attacks. *IEEE Internet Things J.*, 7, 874–881.

Rangan, P. (2017). Vehicle speed sensing and smoke detecting system. *Int. J. Comput. Sci. Engineer.*, 4, 27–33.

Refaey, A., Sallam, A. and Shami, A. (2019). On IoT applications: A proposed SDP framework for MQTT. *Electronics Lett.*, 55, 1201–1203.

Zhang, D., Han, Q. and Zhang, X. (2020). Network-based modeling and proportional–integral control for direct-drive-wheel systems in wireless network environments. *IEEE Trans. Cybernetics*, 50, 2462–2474.

14

IoT-Based Water Quality Monitoring System Using Cloud for Agriculture Use

R. Dhanalakshmi and Jose Anand
KCG College of Technology, Chennai, India

Arun Kumar Sivaraman
Vellore Institute of Technology, Chennai, India

Sita Rani
Gulzar Group of Institutions, Ludhiana, India

CONTENTS

14.1 Introduction

In recent times, the growth rates of population have increased and the relative growth rate of the agricultural sector and crop harvests are becoming slow. This has elevated concerns which will not grow sufficient crops and seeds along with other essential commodities to guarantee the forthcoming populations having no problems and are adequately fed. Around 70% of the earth's exterior is enclosed by seawater (Coben & Garrett, 2009). Urban wastewater is seen as the major source of pollution of soil as well as water bodies in our country. This industrial wastewater consists of many heavyweight metals like arsenic (As), cadmium (Cd), etc., with many other types of harmful microorganisms. This causes health hazards to both farmers and consumers (Tchounwou et al., 2014). Scientists are working untiringly to confirm whether the excellence of the utmost treasured resource on earth are highly available. From lagoons and watercourses to seaside water bodies and bays, water-quality observation is a serious run-through that needs to be carried out across the globe. With the World Water Assessment Program (WWAP) reportage to around 2million tons of human left-over is liable into aquatic bodies; hence, possession track on the water excellence is precarious. The purpose of monitoring water quality has the following five major goals.

- The results obtained from monitoring water quality is recycled to track all the deviations that occur in water builds on the defined period for longstanding implementations.
- Real-time observing of water quality is a vital portion of classifying somewhat problems or matters that might arise now or in the upcoming days. For instance, the data are recycled within a past couple of years, upsurges in fertilizers usage, and for food creation increases worldwide nitrogen contamination in the waterways by a total increase of 20%.
- Design and development solutions for contamination deterrence and organization policies to collect data from water-quality observing exertions is highly supportive.
- Nowadays managements, societies, and trade industries are mandatory to encounter a variety of excellent water quality standards. Observing quality based on data is recycled to regulate it or not to regulate the pollutions that are fulfilled with it.
- From natural disasters such as floods and erosion to oil tumbles and radioactive seepages, water quality observing data is essential once emerging spare policies.

Water Quality Monitoring – Water-quality observing data are extremely suitable and are not continuously be informal to get. Authorities in this field have a variety of diverse methods to place together grades, counting attractive examples of biological circumstances, analyzing deposits and by means of soft-tissue excerpts to identify suggestions of metals, oils, pesticides, dissolved oxygen, and nutrients. Physiological circumstances such as temperature, erosion, and flow suggest valued awareness though organic quantities concerning plant and animal life designate the health of marine-based environments (VanLoon et al., 2000). Conclusively, water-quality observing plays a vital portion of taking the globe well and maintainable. This develops to construct metropolises, clear terrestrial for farming, and take other artificial deviations to the ordinary atmosphere; water-quality observing becomes progressively significant and decisive. Land-based accomplishments give a large effect on water arrangements and are serious to understand the problems of water forms, both beyond and beneath the ground level (McMichael et al., 2003).

14.1.1 Urban City Wastewater for Peri-Agriculture

Water usage is emerging in an efficient way with double the amount of inhabitants increasing throughout the latter century. Administration of water possessions are becoming a crucial subject as urban and peri-urban farmer frequently put on water from community sewage, typically in its unprocessed method, cumulative the menace for infections to farmers and clients (Coben & Garrett, 2009). In urban and peri-urban cultivation, nearby modified small-scale irrigation and plant manufacture approaches and structures are conceivable explanations to include water. Reduced cost with water reserves skills such as alternative and drip irrigation upsurges the water effectiveness and also allows safely to use reduced quality on water possessions. Drip irrigation substructures are manmade from present indigenous products, like absorbent ceramic bottles or pipes through which holes inside that water are dripped against the soil into the root zone only. In circumstances of salt-tolerant yields, water is used in localizing irrigation arrangements (Kane et al., 2018). Urban and peri-city horticulture and micro-gardens which include easy hydroponics are applied to feature financial and dietary blessings through securing a year-spherical deliver of clean produce to city populations. Simple hydroponics promotes water financial savings in recycling and decontamination of water and could facilitate the boom of flowers in regions with marginal situations for crop production, which include unfavorable climate, soil, area barriers in cities, water scarcity, and beyond occurrences. At the equal time, hydroponics generates neighborhood markets in delivering meals chains. Hydroponics is taken into consideration a powerful opportunity to be incorporated into meals safety and vitamins rural and peri-city improvement packages with low-aid populations residing below poverty situations (Schnitzler, 2012). As an effect of the re-use of home wastewater, outflow on inorganic inputs with the aid of using farmers might also additionally failure and supply sustainability of water delivery is improved (Mathew et al., 2013). Other city by-products such as organic solid waste residuals have also been seen a significant input for the urban and peri-urban farming (Francesco et al., 2013).

14.1.2 Untreated Water and Human Health

Water, even though an absolute necessity for all lifeforms, is regularly the creation of many illnesses. The prepared availability of water makes viable the non-public hygiene measures which might be crucial to save you the transmission of enteric illnesses. Infectious water-associated illnesses may be categorized as waterborne, water-hygiene, water-touch, and water-habitat vector illnesses. Globally, a vast variety of sufferers broaden a contamination during a health facility stay, with the percentage plenty more in low-earnings countries. Inadequate control of urban, industrial, and agricultural wastewater method the drinking-water of masses of hundreds of thousands of humans is dangerously infected or chemically polluted (McMichael et al., 2003). In many components of the world, bugs that stay or breed in water convey and transmit illnesses which include dengue fever. A character can turn out to be inflamed with dracunculus most effective via way of means of ingesting water infected with the microscopic crustaceans that include the larvae of the pathogen (Lindsey et al., 1992). Other water hygiene illnesses encompass tinea, scabies, pediculosis and pores, and skin and eye infections. Tinea, a pores and skin ailment; trachoma, an eye fixed ailment; and bug infestations, which include scabies and pediculosis arise much less regularly whilst private hygiene and cleanliness are of an excessive standard. Water touch illnesses are transmitted whilst a character's pores and skin are in touch with pathogen-infested water (Jamie & Richard, 1996).

Motivation – The water which is irrigated for human usage can range substantially in best relying on the kind and dissolved amount of salts, pH, and turbidity. Salts seen in irrigation water are highly trivial; however, extensive quantities as they at once affect the electric conductivity. For irrigation, the salts are implemented with the water and continue to be at the back of inside the soil as the water disappears or is utilized by the crop (Rachna & Disha, 2016). The suitability of water for irrigation isn't best decided through the entire quantity of salt gift however additionally the form of salt. Water best or suitability to be used is referred as the capability harshness of issues that are anticipated to increase all through long-time period use of the equal water source (Shabbir et al., 2018). The maximum encountered issues because of water are the ones associated with saltiness, infiltration proportion in water, poisonousness, and a collection of different miscellaneous issues (Booth & Leavitt, 1999).

14.1.3 Water Quality Issues in Agriculture Irrigation

There are several problems that are caused as a result of bad water quality. Additionally, there are different factors which can cause different outcomes when used without proper treatment; some of the common problems are discussed below (Richard & Ivanildo, 1997).

Salinity – Salt present in water lessens water obtainability to the crop to such a volume where normal yield is degraded. A salinity hassle exists if salt deposits inside the vegetation' root in excessive attention that it reasons in its capacity to take in water. In cultivation areas, those salts originate from saline water used for irrigation.

Water Infiltration Rate – The infiltration charge of water into soil differs extensively and are significantly prompted via way of means of the same old of the irrigation water, soil elements like structure, diploma of compaction, natural count content material, and chemical makeup will significantly have an impact on the consumption charge. The commonest water high-satisfactory elements which have an impact on the conventional infiltration charge are the presence of salt and sodium relative to calcium and magnesium.

Specific Ion Toxicity – Ions such as sodium, chloride, or boron from soil or water collect for the duration of a touchy crop to concentrations excessive sufficient to reason crop harm and decrease yields. Toxic issues arise with ions in soil and water are haunted with the aid of using the plant and collect to attentions excessive sufficient to reason crop harm or decreased yields. The diploma of harm relies upon on uptake and crop sensitivity.

Miscellaneous – Excessive vitamins lessen yield or high-satisfactory; given worst on foliage lessen marketability; immoderate corrosion of package will increase renovation and repairs. A unique hassle confronted via way of means of a few farmers working towards irrigation is the deterioration of device because of water-brought about corrosion. Vector troubles from mosquitoes regularly originate as secondary hassle related to an espresso water infiltration fee, to the usage of wastewater for irrigation, or negative drainage (Johnson & Dhanalakshmi, 2019).

14.1.4 Scope of the Chapter

The basic goal of the suggested system is to deliver a digital and automated explanation for water quality surveillance that provides automated supervision of four different parameters about the water quality. The system also provides continuous and real-time monitoring of data with the help of a cloud-based solution. Easy monitoring with the help of website and mobile application interfaces is included. The system has a solution using modern technologies to measure and monitor the water quality with the help of IoT sensors, networks, and cloud services. Finally, the architecture delivers an attentive message to the end-user whenever a slight nonconformity is observed in the water limitations from the pre-defined set of standards.

14.2 Related Literature

This section describes the related articles published in a crisp manner.

14.2.1 Concerned Constraints

Water excellent constraints encompass chemical, physical, and organic homes and may be examined or monitored primarily based totally at the favored water parameters of concern. Parameters which are often sampled or monitored for water excellent encompass temperature, dissolved oxygen, pH, conductivity, oxidation discount potential, and turbidity. However, water tracking can also encompass measuring overall algae, ion sensitivity electrodes (ammonia, nitrate, chloride), or laboratory parameters together with biochemical oxygen demand, titration, or overall natural carbon. However, they no longer have an effect on human fitness, extended tiers of those parameters purpose purchasers to desert progressed water components, regularly in favor of floor water reasserts which are microbiologically contaminated. It was found that the major list of parameters to consider when monitoring water quality are turbidity, electrical conductivity, pH, and temperature by testing water samples from various sources (Sorlini et al., 2013). With a large number of sensor nodes, the water quality is observed with network ability and the scenario is organized in ad hoc monitoring persistence and unwavering pH level, turbidity, and temperature (Rasin & Rizal, 2009). A dynamic threshold method is implemented for pollution occasion exposure in water delivery system and quality measurements and alerts the possibility of event occurrence as a significance of glitches such as unexpected leakage or any faults and this is developed using Genetic Algorithm for tuning various decision variables (Arad et al., 2013).

14.2.2 Wireless Sensor Networks

To provide a real-time system requires accurate and reliable data which can only be obtained through proper and thorough testing of these crucial parameters in the water being tested. This is done with the help of a wireless sensor network (WSN) (Vijaya et al., 2011), which is a framework that takes the benefits of the WSN for instantaneous specialist care on the water eminence quality in aquaculture (Li & Chen, 2012). The layout shape of WSN is to gather and constantly transmit facts to the tracking software program and the configuration version with inside the software program that complements the reprocess and ability of the tracking project. The tracking software program advanced to symbolize the tracking hardware and facts picturing, and examine the facts with professional information to put into effect the car control (Mingfei et al., 2010). The use of WSN for the entire water monitoring process including data achievement, data broadcast, data protection, and decision building. Few optimization algorithms are used in WSN to efficiently convey the sensed information to the receiver station.

14.2.3 IoT-Based Monitoring

The use of traditional sensors in a WSN is not effective or useful as these sensors are only collect and transmit data, whereas IoT sensors (Swetha et al., 2017) are put this data to good use by analyzing this data and making smart decisions based on programmed logic. The power ingesting is a main restraint for IoT solicitations, to solve this by having solar panels and other renewable power sources for the system (Geetha & Gouthami, 2016). The system focuses on providing biological and bodily quantities and permit data to be observed in real-time via the internet by isolated operators. An IoT-based scheme is recycled to ration the water quality factors for home applications for monitoring the acidity, and alkalinity, and the sensed data is processed in real-time using IoT-enabled mobile application (Saif et al., 2020). The efforts spent on monitoring water quality lacking much deliberation to any activities when the superiority of water indicator is out of limits, the IoT based policy to stock and opinion the collected information from dissimilar positions (Ragavan et al., 2016). An advanced commercial perfect to regulator and improve the resources distantly, and track the water characteristics continuously is discussed which lead to improve the water usage effectively using a cloud computing and IoT enabled technologies (Monisha & Anand, 2021).

14.3 System Architecture

An IoT-based solution that provides automated supervision over different parameters such as turbidity, electrical conductivity, pH, temperature of the water quality by providing easy monitoring to concerned authorities through a simple and user-friendly website and mobile application. Additionally, provide automatic notifications to the end-user regarding the current water quality and also provide solutions and suggestions based on it, to improve the water quality. Figure 14.1 illustrates the architecture diagram of the system under discussion.

Charging Circuit – This unit is connected to the controller unit of the system. The charging circuit delivers power to the entire structure. The charging circuit connected to a battery to charge it.

IoT Sensors – Are unified calculating procedures in the form of hardware, mechanical and digital machineries which have the aptitude to handover data over a network lacking needful human-to-human or human-to-computer collaboration, used to collect the data from the sample water.

Micro Controller Unit (MCU) – Small computer on a single chip. The MCU controls the whole systems functionality. It's used for automatic functioning of the system. A microcontroller contains one or more Central Processing Unit (CPU) inside them with memory and programmable input or output peripherals. The MCU is programmed to collect and handle the data of our system and interact with the IoT sensors.

WI-FI Module – A independent scheme on chip with combined protocol stack with a microcontroller for processing and to access the WI-FI network. It's skilled of both presenting a submission or divesting all Wi-Fi networking gatherings from additional presentation processor. This unit provides us through the Wi-Fi connectivity needed to transmit and receive data from the cloud.

Global System for Mobile Communication (GSM) – GSM module or a General Packet Radio Service (GPRS) module is a chip or circuit in order to be used to set up verbal exchange among a cellular tool or a computing gadget and a GSM system. A GSM module is a module that may be incorporated with an equipment. The GSM module provides cellular connectivity to our system to send and receive SMS.

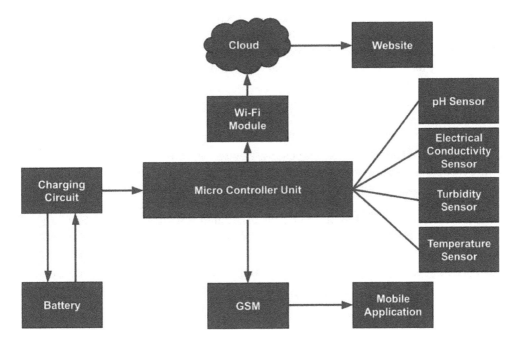

FIGURE 14.1
System architecture.

Website – Developed to provide an easy system interface used to check the results from the system. It provides solutions for various water qualities that have been tested in the module.

Mobile Application – Intended to track on a mobile device, such as a smartphone or tablet. Here the mobile application is used to check the output of the system as well as to control the system remotely, by sending SMS to the GSM module of the system.

The following are the three modules of the system.

    i. Data Collection
    ii. Data Transfer to Cloud
    iii. Access to Cloud Database

Data Collection Module – The IoT Sensors are primarily used for collecting the data from the sample water and transmitting it to the MCU on the system, which then deals with conversions and further analysis of this data.

Data Transfer to Cloud – The acquired data is moved from the microcontroller into the cloud database via the Wi-Fi module.

Cloud Database Access – Cloud services provide distant servers presented on the Internet to stock, accomplish, and development data, somewhat than a local server or a personal computer. This data can be accessed by an endpoint device with the suitable access and authorization, in this case the endpoint application can be a website or a mobile application both of which leverage the use of APIs to access and display the data.

Unified Modelling Language (UML) Diagram – UML with the cause of visually representing a device in conjunction with its most important actors, roles, actions, artifacts or classes, so that you can higher understand, alter, maintain, or report data approximately the device. The UML is explained in three different cases (use case, class and sequence).

Use Case Diagram – A use case diagram at its most effective is an illustration of a customer's interplay with the machine that indicates the connection among the consumer and the exclusive use instances wherein the consumer is involved.

Class Diagram – Describes the shape of a device via way of means of displaying the structure classes, their attributes, operations, and the relationships amongst objects. The details of attributes and operations of a category and additionally the restrictions imposed at the device. The magnificence diagrams are broadly used with inside the modelling of item-orientated structures due to the fact they may be the best UML diagrams, which are mapped at once with item-orientated languages.

Sequence Diagram –Describes object connections with respect to time. It explains the objects and groups given in the scenario and additionally the collection of messages modified among the gadgets required to keep out the practicality of the scenario.

14.4 Hardware Requirements

Node MCU – ESP8266 Wi-Fi System on Chip is used as the node MCU for the proposed system.

DS18B20 Temperature Sensor – A 12-bit configurable module is used, which uses a single wire bus to exchange the information to the processor.

pH Sensor – A thermoplastic-based module to sense the pH value of the water is used in the system.

Total Dissolved Solids (TDS) – TDS is a component and is measured in ppm. Total dissolved solids are typically mentioned best for freshwater systems, as the presence of salt consists of a number of the ions constituting the definition of TDS. The important utility of TDS is to look at of water bodies.

Ultrasonic Sensor – Are dependable, cost-powerful devices for those applications. In operation, the sensor is hooked up over the water. To decide the gap to the water, it transmits a valid pulse that displays from the floor of the water and measures the time it takes for the echo to return. Sometimes structural components, including a small pipe, are positioned with inside the acoustic direction among the ultrasonic sensor and the water. It displays a part of the sound and produces a fake echo that interferes with the cap potential of the sensor to well discover the echo from the floor of the water. Advanced ultrasonic sensors may be adjusted to disregard those fake echoes, which consequently permits them to offer correct water degree measurements.

GSM – This is an ultra-compact and dependable Wi-Fi module. The SIM900A is a Dual-band GSM/GPRS combined module in a surface mount technology module embedded to connect with any client application. The SIM900A module performs at 900/1800 MHz for audio, data, message, and fax. The entire module is available in a 24mmx24mmx3mm packed unit.

ATMEGA2560 Microcontroller – ATmega2560 is an 8-bit CMOS controller with AVR superior RISC architecture and has a throughput of 1 MIPS. It has a self-programmable flash on a monolithic chip and is used for many applications.

14.5 Application Programming

Interface – API is a computing interface used to interact with few software applications. It defines the way of connections are made between end devices to exchange the data. This is closely leveraged in cutting-edge cloud primarily based totally infrastructures to have a greater open and easy–to–use and scalable version. A RESTful API is a software application interface (API) that makes use of HTTP requests to GET, PUT, POST and DELETE information. This is utilized in our proposed device to get the information from the cloud offerings.

Web Hosting – Once a website or web application is developed it needs to be hosted to be able to be accessed by other users or services, this is done by hosting the application on a server, there are several web hosting application available, for this project we will be using Firebase's own hosting services.

Web Application – A internet utility is any laptop software that plays a particular characteristic through the usage of an internet browser as its client. The utility is hosted on a server and accessed from a browser. In this method it's vital to have a web connection to get right of entry to it. They're handy from any browser. It doesn't count number if you're the usage of Firefox, Chrome, Safari or another browser, you may get right of entry to the internet app. They rank in conventional seek engines. As they don't want to be downloaded, you may now no longer locate them with inside the app stores; however, they'll seem as a bring about engines consisting of Google. The forms of internet packages are static internet packages and dynamic internet packages.

In static the pages are pre-rendered, cached, and added to the consumer. This form of internet utility shows little or no content material and isn't very flexible. They are normally evolved in HTML and CSS. However, lively items consisting of banners, GIFs, videos, etc., will also be protected and proven in them. They also can be evolved with jQuery and Ajax. However, enhancing the contents of static internet apps isn't easy. To do this, the HTML code need to be downloaded, then adjust it and in the end add it once more to the server. These adjustments are handiest be made through the webmaster or through the improvement business enterprise that deliberate and designed. However, in a static website online generator after which a shipping community could make a static website online steeply-priced to construct. Without complicated scripting, a database, parsing content material via templating languages, etc. those websites generally load in a snap. The downside of the usage of static internet packages are tough to update, tough to scale and the continuing preservation price.

Dynamic internet packages are a great deal extra complicated at a technical level. They commonly have a management panel (referred to as CMS) from wherein directors can accurate or adjust the app's content material consisting of textual content and pictures. In this sort of app, upgrading content material is quite simple and the server doesn't even must be accessed whilst enhancing it. Also, it permits the implementation of lots of functions consisting of boards or databases. Both layout and content material may be changed to fit the administrator's preferences. The benefits are dynamic internet packages are powered through databases, this is through connecting a dynamic web website online to a database, you're capable of without difficulty request data in a prepared and based manner to create and show content material relying on how the consumer desires to view it. Second, this will without difficulty hook up with a CMS. The low ongoing preservation price. Since you may join a dynamic web website online to a CMS there are very little ongoing charges except there may be an alternate with inside the primary layout or a further functionality is delivered to the website online. The hazards are the layout boundaries and to incur in advance the constructing charges.

Android Application – The proposed gadget makes use of a custom android utility evolved to utilize APIs to show the values saved with inside the Cloud carrier issuer with the aid of a WebView in the utility. Android utility common sense may be written in both Java or Kotlin, primarily based totally on consumer preference, this venture makes use of Java to deal with common sense and XML to keep data approximately the utility, all of those are treated through the Android studio IDE.

14.6 System Implementation

The proposed system was developed with all the components and is shown in Figure 14.2. The setup consists of the primary filter, often used for water polishing, which refers to a process that removes small particulate material or debris from water sample which can

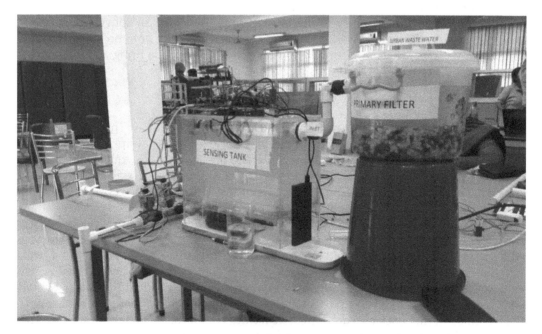

FIGURE 14.2
Experimental setup.

cause damage to the sensors inside the tank. The water is then forwarded through the inlet of the sensing tank, where it is collected from the primary filter for sensing (i.e.) for the measurements of the constraints such as electrical conductivity, pH and turbidity to identify the quality of the water sample using the various sensing modules and controllers present inside the sensing tank.

Once testing is done, the water from the sensing tank is either let out to be used or redirected for treatment based on suggestions. The Hardware system has NodeMCU, it acts the control unit of the whole project. NodeMCU comprises firmware that is executed on the ESP8266 Wi-Fi SoC. Turbidity, pH, and electrical conductivity IOT sensors are enabled to detect the turbidity, pH level and electrical conductivity respectively in the water sample. The sensors gather the data and are forwarded to the NodeMCU (Controller) to check the quality level of the sample of water being tested, if it exceeds the threshold level set based on the available standards then, the system triggers an SMS Alert Notification which is sent to the user. The workflow of this project begins with the user accessing the webapp to get the necessary details about the water quality. Initially, the device uploads the data to the cloud, which is then accessed by the back end of the application when the user is trying to view the details. Consequently, the data is displayed on the front end for the user to see and analyze.

Decision Tree Classifier – The back end of this project uses a decision tree classifier to classify the water based on its parameters into three labels: 'pure', 'impure' and 'unusable'. This classification is based on the range of values obtained from Food and Agriculture Organization (FAO) for agriculture use. The selection tree classifier is one of the maximum normally used class algorithms, selection timber is constructed the usage of a heuristic referred to as recursive partitioning. This method is likewise normally referred to as divide and triumph over as it splits the facts into subsets, that are then break up again and again into even smaller subsets, and so forth and so on till the technique stops while the set of rules determines the facts in the subsets are sufficiently homogenous, or every other preventing criterion has been met. In selection tree class a brand new instance is classed with the aid of using filing it to a chain of checks that decide the elegance label of the instance. These checks are prepared in a hierarchical shape referred to as a selection tree. Decision timber observe divide-and-triumph over set of rules. Using the selection set of rules, we begin on the tree root and break up the facts at the characteristic that effects in the biggest statistics gain (discount in uncertainty closer to the very last selection). In an iterative technique, we are able to then repeat this splitting technique at every toddler node till the leaves are pure. This method that the samples at every leaf node all belong to the identical elegance. In practice, we can also additionally set a restriction at the intensity of the tree to save you overfitting. We compromise on purity right here fairly because the very last leaves can also additionally nevertheless have a few impurities. Generally, a selection tree accommodates of 3 fundamental segments which includes a root node, some hidden nodes, and numerous terminal nodes (referred to as leaves). An illustrative case of a selection tree shape is depicted in Figure 14.3. As demonstrated, for every hidden and terminal node (known as toddler node), there need to exist a determine node demonstrating the facts source. In the interim, with recognize to the basis node and every hidden node (referred to as determine hub), at the least toddler nodes are made from those determine nodes depending on special selection rules. This work uses the training data generated based on the range of standard values given by FAO for pH, electrical conductivity, and turbidity. The value ranges taken are: from 6.50 to 8.40 pH (Scale of 1 to 14), from 2.50 to 5.00 ppm,

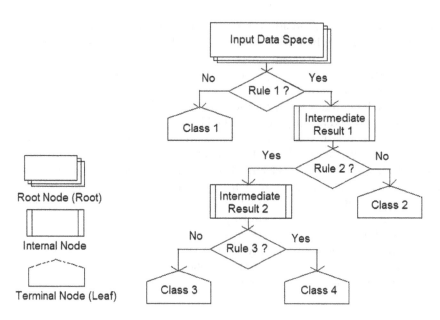

FIGURE 14.3
Decision tree classifier.

from 0.00 to 0.70 mS/cm and less than 33 °C for pH, electrical conductivity, turbidity, and temperature respectively. This training data covers a majority of the possible outcomes of the resulting water quality with over a thousand sample data generated dynamically, and it also contains the respective label marking the quality corresponding to a given set of values. This training data helps to train the decision tree classifier module based on Python Programming Language.

14.7 Result and Discussion

Test Cases – The water samples taken from different sources act as the test cases used for testing the experimental prototype setup. These sample test cases were chosen to highlight the individual possibilities of the water samples quality, which were targeted in this system design.

The constraints such as turbidity, electrical conductivity and pH are measured using appropriate IoT-based sensing modules. The values obtained are shown in the form of tables and the observed results of various water samples taken are shown in the form of charts with respect to time. These water samples were taken for testing from three different sources having different qualities of water, this is unknown to the system and it classifies these unknown water samples based on testing and outputs the purity of the water sample tested.

Sample 1 – Pure water: The values for pH, turbidity and electrical conductivity for a pure water sample which provides the values of the critical parameters. The safety level of water usability has been derived from the critical parameters. The values represent that the pH values falling between 6.50 and 8.40, and turbidity value falling between 2 and 5 and electrical conductivity falling between 0.00 and 0.70 makes the water suitable for use.

Sample 2 – Impure water: The values pH, turbidity, and electrical conductivity for an impure water sample, which provides the values of the critical parameters. The safety level of water usability has been derived from the critical parameters. The values represent that the values of pH, turbidity, and electrical conductivity are not within the suitable range for use, but can be treated using the suggestions and then used, making them impure but treatable.

Sample 3 – Unusable water: The values for pH, turbidity, and electrical conductivity for an impure water sample, which provides the values of the critical parameters. The safety level of water usability has been derived from the critical parameters. The values represent that the values of pH, turbidity, and electrical conductivity are not within the suitable range for use and cannot be treated making them impure and unusable.

14.8 Conclusion and Future Scope

The proposed project mainly focuses on monitoring the quality of water in real-time for agricultural use and provides suggestions and notifications to the user about the water quality. The water quality was determined created on the turbidity, pH, electrical conductivity, and temperature of the water, using a decision tree classifier which classifies the water into three main categories which help us in deciding when and what suggestions and notifications need to be sent to the user. This automated approach can reduce the cost and time spent on testing the water quality regularly and also prevent any damage that might be caused to the crops when untreated water is used.

In the upcoming days, this effort can be prolonged to use multiple sensors and implement blockchain technologies to further help in historical analysis of the water quality globally by government or private bodies. Additionally, the functionality and scope of this project can be expanded based on the needs of the customer, leading to a more versatile product.

References

Arad, J., Housh, M., Pereiman, L., and Ostfeld, A. (2013). A Dyynamic Threshold Scheme for Contaminant Event Detection in Water Dist. System, *Water Research*, 47(5), 1899–1908.

Booth, D.B., and Leavitt, J., (1999). Field Evaluation of Permeable Pavement Systems for Improved Stormwater Management, *Journal of the American Planning Association*, Summer, 314–325.

Coben, M., and Garrett, J. (2009). *The Food Price Crisis and Urban Food Insecurity.* International Institute for Environment and Development, London.

Francesco, O., Remi, K., Remi, N., and Giorgio, G. (2013). Urban Agriculture in the Developing World: A Review, *Agronomy for Sustainable Development*, 33, 695–720.

Geetha, S., and Gouthami, S. (2016). Internet of Things Enabled Real-Time Water Quality Monitoring System, *Smart Water*, 2(1), 1–19.

Jamie, B., and Richard, B. (1996). *Water Quality Monitoring – A Practical Guide to the Design and Implementation of Fresh Water Quality Studies and Monitoring Programmes*, UN Environment Programme and WHO.

Johnson, M., and Dhanalakshmi, R. (2019). Predictive Analysis based Efficient Routing of Smart Garbage Bins for Effective Waste Management, *International Journal of Recent Technology and Engineering*, 8(3), 5733–5739.

Kane, A. M., Lagat, J. K., Fane, T., Langat, J. K., and Teme, B. (2018). Economic Viability of Alternative Small-Scale Irrigation Systems used in Vegetables Production in Koulikoro and Mopti Regions, Mali, *Handbook of Climate Change Resilence*, Springer, 1–32.

Li, D., and Chen, Y. (2012). Design and Development of Water Quality Monitoring System based on Wireless Sensor Network in Aqaculture, *14 International Conference in Computer and Computing Technologies in Agriculture*, 6th IFIP WG, CCTA.

Lindsey, G., Roberts, L., and Page, W. (1992). Inspection and Maintenance of Infiltration Facilities, *Journal of Soil and Water Conservation*, 47(6), 481–486.

Mathew, K., Reddy, V. R., Ton, D., and Damir, B. (2013). Wastewater Re-use for Peri-Urban Agriculture: A Viable Option for Adaptive Water Management, *Sustainability Science*, Springer, 8, 47–59.

McMichael, A. J., Campbell-Lendrum, D. H., Corvalan, C. F., Ebi, K. L., Githeko, A. K., Scheraga, J. D., and Woodward, A. (2003). *Climate Change and Human Health: Risks and Responses*, World Health Organization, Geneva.

Mingfei, Z., Daoliang, L., Lianzhi, W., Daokun, M., and Qisheng, D. (2010). Design and Development of Water Quality Monitoring System based on WSN in Aquaculture, *International Conference on Computer and Computing Technology in Agriculture*, 629–641.

Monisha, V. A., and Anand, J. (2021). Analysis of Dynamic Interference Constraints in Cognitive Radio Cloud Networks, *International Journal of Advanced Research in Science, Communication and Technology*, 6(1), 815–823.

Rachna, B., and Disha, J. (2016). Water Quality Assessment of Lake Water: A Review, *Sustainable Water Resource Management*, 2, 161–173.

Ragavan, E., Hariharan, C., Aravindraj, N., and Manivannan, S. S. (2016). Real Time Water Quality Monitoring System, *International JournalPharmaceutical Technology*, 8(4), 26199–26205.

Rasin, Z., and Rizal, A. M.2009. Water Quality Monitoring System using Zigbee based Wireless Sensor Network, *International Journal of Engineering and Technology*, 9(10), 14–18.

Richard, H., and Ivanildo, H., (1997). *Water Pollution Control – A Guide to the Use of Water Quality Management Principles*, UNEP, WSSCC, WHO.

Saif, A. H. A., Mohamed, K. H., and Mohamed, H. M. (2020). Real Time Internet of Things (IoT) based Water Quality Management System, *30th CIRP Design*, Science Direct, 478–485.

Schnitzler, W. H. (2012). Urban Hydroponics – Facts and Vision. *Conference AVRDC World Vegetable Center*, Chiang Mai, Thailand.

Shabbir, A. S., Mohammad, Z., and Lee, H. (2018). *Introduction to Soil Salinity, Sodicity and Diagnostics Techniques, Guideline for Salinity Assessment, Mitigation and Adaptation using Nuclear and Related Techniques*, Springer, Cham, 1–42.

Sorlini, S., Palazzini, D., Sieliechi, J., and Ngassoum, M. (2013). Assessment of Physical-Chemical Drinking Water Quality in the Logone Valley (Chad-Cameroon), *Sustainability*, 5(7), 3060–3076.

Swetha, S., Suprajah, S., Kanna, S. V., and Dhanalakshmi, R., (2017). An Intelligent Monitor System for Home Appliances using IoT, *Proceedings of International Conference on Technical Advancements in Computers and Communication*, Melmaurvathur, India, 106–108.

Tchounwou, Paul B., Yedjou, Clement G., Patlolla, Anita K., and Sutton, Dwayne J.(2014). Heavy Metals Toxicity and the Environment, *HHS Public Access*, PMC, 26.

VanLoon, G., Anderson, B. C., Watt, W. E., and Marsalek, J. (2000). Characterizing Stormwater Sediments for Ecotoxic Risk, *Water Quality Research Journal of Canada*, 35(3), 341–364.

Vijaya, R. V.Hemamalini, R. R., and Anand, J. (2011). Multi Agent System Based Upstream Congestion Control in Wireless Sensor Networks, *European Journal of Scientific Research*, 59(2), 241–248.

Index